PUBLICATIONS OF THE NEW CHAUCER SOCIETY

THE NEW CHAUCER SOCIETY

Studies in the Age of Chaucer, the yearbook of The New Chaucer Society, is published annually in May. Each issue contains a limited number of substantial articles, reviews of books on Chaucer and related topics, and an annotated Chaucer bibliography. Articles explore such concerns as the efficacy of various critical approaches to the art of Chaucer and his contemporaries, their literary relationships and reputations, and the artistic, economic, intellectual, religious, scientific, and social and historical backgrounds to their work.

Manuscripts, in duplicate, accompanied by return postage, should follow the *MLA Handbook for Writers* (1977). Unsolicited reviews are not accepted. Authors receive free twenty offprints of articles and ten of reviews. All correspondence concerning manuscript submissions for Volume 5, subscriptions to The New Chaucer Society, and information about the Society's activities should be directed to John H. Fisher, Department of English, University of Tennessee, Knoxville, Tennessee 37996.

Studies in the Age of Chaucer

Studies in the Age of Chaucer

Volume 4
1982

EDITED BY ROY J. PEARCY • PUBLISHED
ANNUALLY BY THE NEW CHAUCER SOCIETY

The frontispiece design, showing the Pilgrims at the Tabard Inn, is adapted from the woodcut in Caxton's second edition of *The Canterbury Tales*.

ISBN 0–933784–03–1

ISSN 0190–2407

CONTENTS

ARTICLES

Chaucer's Fifteenth-Century Audience and the Narrowing of the "Chaucer Tradition"
Paul Strohm — 3

Pronuntiatio and its Effect on Chaucer's Audience
Beryl Rowland — 33

'We ben to lewed or to slowe': Chaucer's Astronomy and Audience Participation
J. C. Eade — 53

Punctuation and Caesura in Chaucer
George B. Killough — 87

Theban History in Chaucer's Troilus
David Anderson — 109

REVIEWS

Judson Boyce Allen and Theresa Anne Moritz, *A Distinction of Stories: The Medieval Unity of Chaucer's Fair Chain of Narratives for Canterbury* (Derek Pearsall) — 135

Stephen A. Barney, ed., *Chaucer's* Troilus: *Essays in Criticism* (S. S. Hussey) — 140

Robert G. Benson, *Medieval Body Language: A Study of the Use of Gesture in Chaucer's Poetry* (Barry Windeatt) — 144

Caroline D. Eckhardt, ed., *Essays in the Numerical Criticism of Medieval Literature* (Edmund Reiss) — 146

Sigmund Eisner, ed., Gary Mac Eoin and Sigmund Eisner, trans., *The Kalendarium of Nicholas of Lynn* (Owen Gingerich) — 149

Joseph Gibaldi, *Approaches to Teaching Chaucer's* Canterbury Tales (Gerald L. Evans) — 152

Richard Firth Green, *Poets and Princepleasers: Literature and the English Court in the Late Middle Ages* (Nicolas Jacobs)　　154

N. R. Havely, ed. and trans., *Chaucer's Boccaccio: Sources of Troilus and* The Knight's *and* Franklin's Tales (Thomas A. Van)　　159

Donald R. Howard, *Writers and Pilgrims: Medieval Pilgrimage Narratives and Their Posterity* (Penn R. Szittya)　　161

Anthony Jenkins, ed., *The Isle of Ladies or The Isle of Pleasaunce* (E. Ruth Harvey)　　165

Terry Jones, *Chaucer's Knight: The Portrait of a Medieval Mercenary* (David Aers)　　169

Traugott Lawler, *The One and the Many in* The Canterbury Tales (John Norton-Smith)　　175

Robert A. Peters, *Chaucer's Language* (Walter S. Phelan)　　178

D. W. Robertson, Jr., *Essays in Medieval Culture* (Maxwell Luria)　　181

Theodor Wolpers, *Bürgerliches bei Chaucer* (Karl Heinz Göller)　　190

BIBLIOGRAPHY

John H. Fisher, *An Annotated Chaucer Bibliography 1980*　　193

　　Classifications　　194

　　Journal Abbreviations　　196

　　Citations　　197

　　Author Index　　244

VARIA

　　Letter from the Editor　　247

　　Abbreviations for Chaucer's Works　　249

　　General Index　　251

Studies in the Age of Chaucer

Chaucer's Fifteenth-Century Audience and the Narrowing of the "Chaucer Tradition"

Paul Strohm
Indiana University

THE PRINCIPAL responsibility of any theory of literary history is to account for stylistic change.[1] The shortcoming of a wholly enclosed history of the interrelations of literary texts is that it has no persuasive way to account for the challenge or supplantation of tradition by counter-tradition, for the replacement of one form or genre by another, for the revival of a form or style whose time might seem wholly to have passed. Presumably, none of us still believes in the "evolutionary" model of the progression of texts, in which forms and styles pass from youthful vitality to full maturity to senescence, are born and die out, according to some imperative inherent in their own genetic structure. Yet, in its failure to produce a more satisfactory account of stylistic change, the self-enclosed history of texts causes us to behave as if this evolutionary model still possessed explanatory force. If we are to develop more efficacious models, we must enlarge the scope of our consideration from the interrelationships of literary texts to include the historical and social environments in which they were composed or written, heard or read.

One promising link between literary works and their environments is through the aesthetics of reception, with its interest in the relationship between artistic styles and their literary publics. Hans-Robert Jauss has demonstrated the pertinence of reception-aethetics to the analysis of medieval literature, in his theory that a literary work is received by contemporary readers or hearers within their historically-conditioned

---

[1] I am paraphrasing a comment made by Ralph Cohen at an Indiana University symposium on narrative, October 1980.

"horizon of expectations."[2] Still more relevant to a discussion of stylistic change are the theories of Arnold Hauser, with his recognition that audiences of different social composition (and different expectations and tastes) may co-exist or overlap or succeed each other.[3] In his view, writers within a period and even individual writers within their careers engage in various stylistic experiments, but a particular style is perpetuated when it finds its "point of attachment" in the encouragement of a socially-defined class or group of readers. So long as the position of this group is secure, the style it encourages is likely to persist; displacement of the group may have consequences for artistic style. One corollary of this view is that the emergence of a new style is likely to be associated with the emergence of a new group. Another is that the eclipse of a style is likely to be associated with a major deterioration in the position of the group. Hauser's is essentially a theory of reception. To be sure, his hypothesis of a connection between stylistic tendencies and the different social levels of a society has possible implications for the genesis of works, if we were to seek them.[4] Finally, though, he has most to tell us about why some styles, once available, flourish, while others, equally available, decline.

These introductory comments are meant to frame the discussion of a particular issue in literary history: the striking narrowing in the decades immediately following Chaucer's death of what has been called the

[2] "Literary History as a Challenge to Literary Theory," in *New Directions in Literary History*, ed. Ralph Cohen (Baltimore: Johns Hopkins UP, 1974), pp. 11–41.

[3] "Art History Without Names," in *The Philosophy of Art History* (Meridian Books, 1963), pp. 207–36, 253–76.

[4] Implicit in Hauser's theory is the notion that the work of art does not merely "copy" or "reflect" economic conditions, but that it is a socially-conditioned creation co-ordinate with other social creations. In this he anticipates such neo-Marxian theorists as Raymond Williams (who believes that works of art participate in patterns of hegemonic expression, which embrace the broadest range of social and cultural creations) and Fredric Jameson (whose theory of structural causality presumes the simultaneous existence within works of art of a wide variety of impulses from contradictory modes of cultural production). See Raymond Williams, *Marxism and Literature* (Oxford Paperbacks, 1977), pp. 108–14, and Fredric Jameson, *The Political Unconscious* (Ithaca & London: Cornell UP, 1981) pp. 74–102. All these formulations resist the simple assertion that an artist writes or paints in a particular way 'because' he or she is a member of a particular social group. Yet at a broad level these formulations suggest a connection between the social and cultural assumptions shared by a group, the works of art produced by those belonging to it or identified with it, and the works of art enjoyed or encouraged by its members.

"Chaucer tradition."[5] His literary legacy upon his death in 1400 was, after all, an almost incomparably rich one, encompassing the courtly *dits* and lays and love-visions of his early period; the morality and good counsel of Boethius and *Melibee* and *The Parson's Tale*; such richly reflective narratives as *Troilus* and *The Knight's Tale*; and finally the full stylistic variety inherent in the bold formal and thematic juxtapositions of *The Canterbury Tales*. Further, he did not lack for would-be and self-proclaimed followers and disciples, some of whom were to produce substantial quantities of verse. Yet one must be struck by the apparent inability of his artistic legatees to claim more than a small portion of their inheritance. As frequently noted, Chaucer's fifteenth-century followers neglect his mature works of greatest formal and thematic complexity, in favor of a comparatively narrow range of *dits amoureux* and visions in the manner of continental France. To be sure, manuscripts of *Troilus* and *The Canterbury Tales* were in active circulation throughout the period. Yet from the point of view of literary influence, these major works were, as R. H. Robbins has pointed out, essentially *sans issue*.[6]

General explanations for the inability of the writers of the early fifteenth century to draw upon the full Chaucer legacy have, of course, been offered. A particularly frequent observation is that no writer of Chaucer's genius was available to succeed him—a point which is undoubtedly correct, but still insufficient to explain the near-absence even of feeble attempts to emulate his confident juxtaposition of a full range of styles and themes. Other explanations at a broad level of generality involve such considerations as national and local turmoil and brigandage associated with the dynastic struggles of the century—but one doubts that writers of potential talent spent all or even any of their time worrying about which side to choose in the shifting factional struggles of Lancaster and York. My own thesis is that the first place to look in order to understand the vicissitudes of the Chaucer tradition in the early years of the fifteenth century is to the individual and collective histories of those fourteenth-century readers who most immediately encouraged his literary talent. In general harmony with the theories of Hauser, I would

---

[5] The phrase is taken from Aage Brusendorff, *The Chaucer Tradition* (Oxford: Clarendon, 1925).

[6] "The Vintner's Son: French Wine in English Bottles," *Eleanor of Aquitaine: Patron and Politician*, ed. William Kibler (Austin, 1976), p. 164.

5

expect the long-term fortunes of a particular kind of poetry supported by a definable social group to be affected by any marked alterations in the composition or situation of that group.

I. The Dispersion of Chaucer's Primary Audience

In the last few years, several persons have independently arrived at new and remarkably similar conclusions about the social composition of Chaucer's primary or immediate audience. In "Chaucer's Audience," I argued that his immediate public or "point of attachment" was a group of persons in social situations rather comparable to his own—knights and esquires of the household of Richard II or otherwise prominent in court circles (such as Clifford, Clanvowe, Vache, Scogan, and Bukton), together with a handful of lawyers, chancery figures, and other civil servants (including Gower, Strode, and in some qualified respects Usk and later Hoccleve).[7] My argument was not that *all* of Chaucer's immediate readers came from such a milieu; one must concede the connections between *The Book of the Duchess* and the household of the aristocratic John of Gaunt and the possible interest of Richard II and Queen Anne in *The Legend of Good Women*, as well as the possibility that certain of Chaucer's acquaintances among the merchant classes of London would have admired his work. Yet the unusual *concentration* of members of Chaucer's immediate audience in this one 'circle' of courtiers and civil servants seemed to me quite clearly illustrated by references within his own poetry, by literary imitations (like John Clanvowe's *Boke of Cupide*), and by other explicitly literary activities (such as Lewis Clifford's interaction with both Deschamps and Chaucer). A very similar analysis of the social composition of Chaucer's immediate public was simultaneously advanced by Derek Pearsall, in two different publications. In "The 'Troilus' Frontispiece and Chaucer's Audience" he argued that "We might do well to look beyond the entourage of king and nobility for Chaucer's audience, to the multitude of household knights and officials, career diplomats and civil servants, who constitute the 'court' in its wider sense, that is, the national administration and its metropolitan milieu."[8] This argument was further developed in "The Chaucer Cir-

---

[7] *Literature and History*, 5 (1977), 26–41.
[8] *YES*, 7 (1977), 73.

cle," a subchapter of *Old and Middle English Poetry*, with particular
reference to the so-called 'Lollard Knights,' to government and city
officials like Hoccleve and Usk, and to London intellectual circles.[9]
Additional support for the notion of such an immediate public has been
offered in studies of Chaucer's epistles to Scogan and Bukton by Alfred
David and R. T. Lenaghan, with their emphasis on the implied social
relationship between Chaucer and the recipients of his good-humored
verses.[10] Anne Middleton has endorsed essentially the same view in her
"Chaucer's 'New Men' and the Good of Literature in the *Canterbury
Tales*," pursuing an analysis of the views of those pilgrims who held most
in common with the position of his presumed audience.[11]

Given the amount of independent agreement on this view of Chaucer's
audience, both in recent studies and in such background studies as those
of T. F. Tout,[12] I feel justified in treating it as an established position.[13]
On the reflection of several years, I would propose just one adjustment in
the frame, involving a recognition of the rather large difference in the
social situations of the Chamber knights (and especially the propertied
ones like Montagu) and such lesser officials and clerks as Usk and
Hoccleve. I would still assert the essential homogeneity of this group,
especially since most of the Chamber knights attained landed security
only through marriages related to their Court service. Yet the social
profile of this group might best be expressed through R. T. Lenaghan's
'two-tiered' characterization of the social context of *Lenvoy a Scogan* as
"the civil service of Richard II, a bureaucracy of clerks and a fellowship of
gentlemen" (p. 46). With Montagu and Clifford and Beauchamp we
encounter gentlemen who were something more than clerks, and with

---

[9] (London: Routledge & Kegan Paul, 1977), pp. 194–97.

[10] *The Strumpet Muse: Art and Morals in Chaucer's Poetry* (Bloomington: Indiana UP,
1976), p. 122; "Chaucer's *Envoy to Scogan*: The Uses of Literary Conventions," *ChauR*, 10
(1975–76), 46–61.

[11] *Literature and Society: Selected Papers from the English Institute*, 1978, NS, No. 3, ed.
Edward Said (Baltimore: Johns Hopkins UP, 1980), 15–56.

[12] "Literature and Learning in the English Civil Service in the Fourteenth Century,"
Speculum, 4 (1929), 365–89.

[13] Richard Firth Green, *Poets and Princepleasers: Literature and the English Court in the
Late Middle Ages* (Toronto: U of Toronto P, 1980) has recently reasserted the importance
of Richard II as a sponsor of Chaucer's efforts, though his argument requires that he
concentrate his attention on works apparently advisory to princes, such as *Melibee* and
Boethius (see pp. 143, 166).

Usk and Hoccleve we encounter clerks who were just barely gentlemen. Yet, in a broad sense, all were civil servants of the court of Richard II or its environs. All or most would have been at least glancingly acquainted. All—with the possible exception of Montagu and one or two others—were primarily committed to English in a court which was still French-speaking in its highest social reaches.[14] All finally constituted a social and literary 'circle' in an unusually pronounced and verifiable sense.

If one accepts the proposition that the existence of such a sympathetic social and literary circle had something to do with the breadth and confidence of Chaucer's mature poetic achievement, then one must also suppose that its dispersion would have had something to do with the failure of the transmission of Chaucer's achievement through the first decades of the fifteenth century. Certainly, such a dispersion took place, in the years immediately preceding and following Chaucer's death in 1400—not for any single reason, but for a combination of reasons.

One is always tempted to invoke the broadest political and cultural terms to explain a general phenomenon like the dispersion of a literary public. Here, for example, my own first impulse was to suggest that the dynastic uncertainties of the century had an unsettling effect on cultural life, or that the economic depression of the century somehow eroded the capacity of the lesser gentry for the enjoyment of *belles lettres*. Such broad theories turn out, however, to be of minimal assistance in addressing the particular problem of the dispersion of Chaucer's audience. After all, dynastic uncertainties did not prevent Henry VI and others from endowing colleges at Cambridge and Oxford, or Humphrey Duke of Gloucester and others from patronizing classic letters, nor did the economic constraints of the century limit the copying and circulation of manuscripts of *The Canterbury Tales* or of Shirley's genteel anthologies. Clearly, a phenomenon as delicate as the status of a social and cultural group is

---

[14] Although Rossell Hope Robbins has cogently argued that Richard II's court was French-speaking, I would offer the counter-suggestion that, while its aristocratic members were mainly French-speaking, its knights, esquires, and other gentle members were probably mainly English-speaking. Of course, Chamber knights such as John Montagu might have been exceptions to such a rule. Still, even a generalized linguistic as well as social stratification of the sort I am suggesting would have further defined Chaucer's circle as a distinct circle. See Robbins, "Geoffroi Chaucier, Poète Français, Father of English Poetry," *ChauR*, 13 (1978), 101. On the English wills of the Lollard Chamber knights, see K. B. McFarlane, *Lancastrian Kings and Lollard Knights* (Oxford: Clarendon, 1972), 209–10.

best addressed not at the 'macro' level of general causes, but at the 'micro' level of individual careers.

Even when considering the watershed year of 1400, in which Henry IV consolidated his rule, one finds considerable variation in the situations of the members of Chaucer's circle. Some were old men, obviously ready in any event to retire from the political and cultural scene; some were dead already; some were forced into retirement as a result of the dynastic change; others—including Chaucer himself, in the last months of his life—made the transition smoothly or even advantageously.[15] Finally, I see no alternative but to look case-by-case at their individual circumstances in and around the year 1400. The persons whom I will consider include five Chamber-knights of Richard II (Sturry, Clifford, Clanvowe, Montagu, and Vache); two knights or esquires in royal service, in positions somewhat closer to Chaucer's own (Scogan, Bukton); an Oxford philosopher or London lawyer (Strode); and three fellow poets, one with ties to the rural gentry (Gower) and two civil servants less well placed than Chaucer himself (Usk, Hoccleve).

Richard Sturry was acquainted with Chaucer,[16] and frequently in the company of Clanvowe and Clifford. His literary involvements include his close acquaintance with Froissart and his willingness to act as intermediary between Froissart and Richard II for the presentation of a volume of Froissart's love poems,[17] as well as his own possession of a copy of the *Roman de la Rose*.[18] A half-generation older than Chaucer, he was evidently dead by 1395.[19]

As a subsidiary aspect of his distinguished diplomatic career, Lewis Clifford acted as a literary intermediary between Deschamps and Chauc-

---

[15] Chaucer's "Complaint to His Purse," presumably written immediately after the coronation of Henry IV on September 30, 1399, embodies the Lancastrian theory of Henry's succession "by lyne and free eleccion" (l. 23). For this and all other quotations from Chaucer see *Works*, ed. F. N. Robinson (Boston: Houghton Mifflin, 1957). Chaucer received several key confirmations and grants from Henry IV in 1399 and 1400. See *Chaucer Life-Records*, ed. Martin M. Crow and Clair Olson (Oxford: Clarendon, 1966), pp. 525–34.

[16] Chaucer joined Sturry for at least one visit to France (*Life-Records*, p. 50). When not otherwise annotated, material on the careers of Chaucer's associates is based on the *Life-Records*, on the DNB, on McFarlane, *Lancastrian Kings and Lollard Knights*, and on William Dugdale, *The Baronage of England* (London, 1675).

[17] Froissart, *Oeuvres*, ed. Lettenhove (Brussels: Devaux, 1871), XV, 167.

[18] Cited in McFarlane, p. 185n.

[19] McFarlane, p. 214.

9

er, who sent "par Clifford" the balade to "grant translateur, noble Geffroy Chaucier."[20] His will, in which he left devotional books including his "Book of Tribulacion" to his daughter and to his son-in-law Vache, is printed in Dugdale.[21] Since he was born after 1330, Clifford's withdrawal from the world of affairs would be explicable by age alone—though he evidently did experience at least some difficulty in securing his earlier, highly advantageous grants in the years between the accession of Henry IV and his own death in 1414.[22]

John Clanvowe, born in or about 1341, was an author in English of a devotional treatise and also of the first poem which might be called 'Chaucerian.' (Thomas Clanvowe, possibly his nephew, has been proposed for authorship as well, but the early fifteenth-century dating by Furnivall and Skeat based on the assumption that its title was borrowed from a work by Hoccleve seems unconvincing.)[23] Accepting the arguments of V. J. Scattergood, I would place its *terminus a quo* at about 1386, based on its imitation of *The Knight's Tale*, *The Parlement of Foules*, and *The Legend of Good Women*, and the *terminus ad quem* at 1391, the year of his death near Constantinople.[24]

John Montagu was born in 1351, and became the one undeniable aristocrat of the group when he was elevated to the Earldom of Salisbury in 1397. An author himself, he was praised by Christine de Pisan as not only a lover of poetry but a "gracieux ditteur," and his relations with her included an arrangement to raise her son Jean in his own household.[25] His own poems were presumably written in French, appropriately reflecting the fact that the King and the aristocracy of the court (as opposed to most of the Chamber knights and the remaining members of Chaucer's immediate circle) were almost undoubtedly speakers of French in preference to English, rather than the reverse.[26] All his poems are now

[20] *Oeuvres*, ed. Le Marquis de Saint-Hilaire and G. Raynaud, SATF, II, 138–39; D. S. Brewer, ed., *Chaucer: The Critical Heritage*, (London: Routledge & Kegan Paul, 1978), I, 39–42.

[21] I, 341–42.

[22] McFarlane, p. 190.

[23] *The Complete Works of Geoffrey Chaucer*, (Oxford: Clarendon, 1897), VII, lvii–lviii.

[24] "The Authorship of 'The Boke of Cupide,' " *Anglia*, 82 (1964), 137–48. On his death see Higden, *Polychronicon*, ed. J. K. Lumby, Rolls Series, 9 (1886), p. 34.

[25] *Lavision-Christine*, ed. Sr. Mary Louis Towner (Washington: Catholic UP, 1932), p. 165.

[26] See above, n. 14.

lost, or at least lost in anonymity. Montagu was the one member of Chaucer's circle who may be said not to have made the transition to Henry's reign at all; at liberty through Henry's general policy of amnesty toward Richard's former dukes, Montagu lost his head as a result of his participation in the abortive uprising of January, 1400[27]—an event bitterly reported by Christine.

Clifford's son-in-law Philip de la Vache was the dedicatee of Chaucer's short poem of consolation "Truth," in which a certain warmth and a pun on the name Vache relieve the stern Boethian message. Vache was born in 1346, was a Chamber knight by 1374, and was active in Richard's service; the poem may have been written in response to reversals he suffered during Richard's eclipse, 1386–89.[28] While the summit of his career was probably his elevation to Garter knight in 1399 (following Clifford in 1398), he appears not to have suffered unduly by Henry's seizure of the crown. Rickert notes that "During the first part of Henry's reign, he seems to have been in active service, though there is no sign of any very close connection with the Court" (p. 220). He was exempted from formal duties, entering into a life of retirement in 1403, and died in 1408.

Henry Scogan, a Norfolk squire born about 1361, was (along with Bukton and Vache) addressed in one of the short balades which are so valuable for giving us a glimpse of the intimate and playfully serious manner in which Chaucer addressed his familiars. At any rate, Scogan was certainly closer to Chaucer's station than the Chamber knights— though even he was somewhat better situated than Chaucer, as suggested by Chaucer's Envoy in which Scogan is seen as kneeling "at the stremes hed," while Chaucer waits downstream. Also a poet of sorts, Scogan wrote a gravely serious "Moral Balade," apparently addressed to the sons of Henry IV and quoting Chaucer's "Gentilesse," three times identifying him as his 'mayster' in terms presumably less conventional than such epithets usually are.[29] The tradition has grown up, apparently

[27] E. F. Jacob, *The Fifteenth Century: 1399–1485* (Oxford: Clarendon, 1961), p. 25.

[28] Edith Rickert, "Thou Vache," *MP*, 11 (1913–14), 209–25.

[29] The tradition that the balade is addressed to the sons of Henry IV is based on manuscript headnotes, of the sort provided by Shirley in Ashmole 59: "Here folowethe nexst a moral balade to my lord the Prince, to my lord of Clarence / to my lord of Bedford and to my lord of Gloucestre . . . ," in *Chaucer According to William Caxton*, ed. Beverly Boyd (Lawrence, Kansas: Allen, 1978), p. xi. Since this headnote is confirmed by the opening lines of the text, we might choose to believe the usually unreliable Shirley.

from Scogan's reference to "My noble sones, and eek my lordes dere," that he was the tutor of Henry's sons, though no definitive evidence in such forms as issue rolls seems to exist.[30] Whatever our final conclusion on this point, he certainly seems to have flourished in the period between the accession of Henry and his death in 1407.

The debate has continued as to whether the Bukton who received Chaucer's good-humored balade on "the sorwe and wo that is in mariage" and who evidently knew other works including *The Wife of Bath's Prologue* was Sir Peter Bukton of York (1350–1414) or Sir Robert of Suffolk (d. 1408).[31] The points at dispute are admirably summarized by Robinson in his edition of Chaucer (p. 864), but need not be settled here. For this present purpose of determining the situation of Chaucer's audience around and after 1400, we might note only that each continued to flourish into the early years of the new century—though Sir Peter was more about the Court during Henry IV's reign than Sir Robert, most of whose activities centered in Suffolk.

Uncertainty likewise prevails as to whether Chaucer's "philosophical Strode" from the Envoy to *Troilus* was the Oxford philosopher (a fellow of Merton College before 1360 who took part in controversy with Wyclif), or the successful London lawyer who was sergeant of the City of London 1375–85 and who died in 1387, and whether these were in fact the same person. Ernest Kuhl has argued that they were, pointing out that Wyclif was associated in business dealings with the London lawyer, and that "Ralph Strode of Oxford disappears when a Ralph Strode of London appears on the records."[32] I am more inclined to agree with T. F. Tout, who points out that "if the one Ralph Strode did all these things he was a very remarkable man."[33] My own suspicion is that the two were separate, and that Chaucer's relations were with the London lawyer who was his associate in the Brembre faction.[34] Why then "philosophical Strode"? The answer to this question may reside in the characteristically wry tone of Chaucer's envoys and dedications. Occurring at the point of

[30] See Skeat, *Works*, VII, xlii and 237–44. G. L. Kittredge cautiously witholds comment on this tradition in "Henry Scogan," [Harvard] *Studies and Notes in Philology and Literature*, 1 (1892), 109–17.

[31] See E. P. Kuhl, "Chaucer's Maistre Bukton," *PMLA*, 38 (1923), 115–31; James Hulbert, *Chaucer's Official Life* (1912; rpt. New York: Phaeton, 1970), pp. 75–76.

[32] "Some Friends of Chaucer," *PMLA*, 29 (1914), 273.

[33] "Literature and Learning," p. 388.

[34] "Some Friends of Chaucer," p. 274.

Chaucer's tonally-mixed withdrawal from his own poem, the dedication to "moral Gower" and "philosophical Strode" might well involve affectionate play. (Certainly, as Alfred David has pointed out to me in conversation, the reference to "moral Gower" may be consistent with his light twitting of Gower in the Prologue to *The Man of Law's Tale*.) Perhaps the reference to "philosophical Strode" is therefore intended in a spirit of partial jest to associate his lawyer-acquaintance with the famous academic namesake. Whatever conclusion one draws, however, again has limited applicability to the subject at hand; the lawyer's death in 1387 puts him out of the picture before the end of the century, and the Oxford philosopher (if separate) is unlikely to have lived much longer than that.

"Moral Gower" and Chaucer may or may not have quarreled, as an earlier generation of critics supposed, but they certainly interacted. John Fisher has well shown the influence of Gower on the scope and moral themes of *The Canterbury Tales*,[35] and Alfred David has described the ultimately friendly tonalities running through Chaucer's dissection of Gower's more genteel poetical standards.[36] The slightly competitive currents running through Gower's admonition to Chaucer at the end of the 1392–93 version of the *Confessio* and Chaucer's attribution to the Man of Law of mock dismay at the "unkynde abhomynacions" inherent in subjects treated by Gower are not exactly friendly in the easy vein of Chaucer's poems to Scogan and Bukton, but they certainly argue for an important literary association in the 1380's and 1390's. Of course, Gower was some ten years older than Chaucer,[37] and—with the exception of some revisions to the *Confessio* and some overtly Lancastrian political poems at the end of the century—had finished the most active segment of his literary career by 1390, when he was about 60 years of age. Although he outlived Chaucer by some eight years, these were not eight years of literary activity, or years in which he would have been likely to attract a discipleship. Although Gower had laid a foundation for Lancastrian favor in his 1392–93 revision of the *Confessio* and in the *Cronica* and other poems at the end of the century, by 1400 his literary career was through.

[35] *John Gower: Moral Philosopher and Friend of Chaucer* (New York: New York UP, 1964), pp. 204–302, esp. 301.
[36] *The Strumpet Muse*, p. 125.
[37] Fisher, p. 59.

While more closely aligned with the country gentry than with the court, and hence not exactly of Chaucer's immediate milieu, Gower did share Chaucer's rank of *esquire* and the two may be thought approximate social equals. If one accepts a 'tiered' conception of Chaucer's public, with gentlemen at one extreme and clerks at the other, then both Gower and Chaucer might have fallen fairly near the social middle—though in the final analysis each was more gentleman than clerk. In a lower tier of those who were clerks first and hardly gentlemen at all were Chaucer's disciples and fellow writers Usk and Hoccleve. While each was employed about or by the court, neither was as securely situated as was Chaucer himself. As with Chaucer, neither was primarily a writer; Usk was deeply and rather shadily involved in London faction-politics in the 1380's and Hoccleve was a clerk of Privy Seal from 1387–88 until 1427. Yet each, to a more considerable extent than Chaucer, sought security or advancement from his writing. Writing of Usk in the *DNB*, Henry Bradley notes that "a florid eulogy of 'Troilus and Creseide' is introduced in an awkward manner which suggests that it was written for a special purpose,"[38] and this aura of special purpose clings to the productions of both. Usk's *Testament* did him no good, and he was beheaded in 1388; Hoccleve, nearly two generations younger, may have enjoyed some modest patronage as a result of his writing, but he seems never to have known ease between his birth around 1370 and his death sometime in the 1440's.[39] Each claimed to have been a follower of Chaucer, and Hoccleve claimed to be a friend. While claims of special intimacy may have sprung only from a desire for legitimation,[40] each was nevertheless much influenced by the example of Chaucer's poetry, and Usk in the 1380's and Hoccleve thereafter may be thought to typify one element of Chaucer's literary circle.

Despite the necessary brevity of this survey, it illustrates the instability of any literary 'circle' or 'primary public.' Few members of Chaucer's circle outlived him, and fewer still continued to be active after his death. Sturry was dead by 1395; Clifford was inactive after 1400; Clanvowe died in 1391; Montagu was beheaded in 1400; Vache was inactive after

[38] *DNB*, XX, 61.

[39] *DNB*, V, 950–51.

[40] Jerome Mitchell, "Hoccleve's Supposed Friendship with Chaucer," *ELN*, 4 (1966–67), 9–12.

14

1403; Scogan wrote his "Moral Balade" during the reign of Henry IV, but died in 1407; neither Strode is likely to have lived beyond 1387; Gower was inactive after 1400; Usk died in 1388; Hoccleve alone carried on in vigorous fashion after the first decade of the fifteenth century.

The reader might suspect that I am on the brink of the unexceptional observation that one's friends and associates die, many around the time of one's death and all sooner or later. Certainly, the impact of retirement and death on Chaucer's immediate circle is similar to that which we would expect in the case of any writer. But the crucial question is not whether Chaucer's immediate public changed composition in the way that any public must, but whether it or some similarly-composed public *survived at all* into the early years of the fifteenth century. The distinction I am drawing here is between a public which renews itself through reasonable turnover in its membership, and a public which ceases to exist. Available evidence suggests that Chaucer's public did indeed fail to renew itself, and that by the early years of the fifteenth century it had ceased to exist as a public likely or able to provide a setting encouraging to the creation of literary works. The end of the active careers of Chaucer's associates signals also the end of a particular literary milieu.

While the Lancastrian supplantation of Richard II did not eliminate Chaucer's circle overnight, it did create new circumstances which threatened the maintenance of such a circle. Even though Henry IV adopted a policy unusual in its clemency toward former followers of Richard,[41] the years between 1399 and 1408 were nevertheless marked by an unusual number of requests for exemptions from duties of state, and (as Edith Rickert has pointed out) these exemptions include many names of Richard's courtiers.[42] Presumably the high rate of such retirements was assured after the abortive rebellion of the former dukes in which Montagu perished in 1400, but other aspects of Lancastrian rule also assured the supplantation of Richard's followers. As E. F. Jacob has indicated (p.439), the Lancastrians were always a virtual "pauper government" with respect to funds, and poverty undoubtedly contributed to Henry IV's reliance on his own duchy servants for administrative assistance (pp. 30–31). Just as his administrative support tended to

[41] Jacob, *The Fifteenth Century*, pp. 24–25. Page numbers for references to this work throughout the paragraph are given in parentheses in the text.
[42] "Thou Vache," p. 13.

15

come less from the court than his own duchy, so did his counselors tend to come more from the ranks of the nobility of the kingdom than from a palace entourage; Jacob comments (p. 6) that the policy of the nobility in the early years of Henry's reign was "to get the king out of the hands of a courtier or palace entourage, to emphasize his dependence on a ministerial nobility." Reinvolvement of the nobility—as well as the prolonged absences of Henry V in France and the long minority of Henry VI—led to the increasing importance of the continual council of magnates as the true governing authority of the country (pp. 426–36). While the mechanism of a council headed by the king or a lieutenant or a protector turned out to be reasonably efficient, it did not really constitute or encourage a court in any way similar to that of Richard II. A minor aspect of this shift of the institutions of governance away from the court—but a major one for understanding the disappearance of anything resembling a 'Chaucer circle' in the fifteenth century—is the eclipse of the Chamber. According to Tout, even Richard had not sought to use his Chamber knights for autocratic purposes, and from the end of his reign until the establishment of the Tudor monarchy the Chamber was of limited importance in the government of the realm.[43] Thus, throughout most of the fifteenth century, the institution that had been more central than any other in drawing together a group of persons sympathetic to Chaucer's poetry virtually ceased to be.

The breakup of Chaucer's circle undermined the possibility of familiar poetry of the sort that Chaucer wrote for his circle. Whether the familiarity is explicit, as in the good-humored epistles to Scogan and Bukton,[44] or implicit, as in the created voice in which he addresses the audience of the *Tales*, Chaucer normally wrote within a secure sense of an audience of social equals and near-equals who—despite occasional unease with the bolder of his stylistic experiments—constituted a sympathetic and receptive group. Only rarely, as in "Complaint to his Purse" and some of the longer works possibly directed to royalty or aristocracy such as *The Book of the Duchess*, *The Legend of Good Women*, and *Melibee*, can he be said to have written for a 'special purpose.' But, if Chaucer wrote for a generally sympathetic circle, his most immediate

[43] *Chapters in the Administrative History of Mediaeval England*, (Manchester: Manchester UP, 1928), IV, 341–43.

[44] David, p. 122. See also P. M. Kean, "Love Vision and Debate," in *Chaucer and the Making of English Poetry* (London: Routledge & Kegan Paul, 1972), pp. 33–38.

continuators give us the impression of writing from the outside, look-ing in. If Chaucer addressed his clear superiors only occasionally and obliquely, poets of the first decade of the fifteenth century like Henry Scogan and—especially—Hoccleve and Lydgate seem to address them constantly and explicitly. For, as Derek Brewer comments of Hoccleve and Lydgate, "they were merely on the fringes of that courtly centre of power and prestige of which Chaucer was a full member."[45] With Hoccleve's constant quest for security and Lydgate's attempt to become, in effect, England's first professional poet,[46] each seems constantly to write with 'special purpose.' Occasionally, such purposes were a spur to ingenuity, as in Hoccleve's confessional "Male Regle" (in which repen-tant self-disclosure is mobilized as an argument for payment of his annuity, to cure both body and purse) and his arresting "Complaint" (which candidly addresses the subject of his mental illness, in part with the motive of underscoring his return to good health and full capacity). More often, though, writing in the explicit hope of preferment or for noble patrons had the effect of flattening tone and discouraging experi-ment, as in Lydgate's lengthy commissioned translations and composi-tions for Henry V, Humphrey Duke of Gloucester, the Earl of Salisbury, and others.

No one would argue that Hoccleve or Lydgate, however 'encouraged' by a sympathetic literary circle, could have equalled the range and stylistic variety of Chaucer's later poetry. Even if something very close to Chaucer's own circle had continued to exist, it would presumably not have been open to Hoccleve or Lydgate in the particular sense in which it had been to Chaucer, with all his points of professional and social entry to the court. Yet one can still imagine certain benefits to the poetry of Hoccleve or Lydgate if either had been able to find a sympathetic circle. If Hoccleve had chosen to write for his "fellows of the prive seale"[47] or if Lydgate had identified a congenial audience among monks at Bury and

---

[45] "Images of Chaucer 1386–1900," in *Chaucer and Chaucerians* (London: Nelson, 1966), p. 245. Chaucer was not, of course, a 'full' member in the sense of ranking with the King's council of magnates, or other nobles, or even the knights of the household and Chamber; he was, nevertheless, in the household and on easy terms with many of its more distinguished members (not to mention his relation through marriage to John of Gaunt) in a sense which definitely sets him apart from Hoccleve and Lydgate.

[46] Green, p. 211; Pearsall, p. 215.

[47] *The Minor Poems*, in *Works*, ed. F. J. Furnivall, EETS, ES 61 (London, 1892), I, p. 106, l. 296.

clerics at Oxford, their poetry might not have become more 'Chaucerian,' but it would have benefited from some of the confident familiarity of Chaucer's tone.

II. The Broadening of Chaucer's Fifteenth-Century Audience and the Narrowing of his Tradition

The successful author of any century must experience (and endure) the transition from a 'primary' or intended public to a larger, 'secondary' audience which receives and enjoys the author's works in circumstances over which he or she has little control. This transition was, of course, underscored in the case of the later medieval author, who had some first-hand contact with a primary public (whether through oral performance or through loaned or presentation manuscripts) and for whom the wider distribution of works in manuscript form must have been a disjunction indeed. It was further underscored in Chaucer's own case, because of the rapid dissolution around 1400 of his immediate circle, which effectively ceased to be available either as a 'point of attachment' for new work in his manner, or as a continuing locus of his own fifteenth-century readership. Chaucer's works had undoubtedly begun to find their way to an enlarged secondary audience during the last years of his life, but this natural process was abruptly and inevitably accelerated by his death, the dispersion of his primary audience, and the formation of an altered public for literature in the early years of the fifteenth century. The members of Chaucer's secondary audience were at once more widely distributed geographically and more disparate socially than Chaucer's primary audience, and more narrow in their taste for particular facets of Chaucer's poetic achievement. The narrowing of their attraction to particular facets of the Chaucer legacy is (as critics have frequently observed) evidenced both in the kinds of 'Chaucerian' poetry they encouraged and in the elements of Chaucer's own corpus which they apparently enjoyed. Paradoxically, for all their increased geographical and social latitude, the members of this new audience seem to have inclined strongly toward works which they perceived in some usually nebulous sense as 'courtly' or 'of the court.'

While the 'courtly' style of life was obviously something of a fiction in the first decades of the fifteenth century, it by no means ceased altogether. Actually, it was radically decentralized, into the households of the brothers of Henry V, of Queen Margaret, and of magnates such as the Duke of Suffolk. Much of the original poetry written in the period certainly seems courtly in its points of reference, to the extent that it strikes the reader as coterie verse, written for a very small court circle or cluster of court circles—though it remains oddly lacking in evidence of any particular milieu.[48] Robbins, who has spent considerable time reviewing the original poetry of the period, characterizes the court verse of the fifteenth century as comprising two or three hundred short lyrics structured on the lover's salutation or complaint, together with a cluster of longer love poems extending these devices, all composed "for intellectual and social diversion and amorous dalliance among a miniscule elite group."[49] The presumption that such poems were directed at such a group is fortified by the character of the 'Chaucerian' poetry written soon after his death: for example, Hoccleve's "Letter of Cupid" (1402) is directed at a court audience which is figured by the "gentil kinrede" of subject-lovers which he addresses, and Scogan's "Moral Balade" (1406–07) is addressed to the sons of Henry IV. The fact that such noble *ditteurs* as Charles d'Orleans and the Duke of Suffolk were active participants in the perpetuation of this tradition of love-poetry (admixed with small doses of morality and advice to princes) further supports the notion that such verse was composed for and by a very restricted social coterie.

Still, while verse embodying courtly views may have been produced within a coterie, the audience for such verse ultimately extended well beyond such boundaries. Even R. F. Green, who has recently presented an extremely vigorous argument for the courtly locus of production and enjoyment of fifteenth-century poetry, is prepared to concede a merchant-class element within the apparently courtly audience—with the proviso that the taste of the middle-class segment was indistinguishable from that of other, socially-superior members.[50] The most useful conceptualization of the situation which I have encountered is that of Derek Pearsall, who distinguishes between 'court poetry' produced in and for a court environment and 'courtly poetry' reflecting its values but disseminated among an enlarged public."[51] Even though productions of court or

---

[48] Pearsall, p. 218.

[49] "The Structure of Longer Middle English Court Poems," *Chaucerian Problems and Perspectives* (Notre Dame: Notre Dame UP, 1979), p. 245.

[50] *Poets and Princepleasers*, p. 10.

[51] *Old English and Middle English Poetry*, pp. 212–13.

courtly households were undoubtedly seized upon for dissemination, the ultimate audience of 'Chaucerian' poetry in the fifteenth century was undoubtedly 'courtly' in Pearsall's sense rather than strictly 'of the court.' Such an expanded audience is apparently envisioned by John Shirley, who aimed the mid-fifteenth century manuscript compilations of his scriptorium at a general audience of "bothe the gret and the commune" (i.e., the 'commonality' or middle class), and who—while mentioning the nobility in his prefaces—seems to have been well aware of the potential market opening for him in the emerging middle-class reading public.[52]

When this enlarged, socially-mixed audience encountered Chaucer, its affection or nostalgia for the courtly style apparently limited its attraction to many aspects of his work. With Muscatine, I view the essence of Chaucer's mature poetic achievement as a poetic style which "has within it an extraordinary variety, which derives from the great range of Chaucer's themes and the way in which his style supports or expresses them."[53] Certainly, early fifteenth-century writers were not unaware of the breadth of his stylistic and thematic range. While Lydgate and others most typically praise him as a "noble rethor," Lydgate was also capable of describing the range of *The Canterbury Tales* in this fashion:

> Some of desport / some of moralite
> Some of knyghthode / love and gentillesse,
> And some also of parfit holynesse,
> And some also in soth / of Ribaudye. . . . [54]

Yet in point of fact, the range of possible *endytings* described by Lydgate was narrowed in the practice of professed fifteenth-century Chaucerians to some "moralite" (in the form of advice to princes), some "holynesse" (in the form of saints' lives and related genres), and a considerable amount of "knyghthode / loue and gentillesse." "Desport"—let alone

[52] Otto Gaertner, *John Shirley: Sein Leben und Wirken* (Halle: Von Ehrhardt Karras, 1904), p. 63. This view of Shirley has been questioned by Green, who believes him to have been an 'amateur scribe' who produced his manuscripts for "noblemen and courtiers" (*Poets and Princepleasers*, pp. 130–33).

[53] "The *Canterbury Tales*: style of the man and style of the work," in *Chaucer and Chaucerians*, p. 88.

[54] *Siege of Thebes*, ed. Axel Erdmann, EETS, ES 108, Pt. 1 (London, 1911), ll. 22–25.

"ribaudye"—was out the window, and only a very narrow segment of Chaucer's literary heritage was claimed by those to whom he had bequeathed it.[55]

I will not repeat Robbins' and Green's previously-cited characterizations of the conservatism of mid-fifteenth century 'courtly' literature, with its stress on traditional themes and its emphasis on those genres treating *fin amour*, advice to princes, and morality. I might note, however, that a further indication of the conservatism of the audience for courtly literature is the relatively small number of new pieces which actually found their way into circulation. One notices in the Shirlean compilations, for example, how little of his material was recent or written especially for his audience. His assurances to his readers run in the opposite direction, emphasizing virtuous material:

> As wryten haue thees olde clerkis
> That been appreuede in alle hir werkis
> By oure eldres here to fore. . . . [56]

All medieval writers agree that poetry is intended to foster memory of past achievements, but Shirley appears to accept this commonplace in a particularly literal and restrictive sense. The backward-looking quality of Shirley's selections is apparent in all of his manuscripts, such as MS. Addit. 16165 which includes the following works: Chaucer's translation of *Boethius*; a translation of Trevisa's *Nichodemus*; Edward Duke of York's hunting treatise *Master of Game*; a prose *Regula sacerdotis*; Lydgate's *Complaint of the Black Knight*; and "other balades" including Lydgate's *Dream of a Lover*, Chaucer's *Anelida and Arcite* in two parts, Lydgate's *Invocation to St. Anne* and *Departing of Thomas Chaucer* and other short poems. (Closest to contemporaneity on this list is Lydgate, who may have survived as a very old man when the manuscript was compiled. But

---

[55] To be sure, *The Siege of Thebes* announces itself as an additional Canterbury tale, with teller Lydgate cast as a pilgrim on a lean palfrey with a rusty bridle, and the early fifteenth-century *Tale of Beryn* (ed. F. J. Furnivall and W. G. Stone, EETS, ES 105 [London, 1887]) is preceded by a prologue describing certain japes of the pilgrims at Canterbury. The romance which each introduces is not, however, particularly 'Chaucerian' in execution, except for the rather dim sense in which the *Siege of Thebes* may be taken as a deliberate rivalling of Chaucer's *Knight's Tale*.

[56] Gaertner, pp. 21–22; Brusendorff, pp. 207–36, 453–56.

Lydgate was recognized by his contemporaries as a writer in traditional modes, and his major achievements were by this point far behind him.)

Attention to little known works like *Anelida and Arcite* might seem strange, but it is part of a pattern which emerges as we look at the range of Chaucer's pieces in existing Shirlean compilations: *Anelida* is included three times, along with the *Complaint of Mars*, the *Complaint of Venus*, the *Complaint unto Pity, Fortune, Truth, Gentilesse*, and the *Complaint of Chaucer to his Purse*. Needless to say, Shirley shows no desire in such selections to challenge his audience of "all thoo that beon gentile of birthe or of condicions,"[57] but rather to assist their aspirations, to lead them in a reassuring way to an already-existing world of taste and gentility which they seek but have not previously known.

The narrowing of the Chaucer tradition reflected in the short poems chosen for fifteenth-century circulation seems at first to be contradicted by the relatively large number of surviving manuscripts of the complete or nearly-complete *Canterbury Tales*.[58] The existence of some sixty of these manuscripts would seem to indicate at least some continued capacity for enjoyment of the full range of his achievement throughout the century. These manuscripts seem, as well, to have reached a broader social range of readers than ever heard or read his poetry during his lifetime. Yet an examination of the fifteenth-century manuscript tradition of *The Canterbury Tales* raises as much doubt as encouragement about the nature of their reception in the fifteenth century.

The dispersion of Chaucer's late fourteenth-century literary circle is reflected in patterns of manuscript ownership. While no single group or locale can be identified through the evidence of early manuscripts, the six reasonably complete surviving manuscripts of the *Tales* probably written before 1420 all seem to have been owned by persons with social positions more or less similar to those of Chaucer's original circle. Evidence gathered by Manly and Rickert connects El with the Duke of Exeter or the Duke of Bedford (and Hg with the Ellesmere scribe), Ha[4] with a "person of importance who had it made in a shop," Cp and La with the Burley family, and Dd with the Hungerford family, whose mem-

---

[57] William McCormick, *The Manuscripts of Chaucer's Canterbury Tales* (Oxford: Clarendon, 1933), p. 200.

[58] See Daniel S. Silvia, "Some Fifteenth-Century Manuscripts of the *Canterbury Tales*," in *Chaucer and Middle English Studies in Honor of Rossell Hope Robbins*, ed. Beryl Rowland (London: George Allen & Unwin, 1974), pp. 153–61.

bership included the Lord Treasurer Walter Hungerford (d. 1449).[59]
Thereafter, the spread of manuscript ownership through additional
strata of society was rapid. In the second half of the century, owners
range from Richard III (then Duke of Gloucester) through a variety of
merchants, auditors, and clerks. This broadening-out in the direction of
the urban middle classes is most visible in fifteenth-century wills, of
which the first two instances are a bequest of the *Tales* from Richard
Sotheworth to John Stopyndon (both clerks in Chancery) and from John
Frinchele to William Holgrave (both citizens and tailors of London).[60]

Lydgate imagined in his *Troy Book* that adept readers of *Troilus* (who
"konnyng hath his tracis for to swe") might turn up "in borwe or toun,
village or cite."[61] While his is an undoubtedly sentimentalized view, the
fact that fifteenth-century manuscripts of the *Tales* received wide social
and geographical circulation might be taken as evidence of heightened
receptivity on the part of enlightened individuals. Other evidence suggests, though, that the *Tales* were preserved reasonably intact more out
of respect for Chaucer's secure reputation as a founder and upholder of
the institution of English letters, than because the full range of his
literary achievement was necessarily enjoyed. Certainly, all modern
readers are struck by the traditionalism inherent in fifteenth-century
judgments of Chaucer as translator, compiler, rhetorician, and refiner of
the language, and Shirley further develops this view in his headnote for
the mid-century MS. Harley 7333 of the *Tales*, in which he presents
them as "stories of olde tymis passed . . . wiche beon compilid . . . by the
laureal and moste famous poete that euer was to fore him as in themvel-
isshing of oure rude moders englisshe tonge."[62] Of course, the real
question is how individual readers would have responded to individual
tales, or to the mix of tales, and here extremely limited evidence requires
the most cautious evaluation. Only one fifteenth-century reader—Jean
of Angoulême—has actually left traces of his experience, in the form of
comments written in the Paris MS. fonds anglais 39 of the Bibliothèque
Nationale, which was written under his direction. In a separate discussion, I have suggested that his tastes were quite traditional, including a

[59] John M. Manly and Edith Rickert, *The Text of the Canterbury Tales*, Vol. I
(Chicago: U of Chicago P, 1940).
[60] Manly–Rickert, I, 529–31.
[61] Ed. Henry Bergen, Pt. 3, EETS, ES 106 (London, 1910), l. 3532.
[62] McCormick, p. 200.

strong endorsement of *The Knight's Tale* as "valde bona" (presumably for its use of familiar materials and balancing of *solace* and *sentence*) and rejection as "valde absurda" of the more experimental *Squire's Tale* and *Canon's Yeoman's Tale*, as well as other tales more lopsided in the direction either of *solace* or *sentence*.[63] Fortunately, more particular evidence of the taste both of Chaucer's immediate fourteenth-century circle and his enlarged fifteenth-century public has been developed by Charles A. Owen, Jr. and by Daniel S. Silvia.[64]

Basing his conclusions on the number of independent textual traditions of individual tales existing at the time of Chaucer's death or soon after, Owen has gauged the relative popularity of different tales. Allowing for such factors as probable date of completion (with the earlier tales having more possibility of independent circulation), he finds that the most popular tales among Chaucer's contemporaries were *The Franklin's Tale, Prioress' Tale, Pardoner's Tale, Shipman's Tale, Canon's Yeoman's Tale,* and *Miller's Tale*. On the other hand, tales with few independent textual traditions, indicating that they circulated mainly within collections, include *The Man of Law's Tale, Friar's Tale, Summoner's Tale, Melibeus, Squire's Tale, Clerk's Tale, Second Nun's Tale, Monk's Tale, Manciple's Tale,* and *Parson's Tale*. These findings are in sharp contrast to the evidence of fifteenth-century popularity which Owen and more recently Silvia derive from fifteenth-century 'anthologies' of free-standing tales. The most frequent appearances in the course of the fifteenth century belong to *The Clerk's Tale* (6), *Prioress' Tale* (5), and *Melibeus* (5), together with *The Second Nun's Tale* (2), *Monk's Tale* (2), and *Parson's Tale* (2). *The Franklin's Tale* appears only once and *The Pardoner's Tale, Shipman's Tale, Canon's Yeoman's Tale,* and *Miller's Tale* not at all. In his fuller analysis of this fifteenth-century phenomenon, Silvia points out that all the anthologized pieces belong to one of two traditions,

[63] "Jean of Angoulême: A Fifteenth-Century Reader of Chaucer," *NM*, 72 (1971), 69–76.

[64] Owen, "The *Canterbury Tales*: Early Manuscripts and Relative Popularity," *JEGP*, 54 (1955), 104–10; Silvia, "Some Fifteenth-Century Manuscripts," pp. 153–61. Debate continues over the authority of the textual traditions which Owen uses to determine the early popularity of the respective tales, with some holding that the proliferation of some textual traditions is less a result of authorial intervention than of scribal activity after Chaucer's death. Authority aside, however, the number of textual traditions of a tale would still seem to be a sound indicator of its popularity either before, at the time of, or soon after Chaucer's death.

24

which he labels 'courtly' and 'moral' (p. 155). Certainly, a massive shift in taste has occurred, from tales which tend to the generically and thematically problematic to tales which support traditional assumptions both in their firm delineation of genre and in their theme.

Opposing the tales of the Franklin, Pardoner, Shipman, Canon's Yeoman, and Miller to those of the Clerk, Monk, Second Nun, and Parson, and to *Melibee*, one immediately notices several distinctions between the two clusters.

Granting that Chaucer always adjusts his sources in one way or another and is never content merely to translate or adapt, one may still divide his tales according to the relative independence with which he structures them. By this standard, his most 'original' tales would be those of the Squire (even though written in the exotic traditions of *Floris and Blancheflour* and other popular narratives), the Franklin (for all its pretense of following the form of the Breton lay), and the Canon's Yeoman, and perhaps those of the Miller (with its elaboration of the French *fabliau* tradition and its possible new fusion of two pre-existing plots), the Merchant, and Chaucer's own *Sir Thopas* (which, as generalized parody, follows no one analogue). By the same standard, Chaucer's least independent tales would include, in addition to *Melibeus*, those of the Knight, Man of Law, Clerk, Physician, Prioress, Monk, Second Nun, Manciple, and Parson (though, as in *The Miller's Tale*, Chaucer may have fused two free-standing sources in this latter treatise). The point of this distinction is not, of course, to praise or blame Chaucer according to some anachronistic standard of 'originality,' since in *The Knight's Tale* and elsewhere his perspective on very authoritative material is fully original. The point is to say something about the audience's own previous familiarity with the materials of the tales popular in the two centuries. The tales most circulated in the fourteenth century—including those of the Franklin, Canon's Yeoman, and Miller—would have been among Chaucer's most independent, and would have possessed an effect of 'first encounter,' with all the charged excitement which accompanies such an experience. The tales most anthologized in the fifteenth century—including those of the Clerk, Monk, Second Nun, and Parson, as well as *Melibee*—were established in numerous versions, and would have provided the relatively more comfortable experience which accompanies a re-encounter with generally familiar materials.

A parallel observation may be made of the generic boundaries of the tales popular in the respective centuries. Those tales popular in the fourteenth century tend toward deliberate frustration of generic expectations. *The Franklin's Tale* puts more responsibility on its audience than the lays which it purports to follow, including such open-ended questions as, "which was the mooste fre . . . ?" (V, 1620). *The Pardoner's Tale* is contained within a frame which renders its impact deliberately equivocal. *The Shipman's Tale* has a hard satiric edge, less prominent in its analogues, in its insistence on the commercialization of human relations. The list could be extended, but the point is clear; each of these tales pushes against its audience's generic expectations in ways which (depending on the reader) have the potential to stimulate, to challenge, to annoy. The tales popular in the fifteenth century tend, on the other hand, to be among the most generically stable that Chaucer wrote. *The Clerk's Tale* is perhaps more an extended exemplum or simply a 'moral narrative' than the *historia/hystoire* which it is styled in its continental sources, but as an internationally-known tale with an interpreter/narrator who frequently intervenes to help his audience over the rough spots, it would have occasioned no particular interpretive unease for its audience. *Melibee* was likewise an international success when Chaucer took it in hand, and even an audience encountering it for the first time would have found it familiar as a book of good counsel, leavened with certain allegorical/spiritual undertones. The patterning of the tragedies in *The Monk's Tale* is, of course, so predictable that it provokes a revolt in the pilgrim audience. *The Second Nun's Tale* is a mainstream "lif and passioun" of St. Cecilia, following the dictates of the hagiographical genre and rehearsing one of the best-known stories of all. While somewhat more crowded with different kinds of content than the average vernacular sermon, *The Parson's Tale* would still have struck its audience as a coherently-formed 'treatise.' In short, the works popular in the fifteenth century fulfill rather than deny the general horizon of generic expectations with which their audience would have approached them, or which they evoke in their own opening lines.

The scope of this article hardly permits an adequate analysis of the content of these ten tales, but some generalizations seem possible. The tales popular in the fourteenth century all offer alternatives to social hierarchies, sworn oaths, established bonds. Of course, Chaucer's perspective differs considerably from tale to tale. *The Franklin's Tale* is essentially idealized, as *gentillesse* dissolves both the domination/submission inherent in marriage and the formal obligation of the unintended oath. *The Miller's Tale* is comic, with sexual desire acting as a triumphant leveller. In the more critical and satiric *Pardoner's Tale, Shipman's Tale,* and *Canon's Yeoman's Tale,* financial greed overthrows ties of friendship and hospitality and the natural hierarchy of intellect. The tales popular in the fifteenth century tend instead to reaffirm *obeisance* and subordination to the authority of lord and husband (*The Clerk's Tale*) or to Fortune (*The Monk's Tale*) or to God (*The Second Nun's Tale*) or to the domination of one's own reason over unruly impulse (*Melibee, The Parson's Tale*).

From the evidence of these most valued tales, two different sorts of audiences would seem to be implied—the earlier prepared to be surprised by new turns of plot and ways of shaping material and challenged by interrogation of received beliefs and values, and the later drawn more to familiar materials treated within stable generic frames and to thematic reaffirmation of divine, social, and inner hierarchies. The counterinstance to this generalization would seem, however, to be *The Prioress' Tale,* which Owen reports as the second most popular in the fourteenth century and as the most popular in the fifteenth century. The popularity of this one tale with two different audiences may simply stand as a warning of the hazards of generalization, but it may also suggest that different historically and socially defined audiences can esteem a single work of art for different reasons. *The Prioress' Tale* has been controversial in the twentieth century because critics have argued for two essentially different ways in which it can be read. One group of critics has treated the tale as a critique of the Prioress' shallow values, as revealed in the contradiction between her profession of Christian love and her grisly, excessive, and very unloving anti-Semitism.[65] Another has seen it in historically relative terms, as an embodiment of prevalent values and literary conventions of Chaucer's time.[66] In the face of this apparent contradiction, I would suggest that the tale might have been read in two different ways—that Chaucer's immediate circle might have considered

---

[65] See, for example, R. J. Schoeck, "Chaucer's Prioress: Mercy and Tender Heart," in *Chaucer Criticism*, ed. Schoeck and Taylor, (Notre Dame, Notre Dame UP, 1961), I, 245–58.

[66] See, for example, Raymond Preston, "Chaucer, his Prioress, the Jews, and Professor Robinson," *N&Q*, 206 (1961), 7–8. Preston suggests that the Prioress' anti-Semitism occurs within "the frame of an old folk-tale set in a remote continent," and that her denunciations reveal a variety of "childish enthusiasm."

it a deliberate heightening of the devices of the miracle of the Virgin (with the anti-Semitism one of the devices so heightened) in order to expose the narrowness of the Prioress,[67] while his enlarged fifteenth-century audience might have accepted it as a generically stable and fully satisfying instance of such a miracle. Such a divergence would be consistent with other evidence that Chaucer's immediate circle prized his moments of independent perspective on literary tradition, while his fifteenth-century audience inclined more toward those tales which least challenge traditional forms and values.

The obviously narrowed spectrum of taste among Chaucer's fifteenth-century readers separates them both from his primary audience and from academic audiences of today. Yet, the fact that this fifteenth-century audience found works within *The Canterbury Tales* to circulate and enjoy tells us something about the source of Chaucer's continuing appeal. The perpetuation of any work beyond the immediate social context in which it was composed must always depend on its capacity to disclose new sides of itself to subsequent readerships. Seen in this light, the locus of the 'classic' or 'timeless' quality in an *oeuvre* like Chaucer's might not be its capacity to speak in a single voice to subsequent readerships, but its capacity through inner complexity of form and theme to continue revealing new and pertinent aspects of itself. The presence in *The Canterbury Tales* of works which commanded the interest of Chaucer's traditionally-inclined fifteenth-century public reflects a stylistic and thematic breadth which has enabled him to attract loyal followers in each of seven very different centuries.

That Chaucer's fifteenth-century readers sought, and were able to find, different facets of his work than those esteemed by his immediate circle seems apparent enough. The difficult task is explaining *why* this new audience should have sought different values in an established work. Such an explanation must take us outside the work itself, to the social circumstances of Chaucer's fifteenth-century readership. Having earlier expressed a preference for 'micro' explanations, I would prefer to treat the social situations of Chaucer's fifteenth-century readers as the sum of their individual careers. Limitations of space and evidence, however, will compel a more general level of consideration.

[67] I am here accepting Alfred David's "middle ground" interpretation of the impact of the tale and the character of the Prioress. See *The Strumpet Muse*, pp. 205–14.

III. Some Tentative Explanations

According to evidence of the provenance of manuscripts of *The Canterbury Tales* assembled by Manly and Rickert, the mid-fifteenth century audience for Chaucer's work consisted not only of aristocracy, but members of the landed gentry scattered throughout England and Wales, and more than a sprinkling of prosperous merchants of London and other cities.[68] No century offers a unitary experience for all classes of persons in all decades. Most English peasants, for example, modestly increased their prosperity in the course of the century. But for those members of the landed gentry and the merchant classes most likely to read Chaucer, the mid-century was a period of pessimism, hardening class lines, and decreased economic opportunity.

M. M. Postan, whose overview of the field has been corrected in particulars but retains its broad authority, sees the fifteenth century in England as "an age of recession, arrested economic development and declining national income."[69] In the cases of both merchants and gentry, he sees a new self-protectiveness, a new concern for prerogatives, and less of the apparent optimism of their fourteenth-century counterparts. As for the merchants, Postan says that they "responded to the stability and recession of trade in the way of all merchants. They adopted the policy of regulation and restriction, impeding the entry of new recruits into commerce and attempting to share out the available trade."[70] Some features of this new restrictiveness were: monopoly and protective regulation of trade, the closing of ranks by guildsmen against guild membership or control of production by journeymen laborers, and increased middle-class landlordism.[71] These steps and others led to the formation

[68] Manly–Rickert, Vol. I.

[69] "The Fifteenth Century," *The Economic History Review*, 9 (1938–39), 166. Postan's findings have been modified by more recent studies such as Harry A. Miskimin, "Monetary Movements and Market Structure—Forces for Contraction in Fourteenth- and Fifteenth-Century England, *Journal of Economic History*, 24 (1964), 470–90. Miskimin argues, for example, that the consequences of contraction affected different economic sectors differently, with the landed gentry feeling the blow earliest in the century. Postan's broad conclusions have, however, continued to be accepted.

[70] "The Fifteenth Century," p. 166.

[71] Henri Pirenne, "The Stages in the Social History of Capitalism," *American Historical Review*, 19 (1913–14), 509; Harry A. Miskimin, *The Economy of Early Renaissance Europe, 1300–1460* (Englewood Cliffs, N. J.: Prentice-Hall, 1969), pp. 110–11; R. H. Gretton, *The English Middle Class* (London: G. Bell, 1917), pp. 40, 70, 74.

in fifteenth-century English cities of what J. W. Thompson calls an "urban patriciate"—a closed class, practically a legal class, with mercantile and ultimately social and emotional ties with the old landed aristocracy.[72] For their part, the landed gentry responded to economic adversity by a rear-guard action in defense of traditional privileges. As Postan says, "in an age of dwindling agricultural profits seigneurial revenues derived from feudal rights and privileges were all the more valuable and all the more worth fighting for"—a situation which led to much of the "political gangsterism" of the time.[73]

Confronted with the political and economic vicissitudes of the fifteenth century, the urban merchant patriciate and the country gentry did their best to stay out of trouble. Postan pictures the urban merchant classes "in a state of solid conservative prosperity devoid of both the prizes and the penalties of the more adventurous and speculative ages."[74] C. L. Kingsford argues that the Pastons were an unusual case, and that the life of the country gentry is better represented in the Stonor letters, in which "there is little suggestion of anything that broke the quiet tenor of a country gentleman's life."[75] But this kind of tranquility has its price; a price which Kingsford reveals in what he intends as a reassuring account of the life of the Stonors:

> [T]he *Stonor Letters* afford us no evidence to suggest that either social disorder or civil war necessarily affected the lives of those who through their prudence or good fortune were not entangled in either. What we do get is a picture of the country gentleman busy with the management of his estates, taking his share in the work of local administration, living in friendly intercourse with neighbours in like circumstances to himself, growing rich with his profits as a sheep grazier, and spending money on the rebuilding of his house and laying out of his garden. Thomas Stonor had the wit to keep clear of politics; though on two occasions he was summoned for service by Edward IV, he apparently avoided compliance. He had friends in both political camps . . . but during the Lancastrian restoration managed to compromise himself with neither.[76]

[72] *Economic and Social History of Europe in the Later Middle Ages* (New York: Ungar, 1960), pp. 398–403; see also Pirenne, pp. 511–13.

[73] "The Fifteenth Century," p. 166.

[74] "The Fifteenth Century," p. 165.

[75] *Prejudice and Promise in Fifteenth Century England* (Oxford: Clarendon, 1925), pp. 33–34.

[76] *Prejudice and Promise*, p. 63.

Stonor's kind of prudence—together with unabashed self-interest—enabled many urban merchants and country gentry to consolidate their positions despite the hard times of the fifteenth century. It enabled some of them to own libraries and perhaps to read books. These are the people who, after all, were to form the backbone of the public for the printed book before the end of the century. But their social situation evidently disposed them to poetry in a narrower stylistic register, embodying a more restricted range of themes, than that which appealed to Chaucer's primary audience. McFarlane and Hulbert have documented the remarkable upward social mobility of Richard II's Chamber knights and of the esquires of Edward's and Richard's households,[77] and I feel comfortable in connecting the volatility of their social situations to an attraction to stylistic and thematic juxtaposition, to unresolved debate, and to the challenge of the new.[78] By the same reasoning, a readership composed of persons with a demonstrated interest in consolidating their class positions might well have inclined away from stylistic and thematic experiment. At any rate, their choices would seem to indicate a diminished capacity for all sorts of contradiction. *The Franklin's Tale*, with its implied critique of *maistrie*, was supplanted by *The Clerk's Tale*, with its uncritical endorsement of *maistrie* and subordination in all forms; the figurative and literal 'overextensions' of *The Miller's Tale*, in which requittal in all forms is the ethic shared by all, were supplanted by Prudence's plea for measured self-restraint in *Melibee*; *The Prioress' Tale* was probably, as I have already suggested, read at generic face value, in a new and less taxing way. Certainly, the themes embodied in the short tales of Chaucer most popular in the fifteenth century—of mastery and subordination, of self-mastery, of the consistency of divine and earthly law—would seem highly congenial to persons in the process of constituting themselves as members of legally-sanctioned classes. Likewise, the implied continuity inherent in a return to love-visions and other genres firmly established in fourteenth-century precedent would have had its appeal for persons more interested in maintaining than in changing their status in a troubled world.

[77] On the marriages of Richard II's Chamber knights see McFarlane, *Lancastrian Kings*, pp. 172–76; on the careers of Edward III's and Richard II's esquires see Hulbert, *Chaucer's Official Life*, pp. 17–52.
[78] "Chaucer's Audience," pp. 34–39.

IV. Conclusion

Virtually every literary historian writing in the first half of this century suggests that Chaucer 'exhausted' his tradition, or that his tradition had somehow 'exhausted itself.'[79] My own view is that artists do not exhaust traditions, nor do traditions exhaust themselves. If we suppose that Chaucer's experiments with stylistic and thematic juxtaposition were a central element of his legacy to the fifteenth century, we have no reason to suppose that the fifteenth century failed to claim them because they were used up or worn out. We can see from the richly successful experiments with stylistic juxtaposition and multi-leveled plot in fifteenth-century biblical and moral drama and in early Elizabethan tragedies like *Horestes* and *Cambyses* that the exploration of formal possibilities similar to those of Chaucer's later poetry was always subject to independent revival under new and different circumstances. Any kind of exhaustion which occurred at the beginning of the fifteenth century was not in Chaucer's poetic tradition, which remained charged with undiminished potentiality, but in the capacity of audiences to appreciate the full range of his tradition and in the capacity of new artists, working without public esteem or encouragement, to perpetuate that tradition.

Such an exhaustion, not of literary potentiality but of capacity for appreciation of Chaucer's achievement, occurred in the fifteenth century. Its immediate cause was the replacement of a closely-knit primary audience with a far-flung and disparate secondary audience. A related cause was a social situation which evidently caused the members of this secondary audience to seek different qualities in Chaucer's verse than those which had appealed to his fourteenth-century circle, and to encourage different qualities in verse written by others. This secondary audience regarded Chaucer's poetry differently not because of fatigue or capriciousness, but because of real changes in its own composition and its own world.

---

[79] See, as an example of this widely-shared tendency, Herbert Grierson and J. C. Smith, *A Critical History of English Poetry* (New York: Oxford UP, 1946), p. 43.

Pronuntiatio and its Effect
on Chaucer's Audience

Beryl Rowland
York University, Toronto

CHAUCER has four audiences: his contemporary listeners; a hypothetical group addressed as 'ye' in the poems; fictive characters who were auditors within the poem itself; and lastly, all readers of his poetry either then or since. The audience with which I am concerned is the first, composed of those men and women living elegantly and precariously at the royal court in the last decades of the fourteenth century. I shall suggest that the reaction of this audience was unique and essentially different from our own because of the way Chaucer presented his poetry.

The subject of oral delivery, which in the opinion of Bronson more than forty years ago required further exploration, is still being assayed.[1] The contention that the famous Troilus frontispiece is simply iconographic, representing "as a reality the myth of delivery that Chaucer cultivates so assiduously in the poem,"[2] using the vocabulary of art to reflect upon the poem itself,[3] may remind us of our ignorance of the nature and extent of poetic recitals, but no one denies that Chaucer once

---

[1] B. H. Bronson, "Chaucer's Art in Relation to his Audience," in *Five Studies in Literature* (Berkeley: U of California P, 1940), pp. 1–14.

[2] Derek Pearsall, "The Troilus Frontispiece and Chaucer's Audience," *YES*, 7 (1977), 68–74; see also, D. S. Brewer, " 'Troilus and Criseyde,' " in the *Sphere History of Literature in the English Language*, ed. W. F. Bolton (London: Barrie & Jenkins, 1970), I, 196; James H. McGregor, "The Iconography of Chaucer in Hoccleve's *De Regimine Principum* and in the *Troilus* Frontispiece," *ChauR*, 11 (1977), 338–50. The traditional view is expressed, among others, by Nevill Coghill, "Chaucer's narrative art in *The Canterbury Tales*," in *Chaucer and Chaucerians*, ed. D. S. Brewer (London: Nelson, 1966), pp. 135–36.

[3] M. B. Parkes and Elizabeth Salter, introd., *Troilus and Criseyde: A Facsimile of Corpus Christi College Cambridge MS. 61* (Cambridge: D. S. Brewer, 1978), pp. xv–xvii. To Elizabeth Salter the international cultural traditions reflected in the frontispiece preclude

read his poetry aloud before a select audience or that the custom of oral delivery must have influenced poetry.

Yet the critics who have written eloquently on the effect of oral delivery on such matters as style, tone, content, and structure[4] ignore the impact of Chaucer's presence on his immediate listeners. As a result, when they examine Chaucer's ironic stance and its relation to his audience, they fail to consider how the spoken word might have rendered the sophisticated and complex concept of a persona unnecessary. Writers on rhetoric claimed that *pronuntiatio* was to give the interpretation. The irony that a mask created could be achieved without it. "In irony," said St. Augustine, "we indicate by tone of voice the meaning we wish to convey, as when we say to a man who is behaving badly: 'you are doing well.' "[5] *Pronuntiatio* was, to Geoffrey of Vinsauf "totius condimentum orationis,"[6] and because of the attention paid to this fifth part of rhetoric by the rhetoricians, our considerations regarding oral delivery are likely to be incomplete unless we examine the precepts in detail and endeavor to determine the extent of their practice. The subject is unquestionably important, for if Chaucer did indeed employ the techniques described under the rubric of *pronuntiatio*, he would have eliminated many of the opportunities for an autonomous or phenomenological interpretation that we now apply. How he spoke, what kind of voice, gesture, and

---

a historical interpretation. The meeting between the two retinues is based on some version of the *Itinerary* miniatures devised by the Limbourg brothers in the early fifteenth century; the open-air recital upon a preaching group. The frontispiece anticipates Chaucer's invocation to the lovers in the Proheme; the two retinues, the occasion of Criseyde's departure from Troy. Donald Baker, rev. of M. B. Parkes and Elizabeth Salter, introd., *Troilus and Criseyde*, *SAC*, 1 (1979), 187–93, while accepting Salter's account in general terms, supports Pearsall's view that the frontispiece was intended to create the impression of a real occasion and sees the poem "mirrored, foreshadowed, and embraced in the miniature."

[4] D. S. Brewer, "The Relationship of Chaucer to the English and European Traditions," in *Chaucer and Chaucerians*, ed. D. S. Brewer (London: Nelson, 1966), pp. 1–38; A. C. Spearing, *Criticism and Medieval Poetry*, 2nd ed. (London: Arnold, 1972), pp. 18–27, has an admirable introduction on this subject. On structure he observes that the fact that it is a collocation of disparate parts does not imply lack of concern for connective meaning or absence of synthesis.

[5] *De Doctrina Christiana*, *PL* 34, col. 81. "Sed ironia pronuntiatione indicat quid velit intellegi, uti cum dicimus homini mala facienti, 'Res bonas facis.' "

[6] "Documentum de Modo et Arte Dictandi et Versificandi," in *Les Arts poétiques du XIIᵉ et du XIIIᵉ Siècle*, ed. Edmond Faral (1924; rpt. Paris: Champion, 1962), p. 318.

facial expression he used, would have profoundly affected his listeners' understanding of the poem.

Most of the writings on rhetoric in the Middle Ages, whether they are preaching manuals or handbooks on style, make some reference to oral delivery, and the practices which they cite, though modified and sometimes much abbreviated, reflect the advice given by the early rhetoricians. In particular they go back, as Geoffrey of Vinsauf did, to *Ad Herennium* or to Cicero's *De Oratore*. In *Ad Herennium* the speaker is told how to use voice, expression, and gesture in various situations. Dialogue is defined as consisting of assigning language to some person that conforms to his character, and it should be accompanied by tremendous flexibility in tone and manner of delivery. Emotions such as joy, sorrow, and anger are to be conveyed largely through facial expression, and bodily movements are to suit the tone of the address. While the writer advised a use of restraint and decorum, the gestures that a speaker might use to convey various emotions included facial expressions, walking up and down, stamping the right foot, slapping one's thigh, beating one's head, as well as using the hands.[7] Cicero stressed the artistic and psychological importance: "Imitation of manners and behavior, either given in character or not, is a considerable ornament of style, and extremely effective in calming down an audience and often also in exciting it."[8] He advised free use of the voice and even uncontrolled vociferation to amplify the effects required, and emphasized that delivery was the dominant factor in oratory. Delivery was controlled by "bodily carriage, gesture, play of features and changing intonation of voice . . . to this there should be added a certain humor, flashes of wit, the culture befitting a gentleman, and readiness and terseness alike in repelling and in delivering attack, the whole being combined with a delicate charm and urbanity."[9] Although he was concerned with judicial

---

[7] *Ad C. Herennium*, tr. Harry Caplan (1954; rpt. Cambridge, Mass.: Harvard UP, 1964), III, x – IV, lvi. See especially III, xv, 27: "Sin utemur amplificatione per conquestionem, feminis plangore et capitis ictu, nonnumquam sedato et constanti gestu, maesto et conturbato vultu uti oportebit."

[8] *De Oratore*, tr. E. W. Sutton, with introd. H. Rackham (Cambridge, Mass.: Harvard UP, 1959), III, liv, 204–05: "morum ac vitae imitatio vel in personis vel siue illis, magnum quoddam ornamentum orationis et aptum ad animos conciliandos vel maxime, saepe autem etiam ad commovendos; personarum ficta inductio, vel gravissimum lumen augendi."

[9] *De Oratore*, I, v, 17–19; "Accedat eodem oportet lepos quidam facetiaeque, et

oratory, his precepts on delivery were applicable to many kinds of address. He inveighed against the excesses of stage actors more than once, yet when he discussed the tone of voice, observing that it should be shrill and hasty to express anger, but wavering, full, and halting to express compassion and sorrow, he illustrated his points by quoting from the dramatic poets.

In the fourth and fifth centuries, the books of technical rhetoric that were subsequently much studied in the Middle Ages followed the precepts of *Ad Herennium* and the works of Cicero and Quintillian, but dealt comparatively briefly with *pronuntiatio*. The catechetical work of Chirius Fortunatianus, composed during the latter half of the fourth century, defined *pronuntiatio* as voice, countenance, and gesture. It emphasized the need for restraint and omitted *moderatio cum venustate* of the definition in *Ad Herennium*.[10] In the same century Sulpitius Victor briefly and Julius Victor more extensively repeated some of Cicero's pronouncements on *pronuntiatio* that urged moderation.[11] St. Augustine, in the fourth book of *De Doctrina Christiana*, when he set about recovering the true ancient rhetoric for the new generation of Christian orators, mentioned delivery only incidentally, but what he said was often repeated. Quoting Cicero, he declared that the man who is eloquent can say "little things in a subdued style, moderate things in a temperate style, and great things in a majestic style."[12] Here the modesty topos so widely used by writers in medieval times had its place, but the speaker also had to dominate: his overall purpose was to move and to subdue the audience by the power of eloquence. Martianus Capella, in the fifth century, had more to say concerning facial expression:

> The expression should be varied according to the weight of what one is saying; but it should not be varied according to the extent customary with

---

eruditio libero digna, celeritasque et brevitas et respondendi, et lacessendi, subtili venustate, atque urbanitate coniuncta."

[10] "Artis Rhetoricae," in *Rhetores Latini Minores*, ed. C. Halm (Leipzig: Teubner, 1863), pp. 130–34. See also Paul Abelson, *The Seven Liberal Arts* (New York: Columbia UP, 1906), p. 55.

[11] Sulpith Victor, "Institutiones Oratoriae," in Halm, p. 321; C. Iulius Victor, "Ars Rhetorica," in Halm pp. 440–43.

[12] *De Doctrina Christiana*, IV, 104.

actors, who twist their faces about in ridiculous movements for the audience. For it is meaning, and not spectacle, which delivery and expression are meant to enhance. Control of the eyes is important in this field; they move in mirth, in concentration, in an expression of threat. They ought not to be too much closed by frowning eyebrows . . . gestures should not be made too delicately. . . . In sum, the orator should not use gesture to the extent that actors use it to please their audience.[13]

Later writers continued to treat the fifth part of rhetoric as an important subject. Early in the seventh century Isidore of Seville referred to Cicero on *pronuntiatio* and emphasized that the voice should be modified according to the use of the high, middle, and low style.[14] At the end of the eighth century, Alcuin, drawing heavily upon Julius Victor, defined delivery as "the attaining of excellence in words, the adapting of voice to meaning, and the disciplining of the body."[15] In his view propriety was to be achieved by appropriate delivery: "Some materials to be sure should be delivered in the vein of simple narrative, others in the vein of authoritative advice, and still others in the vein of indignation, or of pity, if the voice and the delivery are to befit a particular kind of subject."[16] Alan of Lille was subsequently to stress in extravagant terms the importance of varying facial expression,[17] but Alcuin was more

---

[13] "De Rhetorica," in Halm, pp. 484–85:

"Vultus vero pro sententiae dignitate mutandi sunt, sed non ita, ut histrionibus mos est, qui ora torquendo ridiculos motus spectantibus praestant; significanda enim, non spectanda sunt ista, quae actio vultusque commendat: sed oculorum in hac parte magna moderatio est, qui tum hilaritate, tum intentione, tum minaci moventur aspectu. Nec nimium gravioribus superciliis premendi . . . nec mollius agitandi sunt gestus. . . . Ad summam gestus non is oratori tenendus est, quo scaenae placere videntur actores."

See *Martianus Capella and the Seven Liberal Arts*, trans. W. H. Stahl and Richard Johnson (New York: Columbia UP, 1977), 204–05.

[14] *Etymologiarum sive originum Libri XX*, ed. W. M. Lindsay (Oxford: Clarendon, 1911), I, lib. II, vii. The modesty topos persists: "Inchoandum est itaqua taliter, ut benivolum, docilem, vel adtentum auditorem faciamus benevolum precando."

[15] *The Rhetoric of Alcuin & Charlemagne*, ed. W. S. Howell (New York: Russell & Russell, 1965), p. 138: "Pronuntiatio est verborum dignitas vocis sensibus accommodatio et corporis moderatio."

[16] *The Rhetoric of Alcuin & Charlemagne*, p. 140. "Nam alia simplicitate narranda sunt, alia auctoritate suadenda, alia cum indignatione depromenda, alia miseratione flectenda, ut semper vox et oratio suae causae conveniat."

[17] "Anticlaudianus," in *The Anglo-Latin Satirical Poets and Epigrammatists of the Twelfth Century*, ed. Thomas Wright (London: Longmans, 1872), II, 315.

cautious: the speaker's countenance should not be inexpressive; his eyes should not be fastened on the floor nor his neck be inclined to one side.

Although Alcuin had nothing to say about gesture, some later writers on the art of preaching regarded it as a dramatic ploy to be used in the interest of ethical persuasion. A treatise attributed to St. Thomas Aquinas set forth specific gestures to express emotions appropriate to different Biblical verses—admiration, horror, excitement, irony, derision, elation, weariness, indignation, joy, and hate.[18] To John of Garland gesticulation and mode of delivery were worthless unless the speaker was an admirable man;[19] to William of Auvergne even the efficacy of prayer was enhanced by gesture and by such adjuncts as blushing, weeping, groaning, and sighing.[20] Hugh of St. Victor, Ranulph Higden, and Robert of Basevorn, while repeating some of the traditional views on *pronuntiatio*, were as cautious as Martianus Capella about gesture: by no means was the speaker to roll his eyes like an actor or extend his arms too much (*nimis*).[21]

Others regarded tone of voice as the more important, and took many of their recommendations from Cicero and St. Augustine. The distinction which Henry of Hesse made in his *Ars Predicandi* between *vox acuta* in exposition, *vox austera* in correction, and *vox benevola* in exaltation was often expanded and modified.[22] Robert of Basevorn, referring to Cicero, St. Augustine, and Hugh of St. Victor, observed that:

> *Vocis discretio* . . . is when grand things are spoken grandly, or other things in their own manner, according to Augustine, *De doctrina Christiana*. Some things must be spoken softly, as, for example, those which provoke the hearer especially to love and supplication; some, with a very sharp accent, as for example, those things which touch upon fear, namely,

---

[18] Harry Caplan, *Of Eloquence* (Ithaca: Cornell UP, 1970), p. 129.

[19] *The Parisiana Poetria of John of Garland*, ed. Traugott Lawler (New Haven: Yale UP, 1974), p. 134.

[20] Caplan, *Of Eloquence*, pp. 129–30. See also pp. 56–57 for instructions in late-medieval tractate.

[21] For Hugh of St. Victor, see *PL* 176, col. 948; for Ranulph Hidgen, see "Ars componendi sermones," ed. Margaret Jennings, in *Medieval Eloquence*, ed. James J. Murphy (Los Angeles: U of California P, 1979), IV; see also St. Augustine, *PL* 34, cols. 115–18.

[22] For text, see Caplan, *Of Eloquence*, p. 155.

judgement, death, hell. Sometimes there must be a change from a subdued accent to a very sharp one because this also changes the mind.[23]

As Howell observes, the procedures of Ciceronian rhetoric reappeared in English learning early in the thirteenth century, but the development occurred under the auspices of poetical as opposed to rhetorical theory.[24] Geoffrey of Vinsauf in his *Poetria Nova*, composed sometime between 1208 and 1213, was the first to discuss the art of the poet under the heading of Ciceronian rhetoric, thus creating what Atkins calls "a treatise on rhetoric as applied to poetry."[25] In his section on delivery, Geoffrey followed the general Ciceronian principles, but was more explicit in his description of dramatic recitation:

> In reciting aloud, let three tongues speak: let the first be that of the mouth, the second that of the speaker's countenance, and the third that of gesture. . . . Modulate your voice in such a way that it is in harmony with the subject. . . . Anger, child of fire and mother of fury, springing up from the very bellows, poisons the heart and soul. . . . Under its emotion a caustic voice speaks; an inflamed countenance and turbulent gestures accompany it. . . . If you act the part of this man, what, as reciter, will you do? Imitate genuine fury, but do not be furious. Be affected in part as he is, but not deeply so. Let your manner be the same in every respect, but not so extreme, yet suggest, as is fitting, the emotion itself. You can represent the manner of a rustic and still be graceful: let your voice represent his voice; your facial expression, his own; and your gesture his gesture. . . .[26]

The survival of eighteen manuscripts in England, ten in France, and nine in Germany and elsewhere[27] suggests that the *Poetria Nova* was

[23] *Artes praedicandi*, ed. Th. M. Charland (Paris: Vrin, 1936), p. 320. Translation is from Leopold Krul, in *Three Medieval Rhetorical Arts*, ed. James J. Murphy (Los Angeles: U of California P, 1971), p. 212.

[24] *Logic and Rhetoric in England, 1500–1700* (New York: Russell & Russell, 1961), p. 75.

[25] J. W. H. Atkins, *English Literary Criticism: The Medieval Phase* (London: Methuen, 1952), p. 97.

[26] "Poetria Nova," in Faral, pp. 259–60: "In recitante sonent tres linguae: prima sit oris, / Altera rhetorici vultus, et tertia gestus. . . . nec limite tendat / Vox alio, quam res intendat; eant simul ambae / Vox quaedam sit imago rei . . . " (ll. 2031–39). Translation is from *Poetria Nova*, trans. Margaret F. Nims (Toronto: Pontifical Institute of Mediaeval Studies, 1967), p. 90.

[27] Faral, pp. 27–28.

widely read. Three centuries later his views on *pronuntiatio* were still being expressed. The learned friar Traversagni, who lectured at Cambridge, Paris, and Toulouse, based his *Nova Rhetorica* (1479) on Ciceronian techniques and advised that voice, facial expression, and gesture be appropriate to the subject.[28] William Caxton in his *Mirror of the World*, usually regarded as the first printed account of Cicero's five rhetorical terms to appear in English, described *pronuntiatio* in detail. Unlike those of most medieval theorists, his definitions have the breadth of the early treatises on rhetoric and show how classical learning had become vernacularized and applied to all kinds of oral communication. The voice was to accord with the 'words' and 'science' and possess "strength, sharpness and temperance." Facial expression and gesture were equally important:

> Countenaunce is the orderynge of thy face / as whan thou spekyst of a mery mater to shew a laughyng and mery countenaunce / And whan thou spekyst of a pytefull mater to shew a lamentable countenaunce & a heuy / And whan thou spekest of a weyghty cause or mater to shewe a sad and a solempne countenaunce
>
> Gesture is not only in excersisyng one parte of the body but in euery outward member of the body / as in hede / armes / & leggs / and other vital partes / Therfore to euery mater that thou shalt vtter / thou must haue quement gesture / as whan thou spekest of a solempne mater to stande vp ryghte with lytell meuynge of thy body / but poyntynge it with thy fore fynger /
>
> And whan thou spekyst of any cruell mater or yrefull cause to bende thy fyst and shake thyn arme / And whan thou spekyst of any heuenly or godly thynges to loke vp & pointe towarde the skye with thy finger /
>
> And whan thou spekest of any gentilnes / myldenes / or humylyte / to ley thy handes vpon thy breste / & whan thou spekest of any holy mater or deuocyon to holde vp thy handes./[29]

Fifteen years later, Stephen Hawes in *The Pastime of Pleasure*, a work that shows structural affinities with Geoffrey of Vinsauf's *Poetria Nova*, applied the principles of *pronuntiatio* to English poetry. He converted the

---

[28] Lorenzo Guglielmo Traversagni, *Nova Rhetorica* (St. Albans, 1480), Bk. III.

[29] *The Myrrour: & dyscrypscyon of the worlde with many meruaylles* ([London, 1527?]), sig. D3^r–D3^v. The first two editions of *The Mirror*, which were from Caxton's press at Westminster, ca. 1481, 1490, do not contain this section. The third edition is from the press of Laurence Andrewe.

key terms of Ciceronian rhetoric to the use of poetry even more fully than
Geoffrey had done, devoting fifty-six lines to '*pronuncyacyon*,' and insisting that voice and manner must be suited to the audience:

> . . . pronuncyacyon / with chere and countenaunce
> Conuenyently / must make the utteraunce
>
> With humble voyce / and also moderate
> Accordynge / as by hym is audyence
> And yf there be / a ryght hye estate
> Than under honoure / and obedyence
> Reasonably done / unto his excellence
> Pronounsynge his mater so facundyous
> In all due maner / to be centencyous . . .
>
> The famous poete / who solyste to here
> To tell his tale / it is solacyous
> Beholdynge his maners / and also his chere
> After the maner / be it sad or ioyous
> Yf it be sadde / his chere is dolorous
> As in bewaylynge / a wofull tragedy /
> That worthy is to be in memory
>
> And yf the mater / be ioyfull and gladde
> Like countenaunce / outwardly they make
> But moderacyon / in theyr mindes is hadde
> Pleasure / so that outrage / maye them not ouertake
> I cannot wryte / to moche for theyr sake
> Them to laude / for my tyme is shorte
> And the mater longe / whiche I must reporte[30]

While we are uncertain of the extent to which these precepts were
augmented, we do know that dramatic recital took place at a very early
date in the pulpit. In response to a request from St. Francis, *jongleurs* and
poets in Italy, under the influence of lay brotherhoods of *laudesi*, "framed
rude songs or dramatic pieces on the chief events of the gospel story,"[31]

---

[30] *The Pastime of Pleasure*, ed. William Edward Mead, EETS, OS 173 (1927), 52–53.
[31] F. J. E. Raby, *A History of Christian-Latin Poetry from the Beginnings to the Close of the
Middle Ages*, 2nd ed. (Oxford: Clarendon, 1953), p. 430.

41

and these vernacular verses were incorporated into sermons to be recited rather than read. Friars used such pieces not only to attract the public to listen to their sermons but also to entertain private households.[32] In general, despite ecclesiastical disapproval of *"mimi et ioculatores,"* the clergy and *jongleurs* in many places appear to have collaborated to such an extent that, in Auerbach's view, their functions were combined in one person.[33] As a result, the laity, whether aristocratic or plebeian, was very familiar with pulpit entertainment that consisted of an individual performer either giving a dramatic monologue or reciting while the action was mimed.

Outside the pulpit the vernacular writers of profane poetry were heirs to a tradition that relied largely on oral transmission. Even in the twelfth century and later, much of the poetry that was recited was never committed to writing. If a composition was written down, the text was intended only for performers.[34] 'Stage scripts' that are still extant suggest that the writers clearly conceived of their poetry as a form of dramatic presentation to be enjoyed by their listeners. The dialogue in *débats* and *dits dialogués* sometimes indicates the use of rudimentary impersonation, including the mimicking of manners and the voices of foreigners. E. K. Chambers postulated that the parts might have been played by a single *auctor* with "appropriate changes of gesture and intonation."[35] In France the reciter of fabliaux presumably enhanced his work by reproducing lively and often raucous dialogue, using the argot of peasants, the specialized vocabulary of thieves and gamblers, the courtly diction of the aristocrat, and the mincing speech of his lady.[36] *Dame Sirith*, the only extant fabliau written in English before Chaucer's time, composed towards the end of the thirteenth century, seems to have

[32] See David L. Jeffrey, "Franciscan Spirituality and the Rise of Early English Drama," *Mosaic*, 8 (1975), 25–26. See also Alexandre Clerval, *Les Écoles de Chartres* (Chartres: Librairie R. Selleret, 1895), pp. 314–15, for description of popular preaching in 12th century MS. B.N. Lat. 9376, fol. 89.

[33] Erich Auerbach, *Literary Language and its Public in Late Latin Antiquity and in the Middle Ages*, trans. Ralph Manheim (New York: Bollingen Foundation, 1965), pp. 284–86.

[34] Auerbach, p. 288.

[35] *The Mediaeval Stage*, (1903; 8th impress. Oxford: Oxford UP, 1978), I, 83.

[36] Anatole de Montaiglon and Gaston Raynaud, eds., *Recueil général et complet des Fabliaux des XIIIᵉ et XIVᵉ Siècles* (Paris: Librairie des Bibliophiles, 1872–90), II, 196. On fabliau dialogue, see Charles Muscatine, *Chaucer and the French Tradition* (Berkeley: U of California P, 1969), pp. 64, 257n.

42

been intended for dramatic recital as does the fragmentary *Interludium de Clerico et Puella* some fifty years later.[37]

A widespread misconception, dating from the ninth century and given currency in a commentary of Remigius of Auxerre, that Roman plays were a form of recitation may have encouraged histrionic delivery. Commentaries in tenth-century manuscripts of Terence's plays described them as being in verse and recited by one man. A common medieval image was of a little booth-like *scena*, shaded by trees or curtains, in which the poet performed his work.[38] Nicolas Trevet's commentaries on Seneca's tragedies distinguished three modes of dramatic presentation in which the *scena* was used: a dramatic recitation in which the poet recited *solo*—"*in qua erat pulpitum super quo poete carmina pronunciabantur*"; a recital by the poet, taking all the parts but being accompanied by mime; a mixture of modes with the poet reciting and introducing the actors who then spoke and acted the roles of his characters.[39]

Evidence also suggests that scribes and redactors may have concerned themselves with techniques that contributed to a dramatic presentation of a poem, making marginal signs and textual alterations to enable the reciter to anticipate what would be required of him. W. P. Gerritsen postulates that the intention of the corrector of the mid-fourteenth-century Middle Dutch Lancelot manuscript was to facilitate reading aloud—"From a close study of the corrections and the intonation marks the picture emerges of a man who went warily over the text because he knew that reading it to an audience was a difficult, tricky job. A small oversight might end up in a mess of mutilated sentences and embarrassing silence. . . . The work of the corrector is perhaps more suggestive of a nervous chaplain called upon to read the story of Lancelot for the entertainment of the ladies of the manor."[40]

---

[37] See R. M. Wilson, *The Lost Literature of Medieval England* (London: Methuen, 1952), p. 239; see also Rossell Hope Robbins, "The English Fabliau: Before and After Chaucer," *Moderna Språk*, 64 (1970), 231–44.

[38] Mary H. Marshall, "Theatre in the Middle Ages: Evidence from Dictionaries and Glosses," *Symposium*, 4 (1950), 16–17. On the recital of Terence's plays, see also E. K. Rand, "Early Mediaeval Commentaries on Terence," *ClassPhil*, 4 (1909), 362.

[39] Nicolai Treveti, *Expositio Hercules Furens*, ed. V. Ussani, Jr. (Rome: Athenaeum, 1959), p. 5. An excellent account of Trevet's concept of drama is given by John Norton-Smith, *Geoffrey Chaucer* (London: Routledge & Kegan Paul, 1974), pp. 163–68.

[40] "Corrections and Indications for Oral Delivery in the Middle Dutch Lancelot

Despite the growth of an intellectual 'manuscript' culture that reflected such rich and varied literary traditions, despite the increase in the
number of manuscripts apparently intended not only to be read in small
groups but even individually, the poet's voice was still a speaking voice.
Chaucer must have remained deeply conscious of the popular indigenous
world of oral culture, rendered more sophisticated, to be sure, by the
increase in literacy, but still retaining an emotional communal reliance
on the spoken word. Although he shows an insistent concern with his
readers' response, he implies that words read are words first put in
writing and supplying, as it were, a platform for the spoken word. Time
and again he acknowledges a listening audience as a primary condition of
his writing. When he refers to his art, he uses words associated with
listening and speaking more frequently than those having to do with
reading and writing, and he often indicates his awareness of the special
interaction between himself and his listeners as he stands physically
before them:

> And shortely of this matere for to make,
> This Theseus of hir hath leve ytake.
> And every point performed was in dede
> As ye have in this covenant herd me rede.
> His wepne, his clew, his thing that I have sayde,
> Was by the gayler in the hous ylayde . . .
>
> (LGW, 2136-41)

In the well-known address in the General Prologue he expresses a direct
concern with problems of oral delivery:

> But first I pray yow, of youre curteisye,
> That ye n'arette it nat my vileynye
> Thogh that I pleynly speke in this mateere,
> To telle yow hir wordes and hir cheere,
> Ne thogh I speke hir wordes proprely.
> For this ye knowen al so wel as I,
> Whoso shal telle a tale after a man,

Manuscript The Hague K.B. 129 A10," *Neerlandica Manuscripta, Essays Presented to G. I. Lieftinck* (Amsterdam: A. L. Van Gendt, 1976), III, 39–59.

He moot reherce as ny as evere he kan
Everich a word, if it be in his charge,
Al speke he never so rudeliche and large,
Or ellis he moot telle his tale untrewe,
Or feyne thyng, or fynde wordes newe.
He may nat spare, althogh he were his brother;
He moot as wel seye o word as another.
Crist spak hymself ful brode in hooly writ,
And wel ye woot no vileynye is it.
Eek Plato seith, whoso kan hym rede,
The wordes moote be cosyn to the dede . . .

(725-42)

Note that in order to justify his approach he refers specifically to the speech, not the writing, of the highest authority. The distinction is made particularly apparent when he supports his claim with a written aphorism from Plato, adding "whoso kan hym rede." His ostensible purpose is to transmit the speech and facial expression of his characters and, in doing so, conform to the requirements concerning impersonation laid down in *Ad Herennium* and *De Oratore*[41] and to the recommendation in *Poetria Nova* that even a humble *agrestis* should be imitated according to *vox, vultus,* and *gestus.*[42]

The texts themselves demand the kind of reading that was prescribed. They are conceived dramatically with dialogue that insistently conveys the many sounds of contemporary life, whether from courtly palaces and gardens, kitchen, bedroom, or street. Chaucer's fiction of reproducing "hir wordes and hir chere" comes alive in conversations peppered with stock expression, oaths, and interjections that seem to catch the spirit and idiom of fourteenth-century society. The present-day reciter does not treat the text as though it were a straight narrative. As he reproduces the dialogue between Chanticleer and Pertilote, he alters his voice and expects his audience to catch the subtle nuances of personality from the modulations of tone and enunciation. When he narrates the dialogue between the Summoner and his defenceless victim, he uses a bullying tone for the gutter language of the extortioner and a timid, high-pitched quavering voice for the response:

[41] *Ad Herrennium*, III, xiv, 24; *De Oratore*, III, liii, 205.
[42] *Poetria Nova*, p. 260.

45

> This somonour clappeth at the wydwes gate.
> "Com out," quod he, "thou olde virytrate!
> I trowe thou hast some frere or preest with thee."
> "Who clappeth?" seyde this wyf, "Benedicitee,
> God save you, sire; what is your sweete wille?"
> (*FrT*, 1581–85)

For the Summoner's response to the tale, as he quakes like an aspen leaf "for ire," the caustic voice described by Geoffrey of Vinsauf is appropriate; for the dialogue between the friar and the angel, second and third voices must be added, the one bland and unctuous, the other contemptuous. The reader manipulates the dialogue according to auditory needs, emphasizing the transitions with "quod he" and "quod the angle" to identify the speaker.

Some estimation of the way in which this kind of presentation may influence the listeners' judgment can be gauged from the recent recordings made by Professor Betsy Bowden of forty major scholars reading key passages commonly held to be textually ambiguous and capable of several interpretations.[43] Without prompting, almost every scholar read the passages dramatically and, by varying vocal inflections, conveyed the meaning of the text as he or she perceived it. Of course, we cannot calculate the ways in which the fourteenth-century audience by its very existence must have affected the quality and nature of the recital, but the results of Professor Bowden's experiment do enable us to assume that the living presence, persuading not only by voice but by gesture and facial expression, must have created an experience of the poem that we cannot share. Because we do not know whether the portrait of the Prioress was recited in tones of irony, respect, admiration even, or was accompanied by a rolling of the eyes, a gesture of dismissal, or a tolerant smile, we can delight in the ambiguities that are certainly present in the text and argue over the merits of conflicting interpretations. But the text that we now appreciate for the variety of its meanings must have been less flexible to that contemporary audience. Today we enjoy having to make up our own minds concerning the extent of Criseyde's involvement in the arrangements for the lovers' meeting at Pandarus' house. We know that we are

---

[43] I wish to express my gratitude to Professor Bowden of Camden College, Rutgers University for this information.

being asked to fill in the deliberately inexplicit outline of Criseyde's state
of mind:

> Nought list myn auctour fully to declare
> What that she thoughte whan that he seyde so,
> That Troylus was out of towne yfare,
> As yf he seyde therof soth or no;
> But that withouten awayt with hym to go
> She graunted hym, sith he hire that bisoughte,
> And, as his nece, obeyed as hire oughte.
>
> (*TC*, III, 575–81)

To that first audience, the challenge to use personal judgment was likely
to have been less provocative and less demanding, being undercut by the
poet's own interpretation which he conveyed through his performance.

The presence of the poet on the podium raises questions concerning
the interpretation of the narrative 'I'. Would an immediate audience,
like the scribes of *Libro de Buen Amor* and the early editors of Chaucer's
poems, regard this 'I' as autobiographical? The medieval listener was
familiar with two kinds of 'I', the questing 'I' engaged, like Everyman,
in search of eternal life, and a more personal 'I', purporting to be the
poet. The first kind exists mainly to bring out the allegory; in *The
Parlement of the Thre Ages*, he is the solitary hunter who witnesses a
disturbing vision; in *The Floure and the Leafe* he is the bewildered
early-morning dreamer with whom the audience is supposed to identify
as it receives a moral lesson. In *The Divine Comedy*, what Spitzer calls the
'poetic I,' the visionary 'I' representing the human soul, and the 'I'
purporting to be the poet belonging to the political and social world of
the Florentines become a composite in order to show "a human being
actively experiencing the truths of the Beyond."[44] In Chaucer's poetry,
the focus in general is on the seemingly authentic and personal rather
than on the supramundane. The questing soul in the dream-vision
poems is fused to the quasi-autobiographical 'I' in such a way that the
central figure seems rooted in everyday life as a bookish, frustrated,
empirical, and enquiring maker of poems. In *Troilus*, the first-person
narrator purporting to be the poet may have something of the poetic 'I's'

---

[44] See Leo Spitzer, "A Note on the Poetic and the Empirical 'I' in Medieval Authors,"
Traditio, 4 (1946), 414–22.

visionary power in his perspective of past and future, but he constantly reminds us that he exists in the present, telling a story, and not participating in the action; the role of the poetic 'I' shifts to Troilus and to the audience, the 'ye' who are to share the final epiphany and the lesson of the palinode. In *The Canterbury Tales* the poetic 'I' is largely subsumed in the overall narrator who presents himself in a way that seems to be autobiographical and does not contradict the general facts of his life as far as we know them. Medieval listeners had no reason to question who the 'I' of a poem was. They sometimes even regarded allegorical or spurious details as autobiographical and factual.[45] Modern readers, armed with a knowledge of sophisticated literary conventions, know that the heart dancing to the daffodils is Wordsworth's whereas the Duchess smiling in the portrait is not Browning's. To them, the first level of fiction in *Troilus* is likely to be the presence of the poet himself, acting out a character; he may even be 'inside' the poem, like Gulliver in *Gulliver's Travels*, and bear as little similarity to Chaucer as Gulliver does to Swift. A medieval audience, looking at the poet, did not think of the authorial voice in terms of fiction and non-fiction. However many hoods he donned to act out the roles of various protagonists, the poet was the 'I' behind the poem.

In Chaucer's poetry, this 'I' was the persuasive force governing the interpretation. What some critics regard as a clashing of discordant styles, indicating a lack of consistency in characterization, is a feature of 'live' performance, essential to give variety in the entertainment. It was Chaucer's physical presence that gave shape and unity to the poetry. To those listening to *Troilus*, the narrator was Geoffrey Chaucer who had written a poem from history, from "olde bokes"; he was poet and performer whose delivery gave significances that the printed page could never convey. Addressing his listeners on the podium, perhaps even overwhelming them with the impact of the 'I', he instructed them how

---

[45] See Juan Ruiz, *Arcipreste de Hita, Libro de Buen Amor*, ed. Julio Cejador y Frauca (Madrid: Espasa-Calpe, 1961), pp. xiii–xxv; Giovanni Boccaccio, *Corbaccio*, trans. and ed. Anthony K. Cassell (Urbana: U of Illinois P, 1975), pp. xi–xiii. On Juan Ruiz's recital, see Raymond S. Willis, ed. *Juan Ruiz Libro de Buen Amor* (Princeton: Princeton UP, 1972), pp. xliv–xlvi. On the personal fallacy, see Peter M. Dunn, "De las Figuras del Arcipreste," in *'Libro de Buen Amor' Studies*, ed. G. B. Gybbon-Monypenny (London: Tamesis, 1970), p. 79. For Chaucer, see G. L. Kittredge's criticism of the common nineteenth-century view, *Chaucer and His Poetry* (Cambridge, Mass.: Harvard UP, 1915), p. 45.

they were to interpret philosophically his tale of the tragic mutability of human relationships, and when he said "I blam hire not for pite," they understood that they too were to exercise Christian charity.

In *The Canterbury Tales*, the narrator's personal presence must have achieved similar control over the audience. Yet critics still interpret the text exclusively in terms of silent reading. We are instructed "to read the tale as a dramatic monologue spoken by its teller" on the understanding that "some of Chaucer's attitudes spill into it," and to realize that the tale is primarily an expression of the teller's personality, with Chaucer's artistry allowing for the inclusion of rhetoric, wit, and philosophy beyond the capability of the teller.[46] Certainly we would agree that the tales show a general suitability to the tellers, and a judicious use of high, medium, and low styles even gives an added sense of appropriateness. The Knight tells a tale of romance; the Churls fabliaux; the Prioress recounts the miracle of the Virgin; the Physician settles the traditional score between the medical and legal professions by citing the notorious case of judiciary corruption that initiated the Roman legal system.[47] But the kind of imaginative feat that critics now demand could not have been realized by medieval listeners because, as they watched the man before them, they would be constantly reminded that there was no Knight, no Miller, no Reeve, only the Poet who was telling a tale about tellers and the tales they told. The occasional use of a Scandinavian word to suggest the Reeve's Norfolk origins might inform the audience that the tale which the poet recited was supposed to belong to the Reeve. But the listeners would know that the brilliant mimicry of the northern dialect of John and Aleyn was too sophisticated for the purported teller. As a performer, Chaucer would have realized both the impossibility of sustaining the illusion of the various impersonations and the artistic advantages of allowing his hearers to realize that the teller assigned to the tale was simply a fiction, the creation of the man who addressed them. The question that is now frequently raised, who is doing the talking, would have been irrelevant: the poet does the talking and, as a result, the Miller

[46] Donald R. Howard, *The Idea of the Canterbury Tales* (Berkeley: U of California P, 1976), p. 231.

[47] For varying views, see Huling E. Ussery, *Chaucer's Physician: Medicine and Literature in Fourteenth-Century England*, Tulane Studies in English, 19 (New Orleans: Department of English, Tulane U, 1971), p. 131; Beryl Rowland, "The Physician's 'Historial Thyng Notable' and the Man of Law," *ELH*, 40 (1973), 165–78.

with uncharacteristic wit and subtlety can mock the Knight's seriousness; the Merchant can provide a vivid account of January's lovemaking that belongs to the merciless vision of youth, not to an aged misanthrope. The medieval listener would have been in no doubt about the speaker of the famous crux in *The Knight's Tale*:

> The destinee, ministre general,
> That executeth in the world over al
> The purveiaunce that God hath seyn biforn,
> So strong it is that, though the world had sworn
> The contrarie of a thyng by ye or nay,
> Yet somtyme it shal fallen on a day
> That falleth nat eft withinne a thousand yeere.
> For certeinly, oure appetites heere,
> Be it of weere, or pees, or hate, or love,
> Al is this reuled by the sighte above.
>
> (*KnT*, 1663–72)

Throughout the tale the poet is present, commenting on the tale and showing his authorship as he selects, condenses his material, and passes judgment on the action. He frequently vivifies descriptive passages by the way he draws attention to himself:

> Ther saugh I how woful Calistopee,
> Whan that Diane agreved was with here,
> Was turned from a womman til a bere,
> And after was she maad the loode-sterre;
> Thus was it peynted, I kan sey yow no ferre.
> Hir sone is eek a sterre, as men may see.
> Ther saugh I Dane, yturned til a tree—
> I mene nat the goddesse Diane,
> But Penneus doghter, which that highte Dane.
> Ther saugh I Attheon an hert ymaked,
> For vengeaunce that he saugh Diane al naked.
>
> (*KnT*, 2056–66)

The 'I' that claims to have actually seen the stories painted on the temple's walls does not have to be explained away as a spectral presence, conventional device, or deliberate anachronism. In an age when scenes from the classics and from Biblical lore decorated the interiors of the palace at Westminster and of royal dwellings elsewhere, he and his audience might well have been looking at such tapestries or murals "with colours fyne . . . peynted" during the recital itself.[48] At any moment the poet could break in and speak *in propria persona*, knowing that his physical presence precluded any sense of incongruity.

Chaucer's personal presence made the reaction of the audience different from our own. Throughout a recital, by gesture, tone of voice, and facial expression the poet was able to indicate whom he was portraying and how he expected his audience to react. Some of the demands that the text makes upon us today were undoubtedly there to challenge his contemporaries, with the poet supplying, as it were, an anatomy to be fattened by the audience according to its experience with complex and unpredictable human nature. But what was then a body is now a skeleton, a framework to be filled in with some uncertainty. The first listeners could participate with assurance; the man before them was author, performer, and 'rhethor,' and his evaluation predominated.

We can only surmise about the nature of Chaucer's first recital, bearing in mind that Chaucer probably did make use of voice and body, adopting the mode of delivery which many rhetoricians considered to be of overwhelming importance in the process of communication. But as a result of what we know about *pronuntiatio*, we should be wary of ascribing to that early audience the reactions of that timeless audience which is the subject of many present critical discussions. Because of the way Chaucer delivered his dramatic monologues, the response of the audience may have been more confident and unequivocal than it has been since.

---

[48] See especially Elizabeth Salter, "Medieval Poetry and the Visual Arts," *E&S* 22 (1969), 16–32.

'We ben to lewed or to slowe': Chaucer's Astronomy and Audience Participation

J. C. Eade
Australian National University

EVEN THE SIMPLEST of Chaucer's astronomical allusions tend to play with number or with the apparatus of astronomy in a way that would be obtuse if one did not suppose he thought his audience—or at least some part of it—would keep up with him. The implication of the manner in which these references are presented is that the 'intelligent layman' had a grounding in a common stock of knowledge on which Chaucer could rely; such, perhaps, as later became embedded in works like *Margarita philosophica*.

In what follows I intend to examine some of the ways in which Chaucer called upon his reader's mental agility or his elementary acquaintance with astronomy, and thereafter to show how some passages which we have become accustomed to regard as fiercely difficult, if not impenetrable, will in fact yield to orderly analysis when once the more advanced elements of their technical apparatus have been mastered. Here, then, I will argue that it would be a mistake to suppose that Chaucer wrote with a deliberate intention to mystify. The consequence of supposing, instead, that he wrote to be understood—if sometimes only by the 'experts'—is not to attribute to them minds like computers; instead, it is to give a new emphasis to the way in which these difficult passages should be read. Hitherto, interpretation of them has been based on a detailed elaboration, one that makes specific (in terms of a precise astronomical date or a particular astrological configuration) what Chaucer was content, knowing his business, to leave general. The problem passages in *The Franklin's Tale* and *The Man of Law's Tale*, perhaps the two most difficult of all, will both, in my view, reveal themselves to be considerably more tractable than has been supposed, when one comes to an understanding of the level at which they are pitched.

We may usefully begin by considering the two passages in which Chaucer uses shadow length as a means of telling the time, and the demands they make on the reader. In the Introduction to *The Man of Law's Tale*, we are told that the Host:

> . . . saugh wel that the shadwe of every tree
> Was as in lengthe the same quantitee
> That was the body erect that caused it.
>
> (II, 7–9)[1]

From this shadow length he "took his wit" that the sun was 45° above the horizon. In the Prologue to *The Parson's Tale*, on the other hand, Chaucer himself finds that:

> The sonne fro the south lyne was descended
> So lowe that he nas nat, to my sighte,
> Degreës nyne and twenty as in highte.
>
> (X, 2–4)

He then concludes that it is 4 o'clock:

> For ellevene foot, or litel moore or lesse,
> My shadwe was at thilke tyme, as there,
> Of swiche feet as my lengthe parted were
> In six feet equal of proporcioun.
>
> (X, 6–9)

As is well known, the *Kalendarium* of Nicholas of Lynn carries tables that show the sun's altitude and the shadow of a six-foot man for the daylight hours throughout the year.[2] The two sets of figures are in fact functions of each other (and both sets are mathematically accurate to a degree far beyond the capacity of any contemporary observational instrument).[3]

---

[1] Quotations are from F. N. Robinson's second edition of *The Complete Works of Geoffrey Chaucer* (London: Oxford UP, 1957).

[2] See *The Kalendarium of Nicholas of Lynn*, ed. Sigmund Eisner (London: Scolar Press, 1980), pp. 68–69, 74–75, etc.

[3] Half a degree of arc would be the best one would expect from an instrument, whereas Nicholas' figures work to the nearest minute of arc.

There is, nonetheless, clearly a point in Nicholas' presenting the information in the two ways: a person with an astrolabe or similar device would use his instrument to obtain a solar altitude, whereas a person six-feet tall would simply pace out his shadow. Indeed, someone only five feet tall could use a 'foot' that was ten inches long and measure his shadow by that unit. More crudely one could simply estimate the ratio between the height of an object and its shadow—which is all the Host does, conveniently concluding that shadow and object are equal. He is thus not greatly pressed to conclude that the sun is 45° above the horizon. The point, though, is that no amount of calculation could have led the Host to a time of day unless he had an improbably capacious memory or access to tables. Some of Chaucer's readers may have smiled at the Host when, after all his ponderous calculations, he merely found it was 10 o'clock precisely; others would have observed the fraudulence in the conclusion: "And for that day, as in that latitude, / It was ten of the clokke, he gan conclude" (II, 13–14). A 'conclucioun' is frequently a calculation performed on an instrument or in a set of tables, but it would be difficult to give the verb that degree of technical force here. The implication is that the Host, though not "depe ysterte in loore," was working by his own devices.

A similar problem occurs in the other passage that uses shadow length. Arab navigators, by using their fingers as sights, used to be able to estimate stellar altitudes in units of six or seven degrees.[4] But when Chaucer asks us to accept that he found the sun just not quite 29° above the horizon, he is foisting an absurdity on us, unless we imagine him equipped with some instrument. And if we imagine him with an astrolabe, it would itself give him a time of day and thereby make shadow length redundant. Some other device or *ad hoc* contrivance would still require him to consult tables.

Chaucer does indeed make his figures round in one case and approximate in the other—but the procedural gap is still there. Seasonal variations make the shadow table too complex to be reduced to a crude form that can be memorized. And the same is true of the solar altitudes. Chaucer's easy solution, of course, would have been to imply the use of

---

[4] See, e.g., Gabriel Ferrand, *Instructions nautiques et routiers arabes et portugais des XV⁰ et XVI⁰ siècles* (Paris: Geuthner, 1928), III, 162.

an astrolabe on both these occasions, substituting the use of the *umbra versa* for the shadow scale.[5]

There are other problems in the two passages which are not my immediate concern here: my point is that, at least in these two instances, Chaucer has worked his material in such a way that the learned among his audience would in fact overtake him, would see that he had made a somewhat ill-digested use of the apparatus he adopted.

My example from *The Merchant's Tale* will appear less technically involved, but it does at the same time provide us with an indication of what kind of astronomical knowledge was a prerequisite for playing one of Chaucer's numbers games. After the marriage May kept to her chamber, as delicate custom required:

> The moone, that at noon was thilke day
> That Januarie hath wedded fresshe May
> In two of Tawr, was into Cancre glyden;
> So longe hath Mayus in hir chambre abyden.
>
> (IV, 1885–88)

The length of her stay is expressed as a puzzle, and those who wish to resolve it must know that there are thirty degrees in each sign; that Gemini interposes between Taurus and Cancer; and that the moon's mean daily motion is reckoned at 13°. Before one has had a chance to put 13's into 58 (+), however, the answer is given:

> The fourthe day compleet fro noon to noon,
> Whan that the heighe masse was ydoon,
> In halle sit this Januarie and May.
>
> (IV, 1893–95)

Chaucer's words are precise—the period of time that is at first expressed as a riddle is in the event given a round value: of four days exact. Since, however, we have been arguing that when posing the puzzle Chaucer trades on a certain specific knowledge in his readers, there is a disparity here which has to be accounted for. If we complete the calculation and continue to assume that the moon's mean daily motion is 13°, we find

---

[5] The use of this device is explained in Pt. II, Sec. 42 of Chaucer's *Treatise on the Astrolabe*, ed. W. W. Skeat, EETS ES 16 (1872), pp. 52–53.

that nearly four-and-a-half days are required for a movement which Chaucer says, very deliberately, took only four days precisely. Are we to conclude that Chaucer has bungled the game he was playing? Or that we are examining it altogether too curiously in detecting a discrepancy in it? North has argued that since more than four days are required, the period to which Chaucer refers should be counted from the noon *after* the day of the wedding.[6] This seems to me to run against the plainness of the sense. If the figures tallied, there would be no motive whatever for imagining Chaucer's count does not begin on the day of the wedding. Rather than quarrel with this plain sense, we may take another expedient: this is to say that 13° per day is simply the moon's *mean* motion, so that by definition there will be many occasions when her speed is greater, when (as the astrologers say) she is 'swift of course.' I take it, then, that part of Chaucer's ploy is to present the reader with a puzzle that is complicated to the extent that it seems to promise a fractional answer, but then to stop him short with a round answer. His potential objection that the answer is less than the calculation seems to demand would then be nullified by his having to admit that the answer given is entirely possible, if only it is supposed that the moon is travelling faster than its mean motion.

There are other places where Chaucer toys with his audience, and they too rely for their effect upon particular knowledge. The successive rising of Palamon, Emelye, and Arcite at hours—planetary, not clock hours—appropriate to their destinations is one instance, and the beginning of the General Prologue is another. This latter gives some indication of the precision of Chaucer's phrasing. Every edition will make it clear that the sun's "halve cours" is not the same thing as 'half his course.' Had the latter phrase been used, our natural—indeed, necessary—assumption would have been that the 'half' was the first half. But with the date already defined by the very opening as being in April, and with the sun beginning his course in the Ram on 12 March in Chaucer's lifetime, the "halve cours" must be the *second* half. Since we have no title whatever to suppose Chaucer is being mystifying here, we are surely forced to the recognition that the audience is expected to know: just as they are expected to know who/what 'Zephirus' is, and that the 'Tabard' is a hostelry.

[6] J. D. North, "Kalenderes Enlumyned Ben They," *RES*, NS 20 (1969), 274.

So far we have explored some of the uses to which Chaucer puts his astronomical learning, chiefly those which patently require the reader to draw upon the same stock in responding to the obliqueness by which otherwise mundane details are expressed. To a twentieth-century audience the best councils are a deep breath, a cool head, perseverance, and an assumption that the author is not willfully obscure and not prone to tedious irrelevance. To approach *The Franklin's Tale, The Complaint of Mars*, or *The Man of Law's Tale* in this spirit will, I believe, be found to yield results.

In pursuit of my point I begin with the notorious section of *The Franklin's Tale*:

> His tables Tolletanes forth he brought,
> Ful wel corrected, ne ther lakked nought,
> Neither his collect ne his expans yeeris,
> Ne his rootes, ne his othere geeris,
> As been his centris and his argumentz
> And his proporcioneles convenientz
> For his equacions in every thyng.
> And by his eighte speere in his wirkyng
> He knew ful wel how fer Alnath was shove
> Fro the heed of thilke fixe Aries above,
> That in the ninthe speere considered is;
> Ful subtilly he kalkuled al this.
>
> Whan he hadde founde his firste mansioun,
> He knew the remenaunt by proporcioun,
> And knew the arisyng of his moone weel,
> And in whos face, and terme, and everydeel;
> And knew ful weel the moones mansioun
> Acordaunt to his operacioun,
> And knew also his othere observaunces
> For swiche illusiouns and swiche meschaunces
> As hethen folk useden in thilke dayes.
>
> (V, 1273–93)

Despite the claims that have been made to the contrary,[7] I believe it can be demonstrated that the lunar mansions are absolutely integral to the

---

[7] E.g., by Chauncey Wood, *Chaucer and the Country of the Stars* (Princeton: Princeton UP, 1970), p. 266.

operations the Clerk performs. While Aurelius is still languishing
("Two yeer and moore lay wrecche Aurelyus," V, 1102), his brother
recalls his time at Orleans and a book, "Which book spak muchel of the
operaciouns / Touchynge the eighte and twenty mansiouns / That longen
to the moone," V, 1129–31). He hopes to find at Orleans some old
friend ("som oold felawe . . . / That hadde thise moones mansions in
mynde," V, 1154); such a one could let his brother "han his love."

What wonder, then, that the subtle Clerk occupies himself with the
moon's mansions when he performs his operations? But what exactly is it
that the Clerk does? Do we have any reasonable chance of discovering; or
are we to conclude, with Phyllis Hodgson, that "Fortunately this
passage with its involved and highly technical account of the Clerk's
astrological calculations need not be taken too seriously"?[8]

As a mode of entry into the passage I propose to emphasize its
structure, in particular the conclusions the Clerk is said to make, which
are conveyed by the verbs 'know' and 'find' [my italics]:

> His tables Tolletanes forth he broughte,
> Ful well corrected ne ther lakked nought,
> . . . .
> For his equacions in every thyng.
> And by his eighte speere in his wirkyng
> He *knew ful wel* how fer Alnath was shove
> . . . .
> Ful subtilly he kalkuled al this.
>   When he hadde *founde* his firste mansioun,
> *He knew* the remenaunt by proporcioun,
> *And knew* the arisyng of his moone weel,
> And in whos face, and terme, and everydeel;
> *And knew ful weel* the moones mansioun
> Acordaunt to his operacioun,
> *And knew also* his othere observaunces.
>
>   (V, 1273–91)

It is surely not too much to assert that in its syntactical ordering, and
when reduced to something approaching its bare minimum, the passage
has at least an air of orderliness and at least the appearance of proceeding

---

[8] *Chaucer: The Franklin's Tale*, ed. Phyllis Hodgson (London: Athlone Press, 1960),
p. 99.

sequentially. The task, then, is to flesh it out in such a way (if that is possible) as to preserve the orderliness and purpose that the bare outline seems to convey.

The Clerk begins with his Toledo Tables, his objective being already declared:

> That nyght and day he spedde hym that he kan
> To wayten a tyme of his conclusioun;
> That is to seye, to maken illusioun.
>
> (V, 1262–64)

It cannot be determined whether his 'Toledo' Tables were those produced under the auspices of Alfonso X or the earlier tables, also generated at Toledo, of Arzachel. This difficulty is not insuperable, however, since we find, in the event, that all the terms employed in relation to the Clerk's initial operation are the common parlance of astronomy. If, for example, one examines the standard treatise on the theory of planetary motion, one finds all the terms in use there. Let us examine the first stage of his procedure:

> His tables Tolletanes forth he brought
> Ful well corrected, ne ther lakked nought,
> Neither his collect ne his expans yeeris,
> Ne his rootes, ne his othere geeris,
> As been his centris and his argumentz
> And his proporcioneles convenientz
> For his equacions in every thyng.
>
> (V, 1273–79)

It will assist in the unravelling of this if we assume that the Clerk was performing his operations on a particular date; for convenience we may choose 10 January, 1392.[9] Approaching his tables (no matter which tables they were) the Clerk will have found that he could enter them only by breaking his date down into components. One function of astronomical tables is to plot rate of motion against elapsed time: if a body moved one degree in one year, two degrees in two years, three degrees in three, there would be no need to tabulate its motion. If, however, it

---

[9] This is one of the dates North assigns (p. 262).

moved 9° 51' in one year, it would be useful to be able to determine merely by inspection how far it moved in 43 years. Moreover, there will be certain dates beyond which (backwards) one will have no need to proceed: astronomers often used the Incarnation, this then being their 'root.' Certain other blocks of years can also usefully be gathered together—thousands, hundreds, and twenties. They are each tabulated as 'collect' years. And if twenty is the smallest number of 'collect' years employed, then the 'expans' years will have to run from 1 to 19. The Clerk's year, 1392, could well have been broken down into the Incarnation (root); plus 1000, plus 300, plus 80 (collect years); plus 11 'expans' years complete. He would then need to break 10 January down into 9 days complete, plus so many hours complete.

We are told that the Clerk worked "nyght and day" on his calculations. This is something of an exaggeration, in the sense that a person familiar with the process (or even someone learning it) would not require days on end to arrive at results. Nonetheless, it can be seen already that a good deal of ink and labor was involved. We notice too that the Clerk's tables were "Ful wel corrected." This is another indication of Chaucer's attention to detail and of his familiarity with what was involved. Any set of tables has to be computed for a particular place. This being so, adjustment will clearly have to be made if one is not at the place for which the tables were drawn up. If one is at a different location, then much tedious calculation will be avoided if the necessary adjustments are made once for all. We have warrant, then, for supposing that the Clerk's version of the tables was corrected for Orleans. (We notice that it was the tables that were corrected, not correction that was made to the tables. Whether he further adjusted them for Brittany in his calculations depends on one's view of how hard he was working for his thousand pounds.) Finally, we should notice—since we already have good cause for supposing that Chaucer was not writing merely at a venture—that it was no wonder that his tables "lakked nought"; they would have been useless if they had. This rhyme phrase should therefore be read, perhaps, as an introductory flourish. It introduces two sets of terms: those that relate to the Clerk's need to convert his date (root, collect and expanse years), and those that relate to the procedures he adopted when once that date was reduced. Chaucer's order of presentation, in other words, reflects the logical order of procedure and therefore necessarily reflects a knowledge of what that procedure is. All this is controlled rather than mystifying or designed to blind with science.

The Clerk's "other geeris" are:

> . . . his centris and his argumentz
> And his proporcioneles convenientz
> For his equacions in every thyng.
>   (V, 1277–79)

If we turned to the *Theorica Planetarum* in its capacity as the ABC of the subject, we would find that under each of its main heads, which deal with the moon, the outer planets (Saturn, Jupiter, Mars), and the inner planets (Venus, Mercury), there is a routine order in which the components of the theory are set down. [10] Astronomical tables such as the Clerk used are based (as is our convention of 'Mean' Time) on the fiction that the heavenly bodies move obligingly at even rates. It is these even rates that are tabulated, together with the adjustments that are necessary to convert a 'Mean' position into an actual ('True') position. The *Theorica Planetarum* expounds, with plodding thoroughness and a daunting terminology, the stages by which the motions of the planets may be determined. In all cases (save for the sun and the lunar nodes) the *discipulus* is obliged to include, successively, the planet's 'equation of center,' its 'equation of argument' and the 'proportionals' that must be used to convert the equation of argument from mean to true.

We have no need whatever to understand this language in order to see that the terminology Chaucer employs is of a piece and to apprehend that anyone with some competence in astronomy would recognize that the language was merely workaday—no more than was to be expected of a description of tables that "lakked nought." To us, on the other hand, the lesson is different. One thing we learn is that there are no such things as "proporcioneles convenientz"—rather, there are 'proportionals' for every planet which are 'convenient for his equations (i.e., of argument) in every thing,' viz., in every calculation the Clerk is obliged to make in finding where the planets are.

Thus far, I hope it is clear, there is a straightforward sense in what Chaucer has said. What of the continuation? We should examine the

---

[10] See, e.g., the useful extracts from the *Theorica* in Edward Grant, *A Source Book in Medieval Science* (Cambridge, Mass.: Harvard UP, 1974), pp. 451 ff.

succeeding sentence entire, being guided by the supposition that the grammatical grouping of the lines is not an accident, however ill they have been understood.

> And by his eighte speere in his wirkyng
> He knew ful wel how fer Alnath was shove
> From the heed of thilke fixe Aries above,
> That in the ninthe speere considered is;
> Ful subtilly he kalkuled al this.
>
> (V, 1280–84)

We have seen that in the first phase Chaucer shows us the Clerk converting his date and employing the sections of the tables that deal with centers, arguments, and proportions. (I am aware that Chaucer does not say that the Clerk consulted these sections, merely that the tables did not lack them; but if one understands the procedures that the Clerk was obliged to conduct, one can see that it would be pointless to suppose that he was not consulting them.) In the second phase the Clerk concerns himself, for some undeclared reason, with the position of 'Alnath' in relation to "the heed of thilke fixe Aries." Commentators have seen, or accepted, that "thilke fixe Aries" refers to what is more generally known as 'the first point of Aries.' This 'point' is the place where the celestial equator intersects with the ecliptic. It is the zero of the system used to calibrate the zodiac and the initial point used to define the extent to which the entire sphere of the 'fixed' stars has moved (at its slow rate) from east to west. The distance of any heavenly body from this point when determined by reference to the ecliptic defines its celestial longitude. If the moon is "into Cancre glyden," its celestial longitude is at least 90°, Cancer being the fourth sign and each sign being 30° in extent. (Here, though for expository reasons, not for the purposes of game-playing, it is necessary to employ the same sort of reliance on the reader's capacity for mental arithmetic as Chaucer himself adopted.)

Almost the whole of the published commentary on this tale has been guided by Skeat's assertion that, by finding the distance that Alnath is from the first point of Aries, the Clerk is bent upon determining the extent of precession (the amount by which the fixed stars have moved in an easterly direction in relation to the ecliptic which defines their longitude at a given epoch).[11] Before we accept Skeat's assertion, and the supposition of the great majority of commentators who have followed him, we should attempt to accommodate some other considerations.

One is that the Clerk achieves his result by employing "his eighte speere in his wirkyng." This is ambiguous, but the ambiguity resolves itself. The 'wirkyng' could be either the movement of the eighth sphere itself, or the Clerk's operation. Chaucer's other uses of 'wirkyng' and the succession of the pronoun 'his' strongly suggest, however, that 'wirkyng' refers to the Clerk's operation. The lines may therefore be glossed, on this interpretation, as follows: 'As a result of his operation in connection with the eighth sphere the Clerk knew how far Alnath was from the first point of Aries.' Now, even if 'wirkyng' applies to the eighth sphere, not to the Clerk, the result is essentially the same: 'by finding what was the movement of the eighth sphere the Clerk knew how far Alnath was shove . . .' The point to determine is what this calculation told him. If Skeat was right, what the Clerk would know (by having determined the extent of precession) would be where the whole of the sphere of the stars stood in relation to the 'fixed' sphere by which their position was measured. But why should this be important to him. And why should Alnath be singled out in this operation?

Alnath is the star known since Bayer's classification in 1603 as 'alpha Arietis.' It is *not* of first magnitude as Skeat asserted,[12] there being no first-magnitude stars in Aries; and it was not the star by which the extent of precession was traditionally measured. That was gamma Arietis, not alpha. Why, then, does the Clerk need to know where Alnath is? Not to measure precession, but because, as one of the learned glosses of the Ellesmere MS. indicates, *"Alnath dicitur prima mansio lune."* Hodgson saw the connection and dismissed it as "spurious"; Hinkley saw it and adduced Albiruni, who names the first lunar mansion as 'Alsharatan,' and 'Alnath.'[13] Let us suppose, then, that 'Alnath' is the name of the first lunar mansion, and let us test the supposition. What else can we find that will support it? The very syntax of the passage will. When this sentence is over, a new paragraph begins in the received text; "When he

[11] Skeat, *Treatise*, p. lx: "the precession of the equinoxes (which is what Chaucer here alludes to) . . . ."

[12] *Treatise*, p. lx.

[13] Hodgson, p. 136; H. B. Hinckley, *Notes on Chaucer* (1907; rpt. New York: Haskell House, 1970), pp. 254–55.

hadde *founde* his firste mansioun. . . ." How did he find it ? By discovering where Alnath was in relation to the first point of Aries.

Since so many commentators have followed Skeat's assertion that the Clerk is here involved with the precession of the equinoxes, we need to be clear about what his assertion implies. Precession is a rate of motion by which the stars gradually increase their longitude. As Skeat indicated,[14] precession can be measured by taking the longitude of some prominent star; but to find that star's position in relation to the first point of Aries is only of significance if one *also* has an interval of time to bring into the calculation. Suppose that the Clerk found that the star Alnath was 20° removed from the first point of Aries; he could not then say that precession was 20° in extent, any more than he could say it was 140° in extent by finding that Regulus was at Leo 20°. In other words, finding the longitude of any star, Alnath included, does not in itself determine the extent of precession.

It is possible to find a considerably more convincing purpose for the Clerk's operation. We have noticed that it is "by his eighte speere in his wirkyng" that the Clerk knew how far Alnath was "shove" from Aries. One of the canons in the Alphonsine Tables shows us the procedure. It is entitled: "Loca stellarum fixarum ad quodcunque tempus volueris inuenire", and it indicates that *two* procedures are required. "Scias primo loca earum verificata ad aliquid tempus . . ." and "Scias ergo equationem motus accessus et recessus octaue sphere. . . ."[15] The whole purpose of the operation is to take a given longitude at a given time and to add to this longitude the amount of precession that answers to the interval between that time and yours. If the Clerk was doing this for Alnath (and we have not yet determined what 'Alnath' signifies) his 'working in the eighth sphere' would merely tell him what value to add to an *already determined* position, that value merely answering to the time that had elapsed. In short, this present sentence merely tells us that the Clerk obtained for himself a current value for 'Alnath,' whatever Alnath is.

The succeeding sentence tells us, though only by implication, why the Clerk needed a current value—it was in order to find where to locate the first lunar mansion. I have been insisting that we should trust the flow of the syntax. Here we are faced with a plain choice: either there is a

---

[14] *Treatise*, p. lx.

[15] *Alfontij regis castelle illustrissimi celestium motuum tabule* ([Venice], 1483), sig. b3.

65

complete hiatus, and the Clerk (for reasons that are not substantiated) wishes to know how great precession is and then for reasons best known to himself lurches off in the direction of lunar mansions; or else there is a sequential flow, and his finding Alnath's longitude is re-expressed as his having found the first lunar mansion. It is difficult to believe that when the Ellesmere adds a gloss pointing to the connection, we should do other than pursue it as strenuously as we can.

The Arab lunar mansions were identified by certain star clusters, some of the stars lying within the same traditional constellation figure but nonetheless being assigned to different lunar mansions. The 11th mansion, 'Az-Zubra,' for instance, contained delta and theta Leonis, whereas the 12th, 'As-Sarfa,' contained beta Leonis from the same constellation. In most accounts the sequence begins with 'As-Saratayn,' which denotes beta and gamma Arietis, who gave their name to the mansion entire.[16] Here, then, we encounter a problem. Although Albiruni indicates that 'Alnath' is an alternative name for the first mansion, if we were to argue that by finding the longitude of Alnath (meaning alpha Arietis) the Clerk knew where to begin dividing up the mansions, we would force gamma and beta into the 28th mansion. Chaucer, however, does not say that by 'Alnath' he means a star; we may therefore suppose that the initial value which the Clerk adopted and to which he added his precessional value was not an old longitude for the *star* Alnath, but rather an old value for the initial longitude of the *mansion* Alnath.[17]

Although the star clusters indicate the general region of a given mansion, they are not so evenly spaced that their longitudes exactly coincide with the mansion boundaries. These must be determined schematically, when once an initial point of departure has been determined. In order to make the lunar mansions equal in extent, then, a way must be found of dividing 28 into 360; or rather (since by convention the succeeding three quadrants repeat the divisions of the first) a way must be found of dividing 7 into 90. One of the simplest of the many methods employed was to make six of the seven mansions in a quadrant of 13° and one of the mansions of 12°. This yields 90° after seven mansions, the sequence being symmetrically repeated, such that the mansion of only

[16] See, e.g., Ferrand, *Instructions nautiques*, III, 145–46.

[17] Hinckley (loc. cit.) cited Albiruni as evidence that the first mansion was called 'Alnath.' Haly's work, usually known as *De judicijs astrorum* (Venice, 1485), does the same (Pt. VII, cap. 101; fol. 126a).

12° falls in the same relative place. The 8th mansion will then have a longitude of 90° greater than the 1st, the 15th a longitude 90° greater than the 8th, and so on. By this means, once the first quadrant is partitioned, the remaining three can be determined "by proporcioun"— which is exactly what we are told of the Clerk's method. Begin the first mansion at Aries 20° and the 8th will begin at Cancer 20°, the 15th at Libra 20°, and so on. From the foregoing argument it will be evident not only that the Clerk was not concerned directly with precession, but that 'Alnath' is in any case not here a star; it is the initial boundary of the first lunar mansion to which the star Alnath has lent its name. It is generally acknowledged that the Ellesmere glosses to the tale carry weight. On my interpretation of this passage the comment on Alnath has considerable importance: it is an 'N.B.,' saying 'Alnath is a *mansion*, not a star—if you take it to be a star, all is lost.'

The Clerk now has one other point to determine. Where is the moon? When he has determined the degree of the zodiac in which the moon will rise on his particular day, he will know automatically (now that he has determined his circle of mansions) in which mansion it will be lying. Again we note that the progression of the Clerk's operations is rational and orderly: finding the first mansion leads to the rest of the mansions; finding the rest *and* where the moon is rising leads to finding "ful weel the moones mansioun." At first sight the sequence "his firste mansioun," "the arisyng of his moone," "the moones mansioun," may strike one as a little lame or flat; but an understanding of the principles of what is involved show it to be logical and workaday.

We should emphasize, even so, that when the Clerk does find "the arisyng of his moone" he does more than merely establish for it a particular position on a particular day. The whole point of the Clerk's operation is "To wayten a tyme of his conclusion." By finding a position of rising on what we may call day 1, therefore, the Clerk puts himself in a position to predict on what day thereafter the moon will rise in the mansion best suited to his magical purposes.

It cannot be too strongly stressed that what we are told of the Clerk's efforts is enough for us to reconstruct what he was doing, enough to show that the procedures were grindingly laborious, but such, too, as had no power whatever to effect the magical results he obtained. It is for this reason that the section concludes with the statement that the Clerk:

> . . . knew also his othere observaunces
> For swiche illusiouns and swiche meschaunces
> As hethen folk useden in thilke dayes.
>
> (V, 1291–93)

Chaucer, in other words, is obliged to cheat, to gloss over the gap between what we are told and the miraculous results it achieves. There is a credibility gap which his "othere observaunces" are obliged to fill. This is not to deny, of course, that the Toledo Tables, the lunar mansions, and the rest would mystify a layman—the operations as described are not mundane and plain to every intelligence. But on the other hand, as astronomical and astrological procedures they are indeed commonplace. More than that—they are presented in only the vaguest terms. A layman may be appropriately nonplussed by centers, arguments, and proportions; but an astronomer with Chaucer's competence would not nod wisely if told that a set of tables full well corrected did not omit these ingredients. There is evidence, then, that Chaucer had the measure of his audience: he could expect the laymen to be duly impressed by a flurry of terms; but at the same time he protected himself from the experts by leaving vague just what the "othere observaunces" were.

It is difficult to know how much to make of the point, but it may be observed that the Franklin disclaims any expertise: "I ne kan no termes of astrologye" (V, 1266). In its context this disclaimer follows hard upon his searching for a word to describe the Clerk's efforts:

> . . . to maken illusioun,
> By swich an apparence or jogelrye—
> I ne kan no termes of astrologye—
> That she and every wight sholde wene and seye
> That of Britaigne the rokkes were aweye.
>
> (V, 1264–68)

Neither "apparence" nor "jogelrye" has a specifically astrological ring about it, and to this extent the Franklin's aside could be taken to be simply an apology for being unable to find the right word. On the other hand, we cannot help seeing the line more as an ironic disclaimer than as an apologetic aside, when such a welter of terms follows upon it. The only specifically astrological words in the passage, however, are 'mansion,' 'face,' and 'term.' Are we then to suppose that the Franklin is distinguishing between astronomical and astrological terminology? It is impossible to say, though it should be pointed out in this connection that neither Chaucer nor anyone else could reasonably describe the Toledo Tables as designed for "supersticious cursedness." There is indeed a disparity between the Clerk's result and the means he takes to achieve it.

With *The Complaint of Mars* one has the curious experience of finding that with the benefit of hindsight and perseverance there is a disarming simplicity behind what at first encounter appeared to be opaque and involved.

The narrative section of the *Complaint* appears to be so circumstantial and particular that one readily gains the impression that here, if anywhere, it must be possible to assign a specific date to the astronomical events described.[18] In broad terms the conditions that a specific astronomical date would have to satisfy in order to be taken as the groundwork for the poem are these: Mars makes his complaint on 12 April. At some time before this Venus and Mars must have been in some aspect (angular relationship) to each other, and Mars must then move into Taurus ahead of Venus: he must be met by her there, and be still there when the sun arrives within that sign; whereupon Venus must move on into Gemini, while Mercury must be in, or move into, Aries when Venus is in Gemini.

All this sounds complex, but the possibilities are rapidly narrowed. First, however, one has to determine the period of search. A date around the middle of the 1380's would carry most resonance as then lying close to the probable date of composition. But one would not exclude a completely exact fit merely because it fell in the 1340's, since it would be easy then to imagine Chaucer using an old ephemeris. As a convenience one may scan the entire fourteenth century without much trouble. This

[18] To assign a date is the intention of the article by Johnstone Parr and Nancy Ann Holtz, "The Astronomy-Astrology in Chaucer's *The Complaint of Mars*," *ChauR*, 15 (1981), 255–66. Unaccountably, there is no reference there to North's discussion in 1969 (n. 6), though North uses the same tables and arrives at a date in the same year as Parr and Holtz. In their article there is a flexibility in dealing with the poem's narrative chronology which it is not always easy to detect. They remark, for instance, that Mars lies in Taurus for a month (p. 259)—"actually until the last part of April, by which time . . . Venus had fled into the next sign." In fact, by this time (Mars' move out of Taurus) Venus was at Gemini 20°—two-thirds of the way through the sign. The more subtle of Chaucer's astrological touches make sense, as will appear below, only when manipulating the astronomical data is avoided.

is because the options are rapidly reduced by the fact that Mars lay in Taurus at the same time as the sun on only fifteen occasions during the century.[19] Of these fifteen Venus then also lay ahead of the sun, as we require, on only seven; and of these seven Mercury then lay behind the sun (had a lesser longitude than the sun) on only five: 1321, 1323, 1353, 1383, 1385.

If we inspect these five years more closely we find that 1321 and 1323 fail to qualify since Venus then reaches Taurus ahead of Mars; 1353 fails because Venus had already moved into Gemini by the time the sun reached Taurus; 1383 fails because Venus then lay closer to the sun than the narrative of the poem will allow; and 1385 fails because Mercury lay in Taurus, not Aries, at the critical time. At this stage we would not wish entirely to dismiss all or any of these dates from further consideration. All we have determined is that the events described are relatively rare and that modern tables do not present us with an unambiguous single choice. Before we proceed to modify our criteria, however, and say that ephemerides contemporary with Chaucer might well indicate that our reliance on modern tables is faulty, we may be allowed to examine the text more narrowly and to see whether it offers us any tighter constraints than we have so far taken into account.

Here I revert to a principle stated earlier—that if we wish to read an actual configuration into a passage, then we must be able to satisfy *all* the constraints it imposes. With this in mind, consider the following curious phrase. Chaucer commiserates with Mars after Mars has told Venus to fly from the approach of the sun: "For she that hath thyn herte in governaunce / Is passed half the stremes of thin yen" (110–11). In naturalistic terms the expression 'half the streams of your eyes' is odd, if not uncouth. Skeat described it as "obscure and fanciful," even though he saw that it had an astrological application.[20] As we shall see, however, he scrambled its sense when providing its astrological gloss. He took it to mean that "Venus is already half past the distance to which Mars's beams extend." Before we deal with "half past the distance," we need to

[19] These figures are derived from Bryant Tuckerman, *Planetary, Lunar, and Solar Positions, A.D. 2 to A.D. 1649* (Philadelphia: American Philosophical Society, 1964), pp. 668–717.

[20] Chaucer, *Complete Works*, ed. W. W. Skeat (2nd ed., Oxford: Clarendon, 1900), I, 498.

be clear about what is meant by "the distance to which Mars's beams extend."

The planets were considered to be in significant relation to each other when their angular separation was of a certain particular value. If they were 180° apart on the zodiac they were in 'opposition,' if 90° they were 'square,' or 'quartile,' and so on. The separations considered were zero and multiples of thirty degrees: conjunction, sestile, quartile, trine, opposition. Given that the separation could be read either clockwise or anticlockwise, this meant that at any given time there were at most eight possibilities of significant relation. Astrology, though, was nothing if not flexible in its operation, and it had to deal with any situation at any instant. One of the ways by which it gained the flexibility it needed to meet all contingencies was by extending the principle of 'aspect' so that interpretation of a given situation would not be limited by the necessity of finding such and such a pair of planets *exactly* 30°, or 60°, or 90°, or 120°, or 180° apart before they began to utter their particular messages. This extension was effected by allowing to each of the planets an 'orb,' or 'rays'—a kind of halo of specific extent. Now, if the halo of a given planet is 10° in diameter, it will be obvious that the radius of that halo will be 5°, since the planetary body or disk is not taken into account. If it is approaching another planet whose halo is 12° in diameter (of 6° radius) they will begin to make contact when they are still 11° apart from each other. This will mark the start of what is known as 'platic' aspect, the purer form of aspect, that measured by the actual physical position of the planets, being known as 'partile' aspect. A 'platic' aspect (including conjunction) continues for as long as the two planets concerned are 'joined by half the sum of their orbs.'

Now, in Chaucer's day the 'orb' of Mars was reckoned at 8°, that of Venus at 7°. An astrologer contemporary with Chaucer would therefore have reckoned that the two planets remained in 'platic' conjunction until the distance between them had increased to more than 7½°. We cannot prove directly that Chaucer subscribed to this doctrine, since we have no statement of his on the question; but we can apply this interpretation to the poem and see whether or not any other elements in the narrative coincide with our supposition. We can now return to Skeat's gloss. He thought that Venus was "half past the distance to which Mars's beams extend." But this would mean that Venus was *not* beyond the range of Mars' beams. If, however, we rearrange the words, they will make sense:

'Venus is past half the distance to which Mars' beams extend.' That is to say, the distance to which Mars' beams extend is the *diameter* of the halo; and Venus is past half that distance, the radius. (Given that she cannot be on both sides of Mars at once it is obvious that it must be the radius of the orb that is at issue.) We are not out of the woods yet, though; the convention of platic aspect makes it clear that it is not Venus herself who has passed outside Mars' halo. Rather it is Venus' own halo that has passed beyond contact with the halo of Mars. If it were simply Venus the planet that had moved 4° from Mars (the radius of his orb) then the two would still be in platic aspect, since the whole radius of Venus' halo would still lie inside the radius of Mars' halo. We must assume that Chaucer, understanding the convention of platic aspect, is here asserting that their platic aspect is over—this is why he commiserates with Mars. The two planets have now gone beyond arm's length, as it were. If one or both of the partners stubbornly kept their arms by their sides, the parting gesture would not be very loving.

By these lengthy means we have established that at this point of the narrative Chaucer is giving poetic expression to the fact that Mars and Venus are now 7½° distant from each other. To make so much of the point would not be forgivable unless we could show that a great deal else flows from it—and without strain to the text.

If we suppose that Chaucer's narrative is sequential and orderly, then we will be compelled to the conclusion that Venus is separated from Mars *before* she reaches "Cilenios tour" (Gemini). This is no more than the text says. Chaucer commiserates with Mars in line 111 and two lines later he says: "*Now* fleeth Venus unto Cilenios tour" (113). Is this not sequential? If it is agreed that it is sequential, then it will follow that the end of the platic conjunction between Venus and Mars had taken place while Venus was still in Taurus. What other evidence do we have to bring to bear? Two pieces, both of them based on common astronomical knowledge.

When Mars and Venus first make their tryst to meet in her "nexte paleys" and he goes ahead, she hastens to meet him: "Wherefore she sped her as faste in her weye / Almost in oo day as he dyde in tweye" (69–70). When Mars is full of woe at losing Venus and is threatened by the sun, "He passeth but o steyre in dayes two." (129). At a mundane level both of these statements reflect the fact that Venus' mean daily motion is twice that of Mars. Indeed, there is rather more to it than that. In round terms Mars' motion would be said to be half a degree a day (as line 129 says) and Venus' motion would be said to be one degree even. Chaucer troubles to say, however, that Venus' motion is "almost" twice that of Mars. This suggests either that he is paying close attention to Venus' actual motion as given by an ephemeris, or that he is being particular and using the more accurate mean figure of 59' per day. In either event, there is an attention to detail here which we may extend to the mechanics of Venus' escape.

Since we are regarding the interpretation of "half the stremes" as critical, and since we have argued that the constraint it imposes is that the separation between Mars and Venus should be 7½° before Venus leaves Taurus, we should continue by tracing the escape in reverse. It follows from our reasoning that at most Mars cannot have moved beyond Taurus 22½° while Venus is still within the sign. Chaucer also troubles to tell us that Mars continues to follow "her that is his lyves cure" at the rate of half a degree a day. We have warrant, then, for supposing that Venus is outdistancing Mars by roughly half a degree a day, and from this it would follow that when the flight began the pair were in, or very close to the middle of, the sign. In fact this is more than supposition, since we are also told that when the sun arrives at the gates of the palace:

> Sojourned hath this Mars, of which I rede,
> In chambre amyd the paleys prively
> A certeyn tyme.
>
> (78–80)

Some commentators have supposed, since the first ten degrees of Taurus are a 'face' of Venus, that these degrees are the "chambre."[21] But what would be the consequence of this? Venus would then have at least twenty degrees to travel before she could quit Taurus, and Mars would be within ten degrees of the sun at its first arrival.

Now we should note that though the sun arrives "sturdely," nonetheless he knocks on the chamber door "ful lyghte." There is an element of contradiction here which it is possible to explain if we give an astrological explanation to the sun's conduct. Mars is "in peril to be sleyn" when the sun arrives, but only as yet "in peril." Eventually he will become 'combust' (burnt up)—as we are later told he is when he waxes "feble . . .

[21] See, e.g., North, "Kalenderes . . . ," p. 139.

for hete." In astrological terms, however, this event will not take place until Mars comes within the sun's 'orb' ('combustion' does *not* take account of the rays of the afflicted planet). If we place Mars and Venus even at the end of the first ten degrees of Taurus, then the sun which is gaining on Mars at half a degree a day (just as Venus is retreating at that rate) will burn Mars up within two-and-a-half days, since his rays of combustion were thought to extend for $7\frac{1}{2}°$. Moreover Venus, moving at the same rate as the sun, would still have a long way to travel before she cleared Taurus—in fact she would, at her best speed, not be much past the middle of the sign before Mars got burnt, and under no circumstances could she have yet gained the $7\frac{1}{2}°$ that would mark the end of her platic conjunction with Mars.

In case this appears to be pursuing the text too closely, we may point out that on Chaucer's specific timing of the events, Mars is only "in peril to be sleyn" when his "penaunce" is said to be double because *at that time* Venus has passed half the streams of his eyes. He does not wax "feble . . . for hete" until after Chaucer returns to him, having seen Venus into Cilenius' tower. This much is specific in the narrative (unless, of course, we choose to assume in Chaucer a propensity to be obscure and difficult, not to say confused and irrelevant).

What, then, comes from taking the text at its face value and from supposing that Mars and Venus are precisely "amyd the paleys" when the sun arrives at its gates? His knocking "ful lyghte" may be explained as a reflection of the fact that as yet Mars is only 'under the sun's beams.' These, by convention, extend for twice the radius of his orb. This orb is $7\frac{1}{2}°$ in radius, and Mars, if in the middle of the palace, will by definition be $15°$ away from the sun. On this construction the sun will now have a gap of $7\frac{1}{2}°$ to close, and he will achieve this aim—given the relative rates of motion in the three planets—at precisely the point where the gap between Mars and Venus opens to $7\frac{1}{2}°$. At this critical instant the sun will arrive exactly in the middle of the sign, and Venus will be poised exactly at the end of the sign, ready to pass into Cilenius' tower. Furthermore, she will not have fallen within the fifteen-degree reach of the sun—she will not have been 'seen' by him, as Mars says she must not be ("But bad her fleen, lest Phebus her espye").

This interpretation suffers from the contrary disadvantages, at first sight, of being at once too complicated and too neat. On inspection, however, it *simultaneously* makes sense of the sun's knocking lightly, of the stipulation that Mars and Venus are in the middle of the palace, of the timing of Venus' passing into Gemini, and of the otherwise inexplicable reference to 'half ' the streams of Mars' eyes. We can even detect where Chaucer slides over the passage of time needed for the events to take place in a logical and orderly fashion. In one stanza (99–105) Mars arms himself in fury ("Ful hevy was he to walken over lond"—a marvellous image of military bluster); in the next (106–12) he is "woful Mars"—the change in tone coincides with the lapse in time that the interpretation advanced here would require. It bridges the gap between the moment when Mars, still in the presence of Venus (an astrologer would say joined 'bodily'), bids her depart, and the moment when the platic conjunction has come to an end.

We are now in a position to redefine the constraints that an actual configuration would have to satisfy—that when the sun reached longitude 30–31°, Mars and Venus were at longitude 45° (within a very small margin); and that when the sun had progressed to longitude 45°, Mars was at 52° and Venus at 60° (again within very small margins). Mercury's longitude must also be less than 30° on the later of the two occasions. For convenience we may tabulate the figures for the five possible years we selected earlier:

	SUN	MARS	VENUS	MERCURY
data	30	45	45	—
	45	52	60	30
1321	30	44	58	—
	45	55	76	22
1323	30	58	66	—
	45	69	65	54
1353	30	48	63	—
	45	47	44	65
1383	30	36	26	—
	45	47	44	65
1385	30	51	69	—
	45	60	80	32

Any of these years could be brought into conformity with the text with a little juggling, though the events of 1383 in particular would suggest a rather different story line. The year 1321, on the other hand, would seem to have as much to recommend it as 1385. In any event, no year matches what I take to be the precise and ultimately very simple scheme which the phraseology and the sequence of the astrological narrative indicate.

It is recognized that Chaucer had an expertise in astronomy and frequently argued that he had a respectably wholesome contempt for astrology. Concomitantly, it has often been supposed that where astrology enters his narratives there is a befuddlement and a mystification in the text. I have read the situation differently. I have been at some pains to show that the supposedly irrecoverable passage in *The Franklin's Tale* is in fact logical, orderly, and somewhat mundane.

Anyone who adopts such a position is going to be asked to give his account of *The Man of Law's Tale*, of the section on which North remarked: "Probably more nonsense has been written in the name of astrology in connection with . . . this tale than in the rest of Chaucer criticism combined" (p. 426). The passage reads as follows:

> O firste moevyng! crueel firmament,
> With thy diurnal sweigh that crowdest ay
> And hurlest al from est til occident
> That naturelly wolde holde another way,
> Thy crowdyng set the hevene in swich array
> At the bigynnyng of this fiers viage,
> That crueel Mars hath slayn this mariage.
> Infortunat ascendent tortuous,
> Of which the lord is helplees falle, allas,
> Out of his angle into the derkeste hous!
> O Mars, o atazir, as in this cas!
> O fieble moone, unhappy been thy paas!
> Thou knyttest thee ther thou art nat receyved;
> Ther thou were weel, fro thennes artow weyved.
>   (II, 295–308)

The overall purpose here is to lament the state of the heavens at the time when Constance began her journey to be married. Chaucer goes on to bewail her father's imprudence:

76

Was ther no philosophre in al thy toun?
Is no tyme bet than oother in swich cas?
Of viage is ther noon eleccioun,
Namely to folk of heigh condicioun?
Noght whan a roote is of a burthe yknowe?
Allas, we been to lewed or to slowe!

(II, 309–15)

I take it that the sense and the sentiment of this second passage is more intelligible than that of the first. The question asked in the second line of the second section is purely rhetorical: some times *are* better than others for taking journeys or getting married, and a "philosophre" who understood about "elecciouns" would have been able to tell the Emperor not to despatch his daughter when he did. The drift of the second passage, then, is plain: the wrong time was chosen for the voyage—or rather, the time was wrong because not chosen in accordance with the astrological principles which govern such matters. Since, therefore, we can see the drift, the thrust, of the second passage, we may be able to arrive at the sense of the first merely by supposing that its function is to give grounds to the feeling which the second airs, to provide respectable *and intelligible* cause for the more general part of the complaint which we do understand.

One indication that this is the case can be found in the bare bones of the first sentence of the first section: "O . . . crueel firmament / . . . / Thy crowdyng set the hevene in swich array / . . . / That crueel Mars hath slayn this mariage." Here we should note that Chaucer is entirely unspecific. All we are told is that the heavens are "in swich array" that Mars has doomed the mariage. This, however, is enough: without telling us *how* the heavens were disposed Chaucer tells us that they *were* so disposed that the malign Mars blighted the marriage. This assertion, which we are obliged to take on trust, then issues in the lament that the Emperor did not consult a "philosophre" who could have told him this was what the heavens were declaring.

Chaucer says more, however. He tells us (and this is the drift of the first section) that there had been a time, presumably not long since, when the voyage would have been propitious. The moon (crucial, of course, in the matter of voyages) had been well placed; but the moment has been let slip: "O fieble moone, unhappy been thy paas! / . . . / Ther thou were weel, fro thennes artow weyved." Again we should note that

77

we are not told where the moon was and we are not told where she is now. This is not willfulness: we do not need to be in possession of either particular in order to catch Chaucer's very simple drift: the moon had been well placed (if only the philosopher had been consulted), but she is now ill placed. This is highly unspecific, but entirely intelligible. Attempts to place a coherent organization on the passage by constructing a 'horoscope' out of it are, in my view, reprehensible. They can proceed only on the basis of narrowing a multiplicity of theoretical options and can achieve that narrowing only by arbitrary assumption; they have a tiresome propensity to take on a life of their own and to remove one from the text; and they falsify the tone and intent of the passage, making it appear more difficult and abstruse than it is. If what Chaucer says is taken to be generalized and self-contained, it is not difficult; if it is taken to contain a concealed 'horoscope' it is obscure and vexatious.

So far we have read only the bare bones of this notorious section, have only taken its general drift; Mars has blighted the marriage, and the moon was no better placed either. This general drift, it will be clear, suits entirely with the restatement of the lament in the second section. But what of the more particular components of the first section? Do they suit with this argument, and in particular do they accommodate themselves to the view, adopted here, that Chaucer's audience would be able to assimilate them on the run?

Let us examine these other elements. The first to be accounted for is that which qualifies how the "crueel firmament" put Mars in the position of slaying the marriage:

> O firste moevyng! crueel firmament,
> With thy diurnal sweigh that crowdest ay
> And hurlest al from est til occident
> That naturelly wolde holde another way,
> Thy crowdyng set the hevene in swich array
> At the bigynnyng of this fiers viage,
> That crueel Mars hath slayn this mariage.
>
> (II, 295–301)

Read this against a sentence in the standard and elementary treatise on cosmology, Sacrobosco's *De Sphaera*: "Primus motus omnes alias secum impetu rapit infra diem et noctem terram semel, illis tamen contra nitentibus. . . ."[22] Chaucer's "crowdest" and "hurlest," dramatic enough, have their counterparts in the sober Sacrobosco's "rapit" and "nitentibus." Here, in other words, Chaucer's language reflects no more than a sentiment which can be paralleled in the most commonplace of the handbooks on planetary motion; even the drear *De Sphaera* finds racy language for the cosmic struggle between the planets' daily east-west motion and their progressive west-east motion. Chaucer, I have been insisting, is being entirely unspecific. We can now see that the vague phrase "swich array" is backed up by language that can be paralleled in the most commonplace astronomical treatise.

The crux in my exposition comes in the following four lines:

> Infortunat ascendent tortuous,
> Of which the lord is helplees falle, allas,
> Out of his angle into the derkeste hous!
> O Mars, o atazir, as in this cas!

It is the thrust of my argument that Chaucer wrote to be understood. How can that argument be sustained here? Only, I take it, by the following means: that all of the words used here can be understood on the run—that a reader moderately well versed in astrology would take it on trust that this made sense; that if given time to verify the purported sense of the lines he would find that he had not been cheated. Our problem, however, is more complicated: it is more than likely that "tortuous," "angle," "derkeste hous," and "atazir" will defeat us, even if we have the advantage of knowing what an "ascendant" and its "lord" are in the first place. Let us therefore take our advantage of leisure and look over the shoulder of the competent reader. What would he conclude? He would know that here an "ascendant" was a sign of the zodiac which happened to be rising on the eastern horizon at a particular moment. He would know that its "lord" was that planet whose 'mansion' that sign was. (The moon's [only] mansion is the sign of Cancer, so that if Cancer is rising, the moon is automatically lord [lady] of the ascendant.) He would also know that the "tortuous" signs are those which rise more obliquely to

---

[22] *The Sphere of Sacrobosco and its Commentators*, ed. Lynn Thorndike (Chicago UP, 1949), p. 79.

the horizon than the six which lie opposite them. He would not know, and not be able to deduce instantly, which of the six was in question here; but he might well know that Aries and Pisces are the two most tortuous signs. He might also know that Aries is one of the mansions of Mars, and therefore suppose that Mars was the lord who has helplessly fallen. But if he knew this much, he might also know that if Mars, one of the two malign planets, had been previously in an angle (as he has been told the "lord" was), he would not then have been propitious to the marriage. Given time to think, therefore, the competent reader would *not* conclude that it must be Mars who has helpless fallen from a position that would have been fortunate, since he would conclude that even if in an "angle" (one of the four strong houses), Mars would not have been propitious. Given this time to think he would conclude that the "tortuous" sign must be Pisces, since the "lord" would then be Jupiter, who could have been propitious when in an "angle" and would be "helplees" if fallen into the "derkeste hous." This house he would assume to be the 12th, called 'carcer,' the 'fall' having taken place from the ascendant itself, the chief of the "angles."

At this point I retire with relief to my original point: what Chaucer says in this section is intelligible, or rather acceptable, to someone with the knowledge that allows him to take it on trust. Our problem is that we do not have that knowledge—so much so that we take it on trust when we are told that Mars is the lord of this ascendant, being ignorant of the fact that Mars could never be a benign lord, whereas the text plainly implies that the lord of this ascendant had been propitious earlier, just as the moon had been. I have Chaucer's own authority for this contention. The little he says that has an astrological bearing in the *Treatise on the Astrolabe* includes the following: "Yit saien these astrologiens that the ascendent . . . may be shapen for to be fortunat . . . whan that no wicked planete, as Saturne or Mars or elles the Tayl of the Dragoun, is in the hous of the ascendent, ne that no wicked planete have noon aspect of enemyte upon the ascendent" (II, 4, 30–40). From this it follows that Mars could not be the lord whose fall Chaucer laments, and that someone possessed of the elementary doctrine Chaucer himself employs would not suppose that he was. We, however, are differently placed: because it has been supposed that Mars *is* lord and therefore that Aries is the sign ascending, it has been argued, further, that the "derkeste hous" must be Mars' other sign, Scorpio.[23] But this sign is the one in which astrological convention says that Mars particularly rejoices. It is his 'gaudium,' the place where his influence is strongest. An author who suspected he stood a chance of being thought to refer to Mars' favorite sign when he alluded to the worst of the astrological houses would presumably have found some more cautious way of proceeding.

Any attempt to expound this difficult passage encounters the problem that what is said in exposition of it may then take on the status of being what Chaucer 'really' meant. I wish to argue to the contrary: that it is possible to give a detailed and doctrinally respectable explanation, but that the function of such an explanation is merely to put us in the position of a reader who would take what Chaucer says on trust. My final task, then, is to give this color to the vexatious line: "O Mars, o atazir, as in this cas!" 'Cas' I take to mean 'condition.' The line could be glossed by 'Oh, how I wish Mars . . . had not been in this state.' What, then of 'atazir'? A reader ignorant of what 'atazir' meant would presumably take the word to be in apposition to 'Mars.' But how would it be read by someone who understood it? To discover this we must again proceed patiently. One of the many branches of astrology was concerned with 'directions.' This was a procedure whereby the future of individuals could be predicted by projecting onwards (by purely mathematical means) the original configurations of their birth charts. The procedure was immensely complicated in its details, but in essence, in principle, the method was simple. Five points, the 'hylegiacal places,' were considered: these were the positions of the sun and the moon, the ascendant, the mid-heaven, and 'pars fortunae.' Their positions in the original horoscope at birth were projected onwards to any one of a number of other positions: for instance, the ascendant might be 'directed' to an opposition of Saturn (i.e., the degree of the ascendant might be advanced to a point where it lay directly opposite to the point occupied by Saturn in the horoscope). Alternatively the degree occupied by the moon might be advanced to a position where it lay in conjunction with Mars. If, for instance, the moon was at Aries 10° in the original horoscope, and Mars was at 15°, then advancing the moon by five degrees would place it in the same degree as Mars. Allow one degree to represent one year (though the

[23] Thus, W. C. Curry, *Chaucer and the Medieval Sciences* (rev. ed., London: Allen & Unwin, 1960), p. 172.

procedure was in fact more complex than this), and you would know what to expect when the child was five years old. Now, the common English word for this procedure was 'direction' (Lat. *directio*). The more arcane word (with an Arabic flavor) was 'atazir.' We can see the word in use in a standard compendium of astrology, Albohazen Haly's *De Judicijs astrorum*: "quando sol fuerit hylech scient ab eius athazir vita & impedimeta . . . et quando luna fuerit hylech per sui athazir scient vita. . . ." [24] Anyone who knew the sense of this bizarre word 'atazir' would be likely to know that it could not lie in apposition to 'Mars.' That planet cannot be atazir; in some circumstances Mars could be hyleg, but he cannot serve as one of the 'hylegiacal places' used in taking directions, and so will not stand as atazir for this reason. What, then, of the sense of Chaucer's line? We can see that he laments "Mars . . . as in this cas"; can he lament Mars *and* the atazir "as in this cas"? He can indeed, if we revert to our initial contention—that the first section is simply a technical but unspecific statement of the conditions that form the grounds of the lament in the second. The second section bewails the fact that no philosopher was consulted, the first includes in its lament the fact that no 'direction' was taken—not even (as Chaucer troubles to say later) "whan a roote is of a burthe yknowe."

My point is this: the passage is, to us, fiercely difficult; but we can sadly misapprehend its difficulty if we do not recognize those elements in it which are accessible to one moderately versed in the subject. The difficulty, in other words, lies in the verification of what Chaucer says, not in its intelligibility to one who had enough expertise in the subject to take what he says on trust.

My argument can be seen at its clearest, I believe, in the case of the narrative section of *The Complaint of Mars*. For all the intricacy of its detail, and despite the obliqueness with which the technicalities are presented, the essential scheme is delightful in its elegance and simplicity. In this and other places Chaucer seems to rely upon an alertness and an expertise in at least some portion of his audience.

Appendix: The Host and the 'artificial' day

The first step in the Host's elaborate calculations involves him,

---

[24] Haly, *De judicijs astrorum*, Pt. IV, cap. 8; fol. 62.

supposedly, in determining how far along its track through the sky the sun has progressed. He finds that:

> the brighte sonne
> The ark of his artificial day hath ronne
> The ferthe part, and half an houre and moore.

Anyone with the ability to check this assertion, however, will find that in fact the time is a good hour short of what it is supposed to be; and the point to be determined is whether it is the Host or Chaucer who has bungled the calculation and (if possible) to decide how the error arose.

We need first of all to recognize what it is that the Host is supposedly able to perform. We have no warrant for thinking that he is equipped either with tables or with an instrument—he appears to be using naked eye and native wit. And while on the move he is supposedly able to know (1) where the sun rose; (2) where due south is; (3) what is the sun's trajectory between these two points; (4) where the half-way mark is; (5) how far past this half-way mark another half an hour or so places the sun. In practice, of course, the Host (had he the ability) would work part of this calculation in reverse: he would observe the sun's present position and then notionally move it backwards eight degrees or so. But in which precise direction? Even in the most approximate terms and in very round figures, the calculation is patently not a simple one.

How, then, did Chaucer himself perform it? Either by using tables, or by using an instrument (which would almost certainly have been an astrolabe). Since he gives every appearance of having employed Nicholas of Lynn's *Kalendarium* for the rest of the Host's calculations, it is not difficult to suppose that he also inspected Nicholas' values for the 'Quantitates diei artificialis' in this first part. If he did, though, then he found a single figure (14 hrs. 26 mins.), to which he was obliged to apply a number of numerical adjustments. The figure represents the total time the sun is above the horizon (at latitude 51° 50′) on 18 April. When halved and subtracted from noon it gives the time of sunrise (4.47 a.m.). When quartered and added to the time of sunrise, it would show how much had to be added to bring the time to 10 o'clock. His answer, however, should have been 8 hrs. 23 mins. 30 secs. (8.24 a.m.). We need only suppose a slip that led him to believe his answer was 9.24 a.m., and the anomaly is resolved. On balance this may be the more plausible explanation; but we should examine the alternative, particularly because Sigmund Eisner has recently presented a refutation of it that bears the appearance of being conclusive.

Skeat adopted A. E. Brae's conjecture that Chaucer at this point confused the arc of the artificial day with the arc of azimuth—that he did not measure the sun's track through the sky but rather its path in relation to the local horizon.[25] Brae performed the calculation, finding that the sun rose 22° 30′ north of east and that it was half way at 9.20 a.m. Sigmund Eisner has attempted to refute Brae by using Nicholas as a base and producing figures that can only be derived mathematically.[26] Eisner asserts that in fact the sun rose 24° 26′ 15″ north of east and that the time at half way was 9.04 a.m.

Since I clearly cannot fall back on counter assertion here, I must briefly demonstrate how the calculation is to be performed using Nicholas. His expressed position for the sun on 18 April (Taurus 6° 42′) allows one to derive a right ascension for the sun from his table of houses (interpolation is necessary). The right ascension, in turn, allows one to derive a value for the obliquity of the ecliptic. With these three values one may then calculate the sun's declination: 13° 48′. One now has a figure, derived from Nicholas, to apply to the standard formula for determining azimuth at sunrise:

$$\cos A_r = \frac{\sin \text{delta}}{\cos \text{phi}}$$

where A_r is the azimuth measured from north, *delta* is the sun's declination, and *phi* is the terrestrial latitude (given by Nicholas as 51° 50′). If, however, one uses Eisner's value for sunrise (24° 26′ 15″) in this formula, then *delta* can only be 14° 48′ 43″. But as already indicated, Nicholas' implied value is 13° 48′, Eisner's value not being reached until 21 April. If one applies Nicholas' implied declination and his expressed latitude to the formula, then the sun's azimuth turns out to be 22° 42′—very close to Brae's value.

Further calculation, using the standard formulas for deriving altitude and azimuth, shows that the azimuth will be 56° (half of 22° + 90°) at

[25] Skeat, *Treatise*, pp. l–li.
[26] See the *Kalendarium*, ed. Eisner, pp. 30–31.

9.14 a.m.[27] Performing the equivalent calculations on an astrolabe valid for 52° and a 42-inch celestial globe—a more reliable *because* more approximate means—I have no trouble at all in getting 9.15 (±) as an answer.

There are, then, strong grounds for not dismissing Brae's argument as though it was invalidated by his procedure. Instead, the issue lies between concluding that Chaucer made an error in his numerical calculation or that he made an error in reading his astrolabe. I see no evidence of sufficient weight to choose between the two, but in either case the gap between what Chaucer did and what he gave the Host to do supposedly unaided is wide indeed.

[27] Readers may perhaps wonder whether the application of sophisticated formulas to Nicholas is justifiable. I have, however, checked all 360 values that Nicholas gives for right ascension (pp. 164–75) and find no error of more than 2' of arc. I have also checked the values for oblique ascension at 5° intervals. These are more difficult to derive, but are still accurate to within the same margin.

Punctuation and Caesura in Chaucer

George B. Killough
College of St. Scholastica

U NTIL very recently, Middle English punctuation has received little attention.[1] Since the two most important manuscripts of *The Canterbury Tales*, Hengwrt and Ellesmere, both contain a *virgula suspensiva* (looks like a slash, hereafter called a virgule) in the middle of virtually every five-stress poetic line, they are especially worthy of close examination to determine punctuation practices.[2] The present article is based on a statistical and historical study of the principles governing placement of these virgules, a study which demonstrates that virgule placement is highly regular, that it depends on syntactic and metrical factors, that mid-line poetic punctuation has precedent in grammatical theory and

---

[1] Except for the brief comments in paleographical manuals and facsimile volumes, the scholarship on punctuation in Middle English manuscripts has included only a few articles: A.C. Cawley, "Punctuation in the Early Versions of Trevisa," *London Medieval Studies*, 1 (1937), 116–33; Peter Clemoes, *Liturgical Influence on Punctuation in Late Old and Early Middle English Manuscripts*, Occasional Papers Printed for the Department of Anglo-Saxon, No. 1 (Cambridge, England: 1952); Margery M. Morgan, "A Treatise in Cadence," *MLR*, 47 (1952), 156–64; Elizabeth Zeeman, "Punctuation in an Early Manuscript of Love's *Mirror*," *RES*, NS 7 (1956), 11–18; Peter J. Lucas, "Sense-Units and the Use of Punctuation-Markers in John Capgrave's *Chronicle*," *Archivum Linguisticum*, 23 (1971), 1–24. M. B. Parkes is now working on a full-length study of medieval punctuation that promises to be helpful; the first step in the study, "Medieval Punctuation: A Preliminary Survey," is circulating in xeroxed copies; see also M. B. Parkes, "Punctuation, or Pause and Effect," in *Medieval Eloquence: Studies in the Theory and Practice of Medieval Rhetoric*, ed. James J. Murphy (Berkeley: U of California P, 1978), pp. 127–42.

[2] The virgule also appears with great frequency in the prose tales in Hengwrt and Ellesmere. See the notes on punctuation by A. I. Doyle and M. B. Parkes, "Paleographical Introduction," in *Geoffrey Chaucer, The Canterbury Tales: A Facsimile and Transcription of the Hengwrt Manuscript, with Variants from the Ellesmere Manuscript*, Vol. I of *The Variorum Edition of the Works of Geoffrey Chaucer*, ed. Paul G. Ruggiers (Norman, Oklahoma: U of Oklahoma P, 1979), pp. xxxvii–xxxix.

scribal practice, and that the marks in Hengwrt and Ellesmere must have been placed by the scribe(s)[3] instead of being handed down as part of Chaucer's text.[4]

The mid-line virgules in Hengwrt and Ellesmere have fueled a controversy about Chaucer's meter. Two scholars have used the virgule as evidence for the theory that Chaucer was composing in a kind of native English meter, each verse having a rhythmic half-line movement, somewhat like the alliterative verse of *Piers Plowman*.[5] They argue that the mid-line punctuation in Chaucer manuscripts parallels the mid-line punctuation in manuscripts of alliterative poetry and thus suggests that Chaucer was following the native metrical model. This idea has not been widely accepted: most metrists still hold the orthodox theory, which is that Chaucer used a five-stress line adapted from the French decasyllable.[6] Nevertheless, the native-meter theorists have raised some important questions, which careful attention to the punctuation itself should help to resolve.

If Chaucer was writing, not a native meter, but a five-stress line adapted from the French decasyllable, what kind of caesura did he use? Do the mid-line virgules reveal a metrical pattern that may be called caesura? Chaucer's caesura once received a lot of scholarly attention. Ten Brink, giving careful consideration to the virgules, praised the caesura's movability. Schipper, noting differences in syllable count and instances

[3] A. I. Doyle and M. B. Parkes have recently argued that Hengwrt and Ellesmere were written by the same scribe. See "The Production of Copies of the *Canterbury Tales* and the *Confessio Amantis* in the Early Fifteenth Century," in *Medieval Scribes, Manuscripts and Libraries: Essays Presented to N. R. Ker*, ed. M. B. Parkes and Andrew G. Watson (London: Scolar Press, 1978), pp. 163–210. Roy Vance Ramsey argues that there were two scribes; see "The Hengwrt and Ellesmere Manuscripts of the *Canterbury Tales*: Different Scribes," *SB*, 35 (1982), 133-54.

[4] George B. Killough, "The Virgule in the Poetry of the *Canterbury Tales*," Diss. Ohio University 1978.

[5] James G. Southworth, *Verses of Cadence: An Introduction to the Prosody of Chaucer and His Followers* (Oxford: Basil Blackwell, 1954); James G. Southworth, *The Prosody of Chaucer and His Followers: Supplementary Chapters to Verses of Cadence* (Oxford: Basil Blackwell, 1962); Ian Robinson, *Chaucer's Prosody: A Study of the Middle English Verse Tradition* (Cambridge, England: Cambridge UP, 1971).

[6] See Tauno F. Mustanoja, "Chaucer's Prosody," in *Companion to Chaucer Studies*, ed. Beryl Rowland, 2nd ed. (New York: Oxford UP, 1979), pp. 65–94; Paull F. Baum, *Chaucer's Verse* (Durham, North Carolina: Duke UP, 1961). The best discussion of the metrical debate is Alan T. Gaylord, "Scanning the Prosodists: An Essay in Metacriticism," *ChauR*, 11 (1976), 22–77.

of initial and internal truncation, concluded that Chaucer's lines allow for sixty-four possible kinds of caesurae. Young, looking back on the excessive variation allowed by his predecessors, decided that the doctrine of an almost indefinitely variable caesura cannot really be a rule of prosody.[7] The question remains today: what is the Chaucerian caesura?

Statistical study helps to resolve the metrical questions. Patterns of virgule placement show that these mid-line marks cannot be equated with mid-line marks in native rhythmic poetry. When virgule positions are described by means of the orthodox five-stress scansion, definite patterns emerge. Moreover, these patterns can be used as guidelines to predict virgule placement in unpunctuated transcripts of the manuscripts. The fact that these patterns emerge in data dependent on the five-stress scansion helps to confirm the five-stress scansion itself, and diminishes the likelihood of any rhythmic half-line movement in Chaucer's verse. In short, the punctuation supports the orthodox theory.

However, even though the punctuation does indicate that a metrical caesura was expected, it does not indicate that there was an inherent, essential caesura in the Chaucerian line. To be sure, the evidence shows that the Hengwrt scribe was aiming at the single most important break in every line. He was identifying this break primarily by seeking the most important syntactic boundary, but also by giving emphasis to the middle of the line. The fact that he tried to put a virgule in every line, regardless of syntax, and the fact that he tried to locate this virgule near line-center (after the second stress and the fourth syllable) show that his concern was not exclusively syntactic but also metrical. Nevertheless, because syntax clearly outweighs meter as the governing force in virgule location, the system of the Hengwrt scribe fails to locate a strictly metrical caesura in Chaucer's verse: the virgule sooner or later appears at every metrical position. There is evidence to suggest that the scribe was trying to find an English caesura after the pattern of markings that he

---

[7] Bernhard Ten Brink, *The Language and Metre of Chaucer*, trans. M. Bentinck Smith (London, 1901; rpt. New York: Haskell House, 1968), pp. 218–21; Jakob Schipper, *A History of English Versification* (Oxford, 1910; rpt. New York: AMS Press, 1971), pp. 209–18; George Young, *An English Prosody on Inductive Lines* (Cambridge, England: 1928; rpt. New York: Greenwood, 1969), pp. 87–92. Young not only rejected the doctrine of the almost indefinitely movable caesura but also took a careful look at punctuation, suggesting that it was "the desire to attach some meaning to a slant-mark, found in some of the Chaucer manuscripts, which stereotyped the caesura theory; perhaps originated it" (p. 90).

found in other manuscripts, perhaps of Latin verse. But the Middle English five-stress line simply does not have a metrical mid-point as an essential feature.

These conclusions derive in part from a tabulation of syntactic boundaries or indicators in the 2828 lines of the Hengwrt manuscript *Monk's, Franklin's, Nun's Priest's,* and *Friar's Tales*, a tabulation that takes note of metrical location and the presence or absence of virgules.[8] Table 1 below represents the tabulation for all the coordinating conjunctions in the four tales. This table demonstrates the general principle that coordinating conjunctions receive a preceding virgule in most metrical positions, as illustrated in the lines below. Metrical positions are identified with Roman numerals for stress and Arabic numerals for syllable, so that II4 means *after the second stress and the fourth syllable.*[9]

	II4
Hg *FranT* 749	But hire obeye / and folwe hir wyl in al
	II5
Hg *FranT* 797	His lady certes / and his wyf also
	I3
Hg *FranT* 904	Of vitaille / and of oother purueiance
	III6
Hg *FranT* 1044	How þat I may been holpe / and in what wyse
	I2
Hg *FranT* 1528	To yow / and eek I se wel youre distresse
	III7
Hg *FranT* 875	It doth no good to my wit ⊣/ but anoyeth
	II4 IV8
Hg *FranT* 757	As in my gilt / were outher werre / or stryf

[8] The number 2828 represents the lines in Hengwrt in the four tales *and* their prologues. My access to the manuscripts came through microfilms being used by my teacher Professor Roy Vance Ramsey in his work on the publication of the Hengwrt facsimile.

[9] Metrical positions are described according to the orthodox syllable-stress scansion because this scansion is a fixed measuring device, providing nine definite positions in every line. The strong-stress system is not a fixed measuring device because it allows an indefinite number of syllables per stress and thus a proliferating number of positions (01, 02, 03, 04, I1, I2, I3, I4, I5, I6, II2, II3, II4, II5, II6, II7, II8, and so forth). The

The two positions not represented, O1 and IV9, cannot be expected to take virgules.[10]

Table 1 gives statistics for incidence in each metrical position. The first column of figures labeled *Presences*, represents the numbers of lines that have all coordinating conjunctions preceded by virgules. The second column, *Absences*, represents numbers of lines with at least one absence before a coordinating conjunction. The third column, *Significant absences*, shows the lines that remain after certain discountable absences are subtracted from the lines in the second column. Absences are considered discountable when they occur because stronger forces draw the virgule to another position. Here are three examples of discountable absence:

	I2	II4	
Hg *FranT* 1606	This al and som / ther is namoore to sayn		
	II4	III6	
Hg *FranT* 730	Ther was a knyght ⁻/ þat louede *and* dide his payne		
	II5	IV8	
Hg *FranT* 964	They fille in speche / and forth moore and moore		

These lines have respectively an absence at I2 because of a clause boundary at II4, an absence at III6 because of a subordinating connective at II4, and an absence at IV8 because of a more important coordinating conjunction at II5. Syntactic features like the clause boundary and the subordinating connective have, by means of other tabulations, proven to influence virgule placement in the same way that the coordinating conjunction does, hence the necessity for discounting absences. The significant ratio to notice below is the ratio between the numbers in the first column and the numbers in the third: total presences compared to significant absences. The positions are listed according to the approxi-

danger of circular reasoning, induced by this initial assumption of the orthodox scansion, has been countered by the prediction test, which shows that virgule placement can be successfully predicted according to guidelines derived from the tabulations based on orthodox scansions. See pp. 93–94.

[10] The transcription follows the practice of the *Variorum Chaucer*. Also, it should be noted that attached virgules (⁻/) have proven to be equivalent to free virgules (/) in mid-line. Virgules at IV8, as in *FranT*, 757, are rare and often occur in lines with a second virgule elsewhere.

mate order of their power to command coordinating conjunction virgules.[11]

TABLE 1

VIRGULE INCIDENCE BEFORE COORDINATING CONJUNCTIONS

Positions	Presences	Absences	Significant Absences
II4	170	10	1
II5	45	0	0
I3	24	2	0
III6	88	34	3
I2	28	18	1
III7	27	31	8
IV8	17	114	39
TOTALS	399	209	52

Tables like this have been compiled for several syntactic indicators: series, subordinating connectives, clause boundaries, saying clauses (having to do with direct or indirect quotation), front position tertiaries (conjunctive adverbs), appositives, direct address words, exclamations, and parallel elements. The tables show that all these indicators influence virgule placement. Further counts show that phrase boundaries have substantial though lesser influence on virgule placement. The Hengwrt punctuator was clearly paying attention to syntax and according it substantial importance in his metrical aim of locating the caesura.

The evidence shows that he was indeed trying to punctuate a metrical mid-point at the same time that he was punctuating syntactic boundaries. For one thing, all the tables for syntactic indicators show, just as in Table 1, a higher incidence of virgules near the center of the line than in the extremities. For another thing, a special count shows that fifty-six percent of all the virgules in the four-tale sample occur at II4 or II5, and

---

[11] The order is said to be approximate here because the data are not considered great enough to represent the precise order. II4 is considered the strongest position because II4 is nearly always the strongest position and because II4 here has by far the greatest number of presences as well as a high ratio of presences to significant absences.

eighty-two percent occur at I3, II4, II5, or III6. The punctuator was clearly aiming for line-center. He was also following a general pattern of one-virgule-per-line, as if he were looking for a *single* position. A special count shows that the vast majority, in fact ninety percent, of all the lines in the four-tale sample have a single mid-line virgule; only nine percent have two virgules or more, and only one percent have no virgules.

The peculiar relationship between the punctuator's effort to mark syntactic boundaries and his effort to find a single metrical mid-point can be seen in his treatment of syntactic indicators in the extremities of the line. Notice, for example, in Table 1 the high proportion of absences by coordinating conjunctions at I2, III7, and IV8. The punctuator has indeed left absences at these syntactic boundaries but, in most cases, only because there are other syntactic indicators closer to line-center. That is why there are relatively few significant absences in Table 1 at I2, III7, and IV8; the rest of the absences at these positions have been discounted because the lines have a syntactic indicator (with virgule) closer to line-center. In other words, the main reason for absence is a syntactic attraction elsewhere.

The conclusion to be drawn from all this information is that the punctuator was seeking a single metrical mid-point dependent partly on metrical structure but mostly on syntax. The syntactic patterns in punctuation placement are so strong (elements in series, for example, exacting as many as four virgules in one line) and the variation in metrical position so great (virgules appearing regularly by syntactic indicators in positions I2 through III7) that we must conclude that syntax was indeed the major determinant in the punctuator's quest for the mid-point of the verse.

In confirmation of the patterns shown by tables of virgule presences and absences, these patterns have been used to predict virgule placement in unpunctuated transcripts of the Hengwrt manuscript. Actual Hengwrt punctuation was predicted in eighty percent of the lines of three tales, *The Franklin's, Nun's Priest's*, and *Friar's Tale*s (1572 lines predicted correctly out of 1958 lines) before these tales were tabulated for virgule presences and absences, the statistical patterns having been determined initially from tabulation of *The Monk's Tale*. This eighty percent rate of success not only confirms the patterns deriving from tabulation but also reveals the extent to which the scribal system is regular. The twenty percent rate of prediction failure has proven to result from internal contradictions in the punctuation system, not from any error in the formulation of the rules.[12] Further confirmation of the eighty percent rate of regularity can be found in the high degree of similarity between Hengwrt and Ellesmere. In all four tales, these two manuscripts show virgule disagreement in only twenty-one percent of their lines. This twenty-one percent rate of disagreement is remarkably consistent with the present twenty percent rate of prediction failure. Such consistency suggests that the Ellesmere scribe was operating from a set of principles similar to those that guided the present prediction of virgule placement.[13]

Prediction success and the extent of Ellesmere agreement confirm the system of punctuation shown by the tables of presences and absences. All of this evidence effectively lessens the likelihood that Chaucer's verse was based on a native meter. There is simply no need to bring up the idea of native meter to explain the mid-line punctuation. Instead of depending on some sort of half-line movement, this punctuation depends on the notion that every verse has a metrical mid-point determined for the most part by syntax. Thus, all of the evidence, particularly the success at prediction, favors the orthodox theory of Chaucer's meter over the unorthodox native-meter one. Even further confirmation of the orthodox theory can be found in the history of mid-verse punctuation. Not at all a unique feature of native English verse, it appears at syntactic boundaries in various English meters. The Hengwrt-Ellesmere scribe(s) probably derived the notion of mid-verse punctuation from models (English and perhaps Latin and Italian) that did not use any kind of strong-stress meter at all.

If the mid-line punctuation does not support the theory of native half-lines, then does it represent the presence of caesura in Chaucer's five-stress line? The answer to this question is also *no*. It is accurate to say that the Hengwrt-Ellesmere punctuation system is metrical in the sense

---

[12] For example, the system requires at least one virgule per line, but the system also includes prohibitions against virgule placement in several circumstances; some lines, which contain no spaces permitted to virgules, are thus battlegrounds for the conflict between the one-virgule-per-line tendency and a whole array of prohibitions.

[13] Thomas J. Garbáty, "Wynkyn de Worde's 'Sir Thopas' and Other Tales," *SB*, 31 (1978), 57–67, finds the same rate of punctuation placement disagreement, twenty-one percent of the lines, between the Hengwrt and the Wynkyn de Worde *Sir Thopas*.

that it seeks to put one virgule in every line as close to line-center as possible; but this is not the same thing as saying that the punctuation system reveals the presence of caesura in line-structure. The punctuation suggests instead that there is no metrical necessity for caesura in Chaucer's line. If there were, the punctuator would have had a much easier time developing his system; he would have avoided the ambiguities and contradictions that cause the twenty percent rate of irregularity. If caesura were implicit in line-structure, Hengwrt and Ellesmere would have a much lower rate of punctuation disagreement.

Caesura, then, is not a useful term for discussions of the mid-line punctuation because it suggests a pause implicit in line-structure. In a very vague sense, for example as the word for the single best syntactic boundary in every line, it does no harm. But because the word implies a necessary and predetermined pause in each verse, it is best avoided. Experience at scansion (of the 2874 lines in the four tales) persuades me that caesura is not necessary to poetic composition, whether it means that every line *must* have a mid-line syntactic boundary or that every line *must* have a pause at a fixed metrical position (for example II4). The evidence of virgule placement will not support either of these meanings for caesura. Hence, it is not accurate to say that the virgule marks *the caesura*. It is only accurate to say that the virgule shows the punctuator's attempt to find a caesura, in imitation of the mid-line punctuation he had seen in earlier manuscripts.

Several kinds of evidence provoke doubt about the notion of an inherent caesura. First of all, virgules appear in every metrical position from O1 to IV9. To be sure, most of them appear at or near line-center (II4), but some appear in the extremities. Table 2 below shows virgule distribution in all nine positions in descending order of incidence. The table represents the total 3090 virgules in the four-tale Hengwrt sample.

TABLE 2

VIRGULE INCIDENCE BY METRICAL POSITION

Position	Number	Percentage
II4	1193	39%
II5	538	17%
III6	455	15%
I3	336	11%
I2	260	8%
III7	216	7%
IV8	52	2%
01	38	1%
IV9	2	0%
	3090	100%

Although a very high percentage of virgules appear near line-center, the total distribution is not what one would expect if the virgule marked some sort of essential metrical feature of line-structure. If no position is prohibited to caesura, as in these lines, caesura must have no definite meaning at all.

More evidence against caesura is found in the incidence of multiple-virgule lines. In the Hengwrt sample, nine percent of all the lines have two or more virgules within the line. In the Ellesmere sample, thirteen percent of all the lines have two or more virgules. Although these percentages may seem small, they represent 268 lines in Hengwrt and 374 lines in Ellesmere, respectively. If caesura is supposed to be a single essential pause, there are not likely to be hundreds of lines with multiple pauses.[14]

Another kind of evidence against caesura is the evidence that shows virgule placement to depend more on syntax than on meter. The punctuator was clearly looking for the most important syntactic break instead

---

[14] The multiple caesura is paralleled by the doctrine of multiple caesura in the Latin grammarians (explained below). The grammatical doctrine could have encouraged the use of multiple mid-verse punctuation marks because the grammarians associated caesura with punctuation; but the doctrine, which was essentially a plan for preserving the flow of a hexameter line by preventing the coincidence of word-ends and foot-ends in mid-line (an unwelcome closure), could have had very little influence on English line-structure because the coincidence of word-ends and foot-ends is not significant in English.

of an essentially metrical mid-point. Several patterns reveal this syntactic emphasis in the punctuation system. First of all, the punctuator paid attention to syntactic hierarchies. A line with both a clause boundary and a phrase boundary has its virgule characteristically at the clause boundary. In the following two examples, there are phrase boundaries at metrically central and thus favorable spots (II4 and II5), but the virgules fall in the less favorable spots at the clause boundaries:

		II4	III6
Hg *FrT* 1549	And neer the feend he drogh / as noght ne were		
		I2	II5
Hg *FrT* 1642	And god / that made after his ymage		

The second kind of evidence for the syntactical emphasis in the punctuation system is the way that the central position in many lines is closed off to virgules because of certain syntactic prohibitions. The following six examples show virgules placed at the extremities of the line because the central position (II4 or II5) is not a suitable syntactic boundary for a virgule:

		I2	II5
Hg *MkT* 3345	That was / the wiseste child of euerychoon		
		II4	IV8
Hg *MkT* 3846	Philippes sone of Macidoyne / he was		
		01	II5
Hg *FrT* 1638	Moore / than a maister of dyuynytee		
		II4	III6
Hg *MkT* 3256	And slepynge in hir barm / vp on a day		
		I3	II4
Hg *MkT* 3170	In prose eek ⁻/ been endited many oon		
		I2	II5
Hg *FranT* 1154	That hadde / this Moones mansions in mynde		

These lines show respectively a virgule at I2 (*MkT*, 3345) because the II5 opening occurs between an adjunct and a noun, a virgule at IV8 (*MkT*, 3846) because the II4 opening occurs at the beginning of a genitival phrase, a virgule at 01 (*FrT*, 1638) because the II5 opening occurs at the beginning of a genitival phrase, a virgule at III6 (*MkT*, 3256) because the II4 opening occurs in mid-prepositional phrase, a virgule at I3 (*MkT*, 3170) because the II4 opening occurs between auxiliary and main verb, and a virgule at I2 (*FranT*, 1154) because the II5 opening occurs between an adjunct and a noun. Counts show that the syntactical positions prohibited to virgules in these lines are regularly prohibited to virgules throughout the four-tale sample. The fact that the punctuator observes such prohibitions illustrates his emphasis on syntax over meter.

A third kind of evidence that favors syntax is the punctuation in lines with series. The punctuator pays very careful attention to items in series, providing as many as four virgules in a single line if necessary. The following two lines show the punctuator's practice of including virgules for series at any metrical position, even at IV9 which is normally prohibited to virgules:

	I3	II5	III7	
Hg *MkT* 3839	Of kynges / Prynces / Dukes / Erles bolde			
	I2	II5	III7	IV9
Hg *MkT* 3401	Glorie / and honour / regne / tresor / rente			

Series virgules like these are clearly for syntactic separation, not for metrical necessity.

The final kind of evidence that shows the dominance of syntax over meter lies in a comparison between Hengwrt and Ellesmere. Most lines in these two manuscripts show no disagreements in virgule occurrence or position; in fact, the rate of disagreement is only twenty-one percent. Among the lines that agree in virgule occurrence and position are numerous lines that show disagreements in spelling and wording, disagreements that affect syllable count. In the four-tale sample, there are 172 lines that show punctuation agreement but spelling disagreements that may affect syllable count.[15] There are 56 lines in which the punctuation agrees but in which wording disagreements change the syllable count. In all these lines, the virgules appear between the same words in Hengwrt as in Ellesmere. So syllable count in these lines does not affect virgule placement. Syntax is clearly a more important consideration than meter.

[15] This is expressed tentatively because the normal metrical devices of syncope, apocope, and final -*e* can often cause a line to absorb new spellings without any change in syllable count.

One of the by-products of punctuation study is the discovery that many of Chaucer's lines *cannot* have a pause at a single fixed central position. The fact that over half of all the virgules occur after the second stress raises an expectation for a pause at either II4 or II5 in every line. But many lines have multisyllabic words bridging these positions. And even more lines have these positions blocked by closely knit syntactic structures (note the prohibitions mentioned above). The following two examples illustrate the closing off of the II4 and II5 positions by multisyllabic words:

	II4 II5 III6
Hg *MkT* 3292	He drow out Cerberus / the hound of helle
	I2 II4 II5
Hg *MkT* 3395	This hand / *þat* Balthasar so soore agaste

In the Hengwrt four-tale sample of 2828 lines, at least 565 lines have multisyllabic words or closely knit syntactic structures blocking the II4 and II5 positions. This obstruction is one of the reasons why the punctuator does not always put his virgules in the same metrical location. But more important, the obstruction shows that there is no fixed central pause in the Chaucerian five-stress line. Chaucer clearly generated his verses without paying heed to any rule requiring a fixed pause after the second stress. So, if caesura means a fixed pause, Chaucer's verse does not have it.

Moreover, if caesura means the best syntactic break near line-center, Chaucer's verse still does not have it. Many verses of course do have a syntactic boundary near line-center that is more important than any other syntactic boundary in the line. But numerous lines have no such thing. These lines, identified during the prediction test and labeled as *Uncongenial* to prediction, comprise nineteen percent of the lines in the three tales used for this test.[16] Occurring as they do in this proportion, uncongenial lines constitute very strong evidence against the idea of caesura as a necessary mid-line syntactic break. The lines in Table 3 below are representative uncongenial lines, shown as they appear in the

---

[16] Prediction succeeded in only half the uncongenial lines. A fifty-fifty success rate is expectable because many of these lines present two equally likely positions for the virgule.

TABLE 3

SAMPLE UNCONGENIAL LINES

		Predictions	Corrections
Hg *FranT* 1074	In to / hir owene / dirke Regioun	II5	I2
Hg *FranT* 1278	And / hise *proporcionels* conuenientz	01	none
Hg *FranT* 740	Hath swich a pitee caught ⌐ of his penance	III6	
Hg *FranT* 741	That *priuely* / she fel of his acord	II4	
Hg *FranT* 1021	He to his hous / is goon / with sorweful herte	II4	III6
Hg *FranT* 1377	They pryuely / been stirt ⌐ in to a welle	III6	II4 III6
Hg *FranT* 1323	For madame / wel ye woot ⌐ what ye han hight ⌐	I3 III6	
Hg *FranT* 1588	¶ Yis *certes* / wel and trewely / quod he	I3 IV8	I3
Hg *FrT* 1424	¶ Now by my trouthe / brother deere / seyde he	II5	II5 IV8

prediction test. Dark slashes represent actual Hengwrt virgules and light slashes represent wrong predictions. The first column on the right describes the positions of the predicted virgules, and the second column describes the corrected positions in lines where prediction failed. When the prediction was correct, no entry was made in the second column. *None* means that the line in Hengwrt contains no virgules.

The first two lines are uncongenial because they contain no syntactic break appropriate for a virgule. The absence of an important syntactic boundary should be immediately apparent, but confirmation of this absence can be found even in the practice of the punctuator. Counts show that virgules are normally prohibited in the middle of prepositional phrases, between adjuncts and nouns, and after coordinating conjunctions. Despite these prohibitions, however, the punctuator normally inserted a virgule in lines without any syntactic breaks because he was trying to adhere to his one-virgule-per-line pattern. The first two lines listed here clearly show the conflict between what the punctuator was trying to do and what the Chaucerian line allows: an important syntactic break simply does not occur in these lines.

The next four lines are uncongenial to prediction because they each have an opening at either II4 or II5 as well as a phrase boundary elsewhere (in these lines at III6). Notice that the punctuator inserted a virgule sometimes at II4, sometimes at III6, and sometimes at both II4 and III6. Careful examination has shown that, although the punctuator often put virgules at phrase boundaries, he gave rather small priority to the phrase boundary as an influence upon virgule placement. As a general rule, he gave even less priority to adverbs like *priuely*, which he did punctuate in *FranT* 741 and 1377. Notice all the difficulties presented by the four lines. *FranT* 740 and /41 both have a phrase boundary at III6, but only *FranT* 740 has this boundary punctuated. *FranT* 741 and 1377 both have the same adverb bordering the II4 position and a phrase boundary at III6; but the punctuation differs. *FranT* 1021 has a phrase boundary at II4 and at III6 as well, and only the boundary at III6 receives a virgule. The problem in all these lines is that there is no single, most important syntactic boundary; instead there are two boundaries of some small significance. The punctuator could not treat these lines with absolute regularity because the lines do not yield what he was looking for, the single important syntactic break near line-center. [17]

The last three lines listed here contain important syntactic bound-aries, but each line contains at least two instead of one. The punctuator solved this dilemma, sometimes by inserting two virgules, but usually by inserting only one. These lines are considered uncongenial because there is no way to know whether both boundaries should receive virgules or, if only one, which one. The syntactic features in all these lines have been proven by counts to exert influence on virgule placement in other lines: direct address words (*madame, brother deere*), subordinating connec-tives (*what*), front position tertiaries (*certes*), saying clauses (*quod he, seyde he*), and exclamations (*by my trouthe*). If the punctuator had been trying to follow an entirely syntactic set of guidelines, we could expect virgules for each one of these features. But we find instead that the general pattern of one-virgule-per-line still holds true in most lines with more than one important syntactic boundary. The punctuator continued to seek the syntactic break that was both important and central, despite the fact that many lines simply had no such thing.

A final result of punctuation study that helps to show that caesura (fixed metrical break or strong central syntactic boundary) is not an essential feature of the Chaucerian line is the discovery that the virgules were inserted by scribes, not by Chaucer. If Chaucer had inserted them, we might hesitate to say that they signified nothing essential about line-structure, despite all the above evidence. But a comparison of Hengwrt and Ellesmere, showing as it does that the scribe put in the virgules, removes this problem from the argument. Counts show that the rate of virgule disagreement between Hengwrt and Ellesmere is nearly constant from tale to tale despite differences in textual affiliation. The four tales were originally selected on the basis of their affiliations. According to Manly-Rickert, Hengwrt and Ellesmere are somewhat related in *The Monk's* and *Nun's Priest's Tale*s, are extremely close (that is, have a common ancestor or were copied one from the other) in *The Friar's Tale*, and are definitely unrelated ("have no common ancestor" short of the archetype) in *The Franklin's Tale*. [18] So, if the punctuation were

---

[17] No doubt the incidence of second virgules is at least partly due to the punctuator's frustration. In Hengwrt, nine percent of the lines have more than one mid-line virgule. Some extra virgules can be predicted because they separate items in series, but most extra virgules cannot be predicted; no discernible guideline governs their occurrence or placement.

[18] John M. Manly and Edith Rickert, eds., *The Text of the Canterbury Tales, Studied on*

passed down from Chaucer through the normal process of textual transmission, we would expect virgule disagreement to be low in *The Friar's
Tale* and high in *The Franklin's Tale*. But no such variation appears, and
the slight fluctuations that do appear do not parallel the textual affiliations. Twenty-one percent of the lines in *The Friar's Tale* have disagreements in virgule location or occurrence, and only eighteen percent of the
lines in *The Franklin's Tale* have such disagreements. The fact that
punctuation disagreement thus fails to reflect textual affiliations shows
almost certainly that the virgules were not passed down from Chaucer.
Moreover, the overall rate of punctuation disagreement (twenty-one
percent of the lines in all four tales together) is so close to the present rate
of prediction failure (twenty percent of the lines in three tales) that the
most likely explanation for the placing of the marks is that each scribe (or
the same scribe each time) independently put them in according to the
same basic guidelines being used now for prediction. All the evidence
thus suggests that Chaucer was not responsible for the virgules and thus
that they do not represent any notion he might have had about caesura.

If then the mid-line punctuation in Hengwrt and Ellesmere is neither
an indication of native half-line movement nor an indication of a caesura
inherent in verse structure, why was it inserted? The best answer to this
question is precedent. The scribes were imitating the mid-line punctuation that they found in other manuscripts. Latin verse manuscripts from
the twelfth through the fourteenth centuries often show extensive quantities of mid-line syntactic punctuation. Although this punctuation does
not appear with the line-by-line and leaf-by-leaf regularity of Hengwrt
or Ellesmere, it does often occur in a majority of lines, thus encouraging
the idea that poetry should be punctuated in mid-line.[19]

In the fourteenth century there is mid-line poetic punctuation in
English non-alliterative verse manuscripts preceding the Hengwrt. Below is a transcript from the Vernon Manuscript (Bodleian, English
Poetry a. 1, fol. 124v), considered to have been written between 1380
and 1400. This excerpt is from a poem about the conversion of an

the Basis of All Known Manuscripts (Chicago: U of Chicago P, 1940), I, 148–59; II, 306.

[19] Study is now in progress. For an example, see British Library MS. Arundel 244,
fol. 37ᵛ in Andrew G. Watson, *Catalogue of Dated and Datable Manuscripts* (London:
British Library, 1979), II, plate 196; the text is Alanus de Insulis, *Anticlaudianus*, the ms
is dated 1316, and the plate shows mid-line virgules in 20 of the 24 lines.

adulterous woman, a poem found among the "Miracles of Oure Lady" (Art. 28 in the ms). The mid-line punctuation here, as elsewhere in Vernon, is very constant. Points appear here just as the virgules do in Hengwrt and Ellesmere:

GOd þat al þis world haþ wrouht   1
And formed alle þing • of nouht
Seþþen alle þing • wiþ outen him
Is deþ • and dernesse • and dim •
Graunt vs grace • and space • and miht   5
þat we mowe serue him • so ariht
Whon we out • of þis world wende
To wynne þe Ioye • wiþouten ende[20]

Except for the fact that these verses have four stresses instead of five, the punctuation here is located just as it is in Hengwrt and Ellesmere. In lines 4 and 5, the points come before coordinating conjunctions. In lines 2, 3, and 8, the points appear at phrase boundaries. The line-by-line constancy of these points parallels Hengwrt and Ellesmere, and so does the scribe's willingness to punctuate several positions rather than one fixed metrical mid-point; notice that, although the favorite position for a point is after the second stress, the scribe punctuates the phrase boundary after the third stress in line 2 instead of interrupting a close syntactic relationship after the second stress. In sum, the system found in the Vernon Manuscript is a prototype of the Hengwrt–Ellesmere system.

Beyond the precedent in scribal practice there is also a precedent in grammatical theory. The doctrine of caesura, as it was expressed by the Latin grammarians, was a confusing mixture of metrical and syntactic ideas, a mixture that could very well foster a mid-verse syntactic punctuation. The early grammatical treatises, including the fourth-century writings of Donatus, Diomedes, and Marius Victorinus, have sections on both punctuation and metrics. The writers promote punctuation for sense units, units which they call *cola* and *commata*. Some grammarians define these sense units as if they were metrical units. Sergius, for example, defines the *colon* and *comma* this way:

---

[20] Bodleian Filmstrip Roll 175 C, frame 10.

nam ubi duo liberi pedes sunt, colon dicitur, ut apud Horatium 'terruit urbes'; comma vero, quando post duos pedes vel post tres pedes sequitur syllaba, quae partem terminat orationis, ut est in primo versu Aeneid-orum 'arma virumque cano', item 'arma virumque cano Troiae'.

[For where there are two free feet, it is called a colon, as in Horace *terruit urbes*: but it is called a comma when after two feet or after three feet a syllable follows, which is the ending of a word, as in the first line of the *Aeneid, arma virumque cano*, and also *arma virumque cano Troiae*.][21]

Sergius is here describing the verse *comma* in the way that the pen-themimeral and hephthemimeral caesurae are normally described. He makes the association unmistakable when in his treatment of caesura, elsewhere in his commentary, he uses the same line from the *Aeneid* for an example (Keil IV, 479–80). This association between sense units and metrical units, coupled with the advice to punctuate sense units, is not uncommon among the grammatical writers.

The ancient world really had two doctrines of caesura. One was a metrical doctrine about the relation between word-ends and foot-ends in Homeric verse. The other was a rhetorical doctrine about the Homeric line's divisibility into sense units, *cola* and *commata*. The two doctrines had merged by the fourth century, so we find the grammatical treatises talking about the sense pause as if it could occur at three or more places in one line: the penthemimeral, third trochaic, hephthemimeral, and fourth trochaic caesurae, and the bucolic dieresis. Marius Victorinus stumbles on this problem when he describes the hephthemimeral caesura: "cuius exemplum erit 'quam Iuno fertur terris': nam post tres pedes suprema ris syllaba sensum complet." [An example of this will be *quam Iuno fertur terris*: for after three feet the last syllable *ris* completes the sense.] The trouble with this example is that the last syllable *ris* does not complete the sense. The whole clause (*Aeneid* I, 15–16) is as follows: "quam Iuno fertur terris magis omnibus unam / posthabita coluisse Samo" [which city alone Juno is said to have cherished above all other

[21] *Sergii De Littera De Syllaba De Pedibus De Accentibus De Distinctione*, in *Grammatici Latini*, ed. Heinrich Keil (Leipzig, 1855–80; rpt. Hildesheim: Georg Olms, 1961), IV, 485. The translation is mine. Note that *partem orationis* is translated as *word*, not as *part of discourse*. In the grammatical writings, *pars orationis* is the regular label for what is known in English as *part of speech*.

lands, even more than Samos]. The words *terris magis omnibus* are really so closely connected in sense that there cannot be a sense boundary after *terris*. Marius Victorinus was confusing two doctrines as if they were one.[22]

As a result of the merger of these two doctrines, the Middle Ages inherited a not-altogether precise idea of caesura that was coupled with advice about punctuation. Students of the grammatical treatises would thus be tempted to think that poetry, Latin or vernacular, should have a sense pause or two in mid-line and that this sense-pause somehow arose from metrical necessity and should be punctuated. This does not mean that Latin, Italian, or English verse actually required caesura, either a mid-verse sense-pause or a single fixed metrical break (French, which does have a fixed caesura essential to line structure, is the exception).[23] Instead, it means that the grammatical tradition encouraged the effort to find a caesura and punctuate it, whether it was there or not.

The Hengwrt scribe must have been responding to this kind of encouragement. He was at the least following a system that had appeared already in Middle English manuscripts like the Vernon. No doubt he thought that his marks indicated a kind of caesura, that this caesura contributed to the metrical and syntactic clarity of the text, and that such a caesura belonged in poetry because it could be found in manuscripts from before his time. If we could interview him, he would very likely tell us that he was marking a caesura. And we must admit of course that the poetry did yield to his efforts enough for us to see that he was not marking native half-lines but instead truly trying to find a caesura. Nevertheless, the caesura is not really there: syntactic boundaries are too variously located and too many lines contain no syntactic boundaries for us to say that the line-structure must have an essential pause. The scribe's system, though highly regular, was doomed to fall short of perfection because many lines simply do not have what he was seeking. No requirement for caesura governed the composition of Chaucer's lines.

---

[22] Samuel E. Bassett, "The Theory of the Homeric Caesura According to the Extant Remains of the Ancient Doctrine," *AJP*, 40 (1919), 343–72; the Latin reference is *Ars Grammatica Marii Victorini*, in Keil, *Grammatici Latini*, VI, 66.

[23] See Georges Lote, *Histoire de Vers Français*, (Paris: Éditions Boivin, 1949), I, 233–46; also, Pierre Guiraud, *La Versification*, 2nd ed. (Paris: Presses Universitaires de France, 1973), p. 74.

The study of mid-line punctuation in Hengwrt and Ellesmere suggests two negative conclusions about Chaucer's verse: (1) that the verse is not based on the half-line movement of native meter, and (2) that the verse does not contain an essential caesura. So, although we may admire the Hengwrt scribe for his attempt to punctuate consistently and for his faith that syntax and meter complement each other, it would be imprecise for us to say that he accurately punctuated caesura. Anyone who tries to predict virgule placement discovers very soon that there is no predetermined caesura in line-structure. The scribe was not identifying an implicit feature; instead he was merely seeking something that tradition told him should be there.

Theban History in Chaucer's *Troilus*

David Anderson
University of Pennsylvania

P‍ROMINENT among Chaucer's additions to the narrative of Troilus and Criseyde that he found in Boccaccio's *Filostrato* is a series of references to the war between the Greek cities of Thebes and Argos, and to the royal families of those cities. These interpolations, which appear in every book of the *Troilus* except the first, and which range from brief allusions to extended passages of description, can be traced to Statius' *Thebaid*, a work that also served Chaucer as a model for certain stylistic features of the *Troilus*.[1] That Chaucer made use of the narrative content of the *Thebaid* has long been recognized, but no satisfactory explanation has been advanced for the role of these borrowings in the larger artistic design of his poem. This paper will argue that Chaucer's references to the main action of the *Thebaid* depend for their significance upon an historical perspective that placed the siege and destruction of Thebes shortly before the siege and destruction of Troy, and revealed parallels in the events that led to those two wars. Because of this perspective, Chaucer was able to use references to the Theban war in satirical counterpoint to the main action of the *Troilus*.[2] Though I propose that Chaucer refers to

---

[1] Chaucer's envoy, "Go, litel book," is an imitation of the envoy to the *Thebaid*, and Chaucer's invocations, formal comparisons, and epic diction sometimes show the influence of Statius. See Paul M. Clogan, "Chaucer's Use of the *Thebaid*," *English Miscellany*, 18 (1967), 9–31, esp. 18–25. Some of the conclusions in this paper were anticipated in a general way by Clogan. See also Boyd A. Wise, *The Influence of Statius upon Chaucer* (Baltimore: J. H. Furst, 1911), and the notes to Robert K. Root's edn., *The Book of Troilus and Criseyde* (Princeton: Princeton UP, 1926). My quotations of the *Troilus* are from this edn.

[2] Recent studies have argued persuasively that Chaucer's allusions to the works of Ovid also comment satirically on the characters in the *Troilus*. See esp. John M. Fyler, *Chaucer and Ovid* (New Haven and London: Yale UP, 1979), 115–38; and Mary-Jo Arn, "Three Ovidian Women in Chaucer's *Troilus*: Medea, Helen, Oenone," *ChauR*, 15 (1980), 1–10.

an historical Thebes, linked to Troy by proximity in time and by a degree of conformity to a single historical pattern, I do not mean to suggest that the source for these references was any work other than the *Thebaid*. Medieval *accessus* and glosses to that classical epic define its genre as a variety of historiography.[3] To be sure, Statius was thought to have written in the manner of the poets rather than in the manner of the historians, and the details of his narration were recognized as the products of literary convention and artistic manipulation, but the general outline of events in the *Thebaid* as well as the *dramatis personae* of the epic were thought to be historical.

I

To mention the Theban war during the Trojan war, as Pandarus, Criseyde, Troilus, and Cassandra all do in the *Troilus*, was, in the perspective of Chaucer's age, to speak of events in the very recent past. Influenced ultimately—if very indirectly—by the archaic Greek epic cycles, medieval chronologies of the ancient world placed the destruction of Boeotian Thebes[4] about two generations earlier than the fall of Troy. The two wars were considered not as literary fables nor as events from an indistinct and legendary past, but as landmarks in the history of the ancient gentile kingdoms that historians attempted to locate exactly in time by correlating them with the chronology of events in the Old Testament. The Trojan war generally received more attention from medieval historians, but the war of the Seven against Thebes is rarely absent altogether from their accounts, and it was occasionally described at length.[5]

[3] My study of unpublished *accessus* and glosses in manuscripts of the *Thebaid* was made possible by a Fulbright grant to Italy during the academic year 1978–1979.

[4] Medieval geographers distinguished between the various cities named Thebes, and as a rule medieval writers did not confuse their various histories. In the *Polychronicon*, Ranulf Higden states that different adjectival forms of the word should be used to distinguish between citizens of three different cities: "Et nota quod a Thebis Aegyptiorum dicuntur Thebaei, a Thebis Graecorum Thebani, a Thebis Judeaorum Thebitae" (C. Babington, ed., The Chronicles and Memorials of Great Britain and Ireland, No. 41 [London: Longman, 1865], I, 196).

[5] For example, in the universal chronicle of Paolino Veneto, Biblioteca Vaticana, MS. Vat. Lat. 1960, fol. 56[r-v]. On Boccaccio's reaction to this chronicle, see Aldo Maria Costantini, "La polemica con Fra Paolino da Venezia," in *Boccaccio, Venezia e il Veneto*, eds. Vittore Branca and Giorgio Padoan (Florence: Olschki, 1979), 101–21.

St. Jerome's translation of Eusebius' *Chronicon*, with its tables of parallel reigns from the founding of the biblical city of Babylon to the later years of the Roman empire, was the single most influential model for later medieval chronicles of pre-Christian times, and the entries in the *Chronicon* regarding Thebes and Troy were repeated frequently by later writers.[6] Neither Thebes nor Troy is one of the major empires for which Eusebius lists each ruler and each regnal year. Along with the rest of Greek history, the most notable acts of these cities are correlated with the chronology of the kingdom of Athens. Thus for the first year of the reign of Theseus at Athens, when Thola had ruled the Hebrew nation for eight years, Eusebius records the "septem qui adversum Thebas pugnaverunt" (p. 57[a]). Forty-three years later, during the fourteenth year of the reign of Theseus' successor Menestheus, and the last year of the reign of Iepthae, the *Chronicon* notes the abduction of Helen from the court of Sparta and the beginning of the Trojan war. Ten years further on, an entry states that king Menestheus died while returning to Greece after the Trojan war, and the parallel columns of regnal years in the major kingdoms of the world reveal that his death occurred at the time of the Hebrew judge Labdon. The chronicle itself is interrupted at this point by a relatively long passage headed "Troia capta" (p. 60a). A simplified version of Eusebius' tables for this period of history, showing only the rulers of Israel and Athens and the entries regarding the Theban and Trojan wars, is reproduced below.

The universal chronicles of the later Middle Ages, such as Vincent of Beauvais' *Speculum Historiale* and Ranulf Higden's *Polychronicon*, sometimes differ from Eusebius in detail, but never in substance when treating this period of Greek history. Following Eusebius, whom he cites frequently by name, Vincent of Beauvais places Theseus and the Theban war in a chapter about the events in the time of the judges Thola and Iair, specifying that Theseus fought at Thebes while Thola was judge in Israel.[7] Vincent goes on to devote three entire chapters (60, 62, and 63) of Book II to the Trojan war, which he says—again following Eusebius—began during the last year of the reign of the judge Jepte

---

[6] Eusebius' chronicle ends at A.D. 325. Citations are from *Hieronymi Chronicon*, ed. R. W. O. Helm, 2nd edn. (Berlin: Akademie-Verlag, 1956).

[7] Book II, Chap. 57: "De Gedeone et Abimelech et Thola et Iair." I quote from the Venetian edn. of 1494.

Partial Reproduction of
Eusebius' Tabular Summary of Ancient History

Hebraeorum	Sicyoniorum	Mycenatium	Atheniensium
THOLA (22 years)			
1			
5			THESEUS (30 years)
	SEPTEM QUI ADVERSUM		1
10	THEBAS PUGNAVERUNT		
			5
15			
			10
20			
IAIR (22 years)			15
5			20
10			25
15			MENESTHEUS (23 years)
20			5
IEPTHAE (6 years)			
4			10
ESEBON (7 years)	ALEXANDER HELENAM		15
	RAPUIT		
5			
LABDON (8 years)			20
3	TROIA CAPTA		23

[Iepthae]. Although scores of universal chronicles were written in the thirteenth and fourteenth centuries, the *Speculum Historiale* enjoyed the greatest prestige and influence, with many of the others depending on Vincent's encyclopedic history for all but those periods of time that were of particular interest to their authors. The historical works of Nicholas Trevet, with which Chaucer had some familiarity, well exemplify Vincent's influence.[8]

---

[8] *The Man of Law's Tale* is based on a passage in Trevet's Anglo-Norman Chronicle, written c. 1334; Trevet's *Historia ab Orbe Condito ad Christi Nativitatem*, written in Latin shortly before the Anglo-Norman Chronicle, is particularly heavily indebted to the work

The most important universal chronical compiled in England during the fourteenth century was Ranulf Higden's *Polychronicon*, which was translated twice into English within a century after its appearance. Higden followed the Eusebian chronolgy of ancient Greece with one minor exception. Abandoning Eusebius for a source he identifies as Trogus Pompeius, Higden made a slight alteration in the traditional list of kings at Athens:

> Post Aegeum apud Athenas regnavit filius suus Theseus, qui aliquando cum Hercule profectus Amazones contrivit. Post Theseum Demophon filius eius successit, qui adversus Troyanos Graecis opem tulit.[9]

Whereas Eusebius and Vincent listed Menestheus as Theseus' successor and Demophon as the successor to Menestheus, Higden omits Menestheus and calls Demophon the successor to Theseus and the king of Athens during the Trojan war. It is worth noting that, although Higden does not mention the Theban war *per se*, a reader of the *Polychronicon* would have no difficulty locating that war in time by identifying Theseus as one of the participants in it. Theseus' reign is clearly indicated to have ended just before the Trojan war began, and his son Demophon is said to have fought at Troy.

Chaucer drew on Statius' *Thebaid* rather than universal chronicles when he wove a series of allusions to Thebes and the Theban war into his poetic narrative, but those portions of the *Thebaid* that appear in the *Troilus* were thought of in Chaucer's age as history rather than poetic fiction. Medieval poetic theory defined the subject of epic poetry to be 'historia' and its author to be an 'historiographus' as well as a 'poeta.'[10]

of Trevet's fellow Dominican, Vincent of Beauvais. See Antonia Gransden, *Historical Writing in England, c. 550–c. 1307* (Ithaca: Cornell UP, 1974), 504–05 and n. 165. Karl H. Krüger, *Die Universalchroniken* (Turnhout, Belgium: Brepols, 1976), is a valuable guide to the many unpublished universal chronicles of the Middle Ages.

[9] *Polychronicon*, II, 402. On the composition and circulation of Higden's immense work, see John Taylor, *The Universal Chronicle of Ranulf Higden* (Oxford: Clarendon, 1966), 36 ff.

[10] Alexander Neckham, "Sacerdos ad altare," in C. H. Haskins, *Studies in the History of Medieval Science* (Cambridge: Harvard UP, 1924), p. 372. Guido delle Colonne, *Historia Destructionis Troiae*, trans. Mary E. Meek (Bloomington: Indiana UP, 1974), pp. 1–3; Giovanni Boccaccio, *Genealogie Deorum Gentilium Libri*, ed. Vincenzo Romano (Bari: G. Laterza, 1951), esp. pp. 721–23. Cf. Conrad of Hirsau, *Dialogus super Auctores*, ed. R. B. C. Huygens (Bruxelles: Latomus, 1955), pp. 16, 54 ff. Conrad, while

The difference between historical narrative in the form of an epic poem and historical narrative in its simple form was thought to be the manner of presentation: poets write with more liberty, beginning *in medias res* rather than following a strictly chronological order of events, and introducing anachronisms, such as Dido in the *Aeneid*, to help illustrate the moral stature of an historical personage, such as Aeneas.[11] Epic poets also introduce fictions about the pagan gods into their poems. Fictions about the pagan gods must necessarily be interpreted as allegories, since they cannot represent historical truth.

It is well beyond the scope of this essay to discuss the range of commentaries on and translations of Statius' *Thebaid* in the Middle Ages, but a few passages from the *accessus* and glosses of late-medieval manuscripts of the poem will show how the general distinction between historical and fictional elements in epics was applied to that work. Medieval *accessus* to the *Thebaid* usually begin by interpreting the title to mean "of Theban history," and the titles other than *Thebais* and *Thebaidos* that scribes occasionally give the epic usually elaborate on this definition.[12] A thirteenth-century *accessus* describes the style of the *Thebaid* as follows: "Qualitas carminis est metrum heroicum, et est metrum continens tam divinas quam etiam humanas personas, vera falsis admiscens."[13] The 'heroic style' is one that "contains both human and

---

distinguishing between an historian and a poet, identifies the *materia* of the *Aeneid* and *Thebaid* as *historia*, and the poetic mode of those epics as a mixture of truth and falsehood ("vera cum fictis").

[11] Boccaccio, *Genealogie*, p. 722.

[12] Cf. Dante, *Convivio* IV. xxv. 6: " . . . dice Stazio . . . nel primo de la Tebana Istoria." Quotation is from the edn. of Maria Simonelli (Bologna: R. Patron, 1966), p. 205. For a list of manuscripts containing commentaries on the *Thebaid*, see Robert D. Sweeney, *Prolegomena to an Edition of the Scholia to Statius, Mnemosyne*: supplementum octavum (Leyden: E. J. Brill, 1969), and for a discussion of the scholia that may have been known to Chaucer, see Paul M. Clogan, "Chaucer and the *Thebaid* Scholia," *SP*, 61 (1964), 599–615.

[13] The passage was modelled on the preface to Servius' commentary on the *Aeneid* (ed. E. K. Rand, et al., [Lancaster, Pa.: American Philological Soc., 1946], II, 4). My transcription follows London, British Library MS. Add. 16380, a thirteenth-century manuscript probably copied in England; and Florence, Biblioteca Riccardiana e Moreniana MS. 842 (M. III. 2), a fifteenth-century Italian manuscript. The *accessus* survives in two other copies as well, now in Leyden and West Berlin. Riccardiana 842, fol. 1ʳ; Add. 16380, fol. 144ʳ. When quoting from mss, I expand abbreviations and add modern punctuation.

divine" characters, mixing the true (that is, the 'humanas personas') with the false (the pagan gods). Later in the same *accessus*, Statius' manner is further defined: "Modus materie est tripertitus, que nunc istoriam tangit, nunc figmento subservit poetico, nunc scripto utitur allegorico."[14] The narration is said to shift between history ("nunc istoriam tangit") and poetic fictions, which are now divided into two kinds. The first, simply called poetic fiction ("nunc figmento subservit poetico"), probably refers to the acts of the pagan gods in the poem, while the second ("nunc scripto utitur allegorico") refers to Statius' allegorical descriptions of the 'house of Mars' and the 'house of Sleep' in books VII and X, respectively, passages that are often singled out by glossators in manuscripts of the *Thebaid* and which caught the eye of Boccaccio, who imitated them in his allegorical descriptions of the abodes of Mars and Venus in the *Teseida*.

A fourteenth-century *Thebaid* from Monteoliveto, near Siena, and a similar manuscript of Italian origins now in Wolfenbüttel, contain a number of glosses in the form of long chapter rubrics that specify the fabulous and the historical scenes of the poem much as the *accessus* cited above prescribes.[15] For example, at *Thebaid* I, 197, the gloss reads:

In hoc secundo capitulo describitur quedam conventio deorum ad consilium ex precepto Jovis et interserit auctor hic, relicta ystoria Thebana principali, quandam fictionem poeticum de concilio deorum (Laurenziana Ashb. 1032, fol. 4ʳ).

In the *Thebaid*, Statius has turned from events in the kingdom of Thebes to events in the heavens. Jove has called a council of the gods to discuss king Oedipus' curse on his sons. The glossator comments that Statius has "inserted here" a "certain poetic fiction" and has temporarily left his main narrative of Theban history. Shortly afterwards, at *Thebaid* I, 312, the rubric notes Statius' return to his principal subject:

In hoc tertio capitulo revertitur auctor post transgressionem ad istoriam Thebanam, notando quoniam Pollinices ex conventione cum Etiocle iam exul . . . (Laurenziana Ashb. 1032, fol. 5ᵛ).

[14] Riccardiana 842, 1ᵛ; Add. 16380, 144ᵛ.
[15] Florence, Biblioteca Medicea Laurenziana, MS. Ashburnham 1032, a fourteenth-century manuscript from the library of the monastery of Monteoliveto Maggiore; and Wolfenbüttel, Herzog-August Bibliothek, MS. 52 Gudianus Lat.

Having ended his fictional digression, Statius returns to the events at ancient Thebes, and specifically to the exile of Oedipus' son Polynices.

Admittedly, the meaning of the term 'historia' in these glosses is not perfectly clear. That term had a range of possible meanings in medieval writings, just as it does today.[16] When applying it to the narrative of the *Thebaid*, which is one of the most mannered of classical poems with a structure full of elaborate foreshadowing and symmetry, the glossator has probably not used 'historia' in the same sense he would use it for the Old Testament or even the works of Livy. Statius' poetic manner intrudes too frequently upon his subject matter for all of the details of his narrative to carry authority as a chronicle of actual events. Our glossator has not distinguished, as Isidore does in the *Etymologies*, between 'historia' or things which actually occurred ("res verae quae factae sunt") and 'argumentum,' or verisimilar literary invention ("quae etsi facta non sunt, fieri tamen possunt"), both of which are distinct from 'fabula' or literary inventions that could not be true ("quae non factae sunt nec fieri possunt").[17] Thus, in spite of the detailed exposition we find in this set of chapter rubrics, it is not possible to determine whether certain passages of the *Thebaid* were taken to be history or simply credible literary elaboration. More significantly, however, comparison of the *Thebaid* and its medieval commentaries with universal chronicles and other histories of the ancient world leaves no doubt that Chaucer would have recognized the Theban war, the main protagonists of that war, and the general outline of events from the blinding of Oedipus to the destruction of Thebes as history in the narrowest sense of that word. And it is to the general outline of events, rather than to particular scenes of the *Thebaid*, that Chaucer refers in the *Troilus*.

Other medieval sources suggest that the *Thebaid* was also considered 'historia' in the sense that its main action was exemplary of larger historical patterns. In the late fourteenth-century French translation of

[16] On the use of *fabula* and *historia* as contrasting terms in medieval literary theory, see J. W. H. Atkins, *English Literary Criticism: The Medieval Phase*, 2nd edn. (Gloucester, Mass.: P. Smith, 1961), p. 33. On the concept of *historia* in biblical exegesis, see Henri de Lubac, *Exégèse Médiévale* (Paris: Aubier, 1959), passim; and in the works of Hugh of St. Victor in particular, M.-D. Chenu, *Nature, Man, and Society in the Twelfth Century*, trans. Jerome Taylor and Lester K. Little (Chicago: U of Chicago P, 1968), pp. 165–77.

[17] *Etymologiarum Libri*, ed. W. M. Lindsay (Oxford: Clarendon, 1911), I. xliv.5, and the comments of Giuseppe Mazzotta, *Dante Poet of the Desert: History and Allegory in the Divine Comedy* (Princeton: Princeton UP, 1979), pp. 66–68.

116

Orosius' *Historia Contra Paganos*, a prose version of the *Roman de Thèbes*—
itself a loose translation of the *Thebaid*—is introduced into the discussion
of ancient empires in place of a short reference to Oedipus and his sons. [18]
Orosius' *Historia*, written apparently at the instigation of St. Augustine,
was, with Augustine's own works and Jerome's translation of Eusebius'
Chronicon, an authority to which medieval writers turned for an account
of the ancient world and an interpretation of those events. The French
Orose seems to have been quite popular. Léopold Constans reported in
1890 that he had found "many fifteenth-century manuscripts" (II, cxli
n.3), and there were many early printed editions. The anonymous
translator introduces the prose *Roman de Thèbes* into his work with the
words: "Pour avoir evidente congnoissance des misères du monde, nous
devons noter que Thèbes fut une fort belle cité, de la quelle ung nommé
Layus fut roy . . ." (II, cxliii). Appearing as it does in a treatise on ancient
history, the prose *Roman* is stripped of its poetic fictions, and begins
with the birth of Oedipus rather than *in medias res*, as Statius had, with
Oedipus already blind and his sons contending for his throne. The
translator interpolates moralizing comments throughout his version of
Theban history, giving the narrative a tone and style close to that of
Orosius' *Historia*. As the importance of the Trojan war in the medieval
vision of history might lead us to predict, the *Orose* also contains a
lengthy version of the fall of Troy in place of Orosius' brief references to
that city. [19] The whole of the *Orose* is about twice as long as the Latin
original, because of the bulk of these two interpolated *exempla*.

[18] There is no modern edition of the *Orose*. It is described in Léopold Constans, ed., *Le
Roman de Thèbes*, SATF (Paris: F. Didot, 1890–95), II, cxl ff. The work was printed in
1491, 1503, 1509, 1515, and 1526.

[19] Other works containing prose versions of the *Roman de Thèbes* reinforce the
impression given by the *Orose* that late-medieval tradition placed the literary account of
the Theban war, based on Statius' epic, in the context of ancient history. In "Les
premières compilations françaises d'histoire ancienne," *Romania*, 14 (1885), 1–81, Paul
Meyer first described the compilation of texts which is in some manuscripts called "Les
livres des estoires dou commencement dou mond" and often ascribed to Orosius,
presumably because portions of his *Historia* appear in it. The family of surviving
manuscripts containing the *Livres des Estoires* is large, and includes the original French
versions and subsequent translations into Italian. According to Léopold Constans, *La
Légende d'Oedipe* (Paris: Maisonneuve, 1881), p. 315, John Lydgate's *Siege of Thebes* was
probably based on a prose version of the *Roman de Thèbes* in a copy of the *Livres des Estoires*,
the full contents of which may be summarized as follows: I. The Creation (following, in
part, the *Historia Scholastica* of Peter Comestor); II. The Empires of Assyria and Greece

In the *Orose*, Statius' account of the Theban war is assimilated into a succession of empires stretching from Babylon, the first such empire according to the Old Testament, to Rome. Orosius, following St. Augustine, saw manifest in the recurrent rise and fall of such empires the history of unredeemed mankind, who sought worldly power and possessions rather than wisdom, and who were consequently subjected to the capricious fortune that rules worldly goods. Of course, Eusebius' *Chronicon* and the universal chronicles identify Thebes as part of the succession of pagan empires, but the *Orose* is remarkable for making Statius' version of Theban history a conspicuous example of that historical pattern. The concept of a succession of empires, so common in patristic and medieval histories alike, appears briefly at the end of Chaucer's *Troilus* as well, when, against a background of the imminent fall of Troy, the narrator remarks that " . . . regnes shal be flitted / Fro folk in folk" (V, 1544–45). This concept, and the typological analogies that historians found in the histories of empires in that succession, go some way in explaining the implicit analogy between the fall of Thebes and the fall of Troy that governs Chaucer's use of Theban history in the *Troilus*.

To a vision of history predisposed to identifying correspondences in the histories of cities in the Babylonian succession, the classical accounts of the wars at Thebes and Troy offered some very attractive similarities. According to the *Thebaid*, Polynices gathered an army and attacked Thebes in order to regain a throne that was rightfully his. Eteocles, Polynices' brother, had agreed to share the rule of Thebes, but later went back on his word. As Chaucer has Cassandra describe it in Book V of the *Troilus*, the Theban war began because of Eteocles' 'theft' of the throne of Thebes:

> She tolde ek how Tideus, or she stente,
> Unto the stronge citee of Thebes,

(following the Old Testament and Orosius' *Historia*); III. "Le romant de Edipus filz du roy Layus" (a prose version of the *Roman de Thèbes*); IV. The Amazones, Hercules, and the Minotaur (following Orosius); V. The Trojan War (a prose version of Benoit's *Roman de Troie*): VI. Aeneas and the early history of Rome (following Vergil, among others). In one of the few essays dedicated to Lydgate's *Siege of Thebes*, Robert W. Ayers has pointed out that Lydgate considered his subject to be a chapter from ancient history, and his purpose in writing to show the moral lessons of that history. See "Medieval History, Moral Purpose, and the Structure of Lydgate's *Siege of Thebes*," *PMLA*, 73 (1958), 463–74.

To cleymen kyngdom of the citee, wente,
For his felawe, daun Polymytes,
Of which the brother, daun Ethiocles,
Ful wrongfully of Thebes held the strengthe.

(V, 1485–90)

The Trojan war began in approximately the same way: Paris stole Menelaus' wife Helen, and when the city of Troy chose to defend Paris' theft, Menelaus gathered his allies and besieged the city, much as Polynices had gathered his allies to besiege Thebes. What is more, many of the Greek allies in the first case were fathers and grandfathers to the allies that rallied around Menelaus, as Chaucer notes in Book V of the *Troilus* when he describes the genealogy of Diomede.[20] Classical literature also assigned an antagonistic role to the pagan goddess Juno that is very nearly the same in both wars. When Troilus asks Cupid to keep Juno from being as 'cruel' to the Trojans as she had been to the Thebans (V, 599–602), the irony of his request depends upon this similarity. As Wise pointed out long ago with reference to Troilus' prayer, "in the *Thebaid* Juno is always inimical to Thebes as she is to Troy in the *Aeneid*."[21] From the point of view of the historian, mythological explanations of past events such as crediting Juno with influence on the wars at Thebes and Troy would clearly not have been acceptable. But in the language of the poets, mythological references were permissible, and this particular reference to Juno elaborates on a correspondence between the wars of Thebes and Troy that was thought to have an historical basis.

II

Statius' 'historia Thebana' makes its first appearance in the *Troilus* early in Book II. Pandarus has come to visit Criseyde on behalf of the love-struck Troilus, and finds her in a garden with her three nieces, listening to a young woman read about " . . . the sege of Thebes" (II, 83–84). Enough is said of her book in the course of this scene to identify

---

[20] On the genealogical connections between the Greeks who fought at Thebes and those who fought at Troy, see below, Sec. III, and n. 30.

[21] *The Influence of Statius upon Chaucer*, p. 14.

it as the *Thebaid* or a translation of the *Thebaid*.[22] Pandarus' reaction, when Criseyde tells him what the book is about, reveals a streak of pedantry and another aspect of his character as well:

> Quod Pandarus: "al this knowe I my selve,
> And al thassege of Thebes, and the care;
> For herof ben ther maked bookes twelve;
> But lat be this, and tel me how ye fare;
> Do wey youre wympel, and shewe youre face bare;
> Do wey youre book, rys up and lat us daunce,
> And lat us don to May som observaunce."
>
> (II, 106–12)

His attempt to divert attention from the *Thebaid* is wholly consistent with his inclination, revealed in the course of his interview with Troilus in Book I, to dismiss the siege of Troy as a subject less interesting than the pursuit of "jolite" (I, 554–60). For an audience that imagined an historical Thebes burning only a few years before Troy burned, there must have been poignant satire in Chaucer's use of this particular book in this particular garden.

Leaving for a moment the issue of anachronism that is raised by a copy of the *Thebaid* in a scene set in ancient Troy, let us turn to the other appearance of the *Thebaid* itself in the *Troilus*. The ironic implications of the first scene are made more obvious by the second.

---

[22] By calling the book a 'romance' or translation, Criseyde seems to be describing one of the medieval versions of the *Thebaid*, rather than the Latin epic itself. Statius begins *in medias res* with Oedipus already blind, whereas the *Roman de Thèbes* and its prose redactions begin, as does Criseyde's book, with an account of Oedipus' early life and his murder of Layus. Pandarus' comments, however, suggest that he knows Statius' original, which is divided into twelve books as the *Roman* is not. See Root, p. 438–39. The "lettres rede" at which Criseyde and her companions have arrived in their reading may refer to the chapter divisions so common in late medieval *Thebaid*s. The conventional chapter division at the beginning of Statius' description of Amphiaraus' death is at *Thebaid* VII, 628. In his brief discussion of this scene, Paul Clogan noted that both Criseyde and Pandarus "are unaware of the ultimate consequences of fate as revealed in the story of Thebes," ("Chaucer's Use of the *Thebaid*," p. 22). Alan Renoir has pointed out that copies of the *Roman de Thèbes* and the *Roman de Troie* often appeared in the same manuscript books, and argues that Criseyde could therefore read about herself in the book that appears in this scene. See "Thebes, Troy, Criseyde and Pandarus: An Instance of Chaucerian Irony," *SN* 32 (1960), 14–17. The probable cause of the frequent association of these two works has been discussed above.

120

In Book V, Chaucer included a twenty-seven line summary of the *Thebaid* in a long speech by Troilus' sister Cassandra. No book appears in this scene, but Cassandra's summary recalls Criseyde's book in at least two ways. She summarizes the contents of the *Thebaid* in a way that strongly resembles the passage in the earlier scene in which Criseyde briefly describes for Pandarus the contents of her book. Also, Cassandra's summary is based on a Latin verse-argument beginning "Associat profugum" that appeared in medieval copies of the *Thebaid*. It is a general argument, which condenses the twelve books of the epic into twelve lines of hexameter verse. The "Associat profugum" is properly a part of Chaucer's text as well, as Root (p. 554) has observed: "After line [V,] 1498, all the authorities, except H₄R, contain in the body of the text twelve lines of Latin verse, which summarize the twelve books of the *Thebais* of Statius. . . . Their presence is probably due to Chaucer himself." Modern editors of the *Troilus* have relegated the "Associat profugum" to their notes on the text, but it probably should appear in the middle of Cassandra's speech. The effect of these lines is to identify her digression specifically with the *Thebaid*, for the "Associat profugum" is at once the general argument that medieval readers found in their copies of Statius' epic, and a miniature version of that epic, its twelve lines corresponding to the twelve books of the *Thebaid*.[23]

If there are similarities between these two scenes, they exist to establish a contrast between our view of Pandarus in the first and Cassandra in the second. Chaucer's portrait of Cassandra is conventional in that he identifies her as a prophetess or "Sibille" (V, 1450), and as one of the children of Priam and Hecuba. Her traditional role in the Troy literature as the unheeded prophetess of doom, whose warnings about the imminent fall of Troy were ignored by her family and countrymen, is not stated explicitly in the *Troilus*, but is clearly present by implication in Chaucer's portrait of her. Remarkably, however, Chaucer's Cassandra does not foretell future events by means of oracles or augury. That, in the *Troilus*, is left to Pandarus' brother Calkas (I, 71–72). Instead, she draws attention to the past and explains or suggests its relevance to the present. As she tells Troilus: "If thow a soth of this desirest knowe, / Thow most a

---

[23] Francis P. Magoun, Jr. has shown that Cassandra's summary of the *Thebaid* is based on Latin verse-arguments and the text of the *Thebaid* itself: "Chaucer's Summary of Statius' *Thebaid*, II–XII," *Traditio*, 11 (1955), 409–20.

fewe of olde stories heere, / . . . as men in bokes fynde" (V, 1458–63). 'Stories' in Middle English meant something closer to the Modern English word 'history' than to our word 'story' or fictional narrative,[24] and we soon learn that the 'book' Cassandra wants most to draw to Troilus' attention is the *Thebaid*. Her prophetic powers, it would seem, are of a bookish sort, and derive primarily from her knowledge of recent Greek history.

The relation of Cassandra's digression on the Theban war to the context of her speech is not readily apparent. Troilus has come to his sister for an interpretation of his dream about a "boor with tuskes grete," and Cassandra explains that the boar represents Diomede. Diomede's ancestor Meleager, she tells Troilus, killed a "boor as gret as oxe in stalle," and the animal has remained an emblem for Meleager's descendants (V, 1464–70). Troilus has dreamed that he discovered Criseyde "by this boor, faste in hire armes folde" (V, 1240), and Cassandra concludes simply that the dream means Criseyde is enjoying the embraces of Diomede: "Wepe if thow wolt, or lef; for, out of doute, / This Diomede is inne, and thow art oute" (V, 1518–19). Troilus denies Cassandra's interpretation, and rejects her advice, just as Troy denied her warnings to the city as a whole: "Thow seyst nat soth," quod he, "thow sorceresse, / With al thy false goost of prophecye!" (V, 1520–21). But as Troilus' words echo the foolish cries of the citizens of Troy, we recognize that he, like the Trojans, is refusing to believe the truth.

Cassandra's long digression on the Theban war also recalls her traditional role as the wise prophetess whose city would not heed her warnings. Chaucer does not show us Cassandra in the act of admonishing the Trojans and warning what may befall their city. He has undertaken to recount the story of Troilus' love for Criseyde, not the history of the

---

[24] The Middle English word derived from the medieval Latin word 'historia,' probably by way of the Anglo-Norman 'estorie,' and it retained much of the semantic range of its cognates, with a primary meaning near to the MnE word 'history.' Langland, among other fourteenth-century writers, refers to Peter Comestor, author of the *Historia Scholastica*, a universal chronicle, as the 'clerk of the stories' (*Piers Plowman*, B. VII. 73). Chaucer never uses the noun 'history' and rarely the adjectival form 'historical,' using 'story' instead both in the sense of 'history' and 'legend,' but he does seem to make a distinction between 'story' and 'fable,' the latter carrying the connotation of falsehood and even deceit, whereas the former indicates events that either are true or could be true. See *A Chaucer Glossary*, eds. Norman Davis, et al. (Oxford: Clarendon, 1979), under 'fable' and 'stories'.

Trojan war (V, 1765 ff.), and Cassandra only appears in his narrative in her capacity as an advisor to Troilus about Criseyde. But characteristically throughout the *Troilus*, Chaucer suggests the course of Trojan history by comparing it to the course of Troilus' love for Criseyde, and the speech he gives Cassandra in Book V further elaborates this analogy between Troilus and Troy. It is therefore appropriate that Cassandra, while explaining the sad end of Troilus' love affair, also suggest the analogous outcome of the Trojan war. She does so in both cases by reference to Theban history, but she states the significance of that history only with reference to Troilus' personal affairs, leaving unstated the relevance it may have for the affairs of Troy. However, in the context of Book V of the *Troilus* these implications are fairly obvious.[25] Cassandra's summary of the *Thebaid* also reflects back upon Pandarus as we saw him in Book II. He interrupted the reading in Criseyde's garden at the beginning of Statius' account of the siege of Thebes; Cassandra now gives a summary of the entire war, including the final destruction of Thebes. Pandarus advised a group of Trojan noblewomen to "do wey" their book and dance; Cassandra's speech, by contrast, strongly suggests that Trojans should not ignore the specter of fallen Thebes.

The appearance of the *Thebaid* at the time of the Trojan war would have struck Chaucer's audience as anachronistic. There is no ambiguity in the medieval sources that ascribe the poem to Publius Statius (his agnomen is recorded, incorrectly, as Surculus until the fifteenth century), who lived during the reigns of the Roman emperors Vespasian, Titus, and Domitian. A short "vita Statii" that gives this information is the most frequent introduction to the *Thebaid* in manuscripts of that work, and the biographies of major Latin poets also appear in other medieval writings and were part of the arts courses in medieval schools.[26] An anachronism of this sort does not indicate that Chaucer

---

[25] On the parallels between Cassandra's role in Troilus' personal affairs and her traditional role in the history of the Trojan war, see below, Sect. IV. On the Trojan setting in Book V, see John P. McCall, "The Trojan Scene in Chaucer's Troilus," *ELH*, 29 (1962), 263–75, and esp. 269 ff.

[26] Dante, Boccaccio, and Chaucer were all familiar with some form of the "Vita Statii." See *Purgatorio*, 22; *Amorosa Visione*, 5.34; *HF*, 1460. The text, as it appears in Biblioteca Vaticana MS. Palatinus Latinus 1694, a Caroline manuscript that also contains a very early and authoritative text of Lactantius' commentary on the *Thebaid*, is as follows:

Queritur quo tempore fuerit iste Statius. Sed constat veraciter fuisse eum temporibus Vespasiani imperatoris ac pervenisse usque ad imperium Domiciani fratris

had a vague sense of the chronology of events that form the background of the *Troilus*, or that he chose to ignore that chronology and set his poem in an undetermined time where historical relations are suspended. Chaucer wrote as a poet rather than as an historian, and anachronism is a legitimate resource for poets even when their subject is essentially historical.[27] Although the question of the theory of epic poetry in the later Middle Ages and the relation of this theory to the *Troilus* is a large one that cannot be addressed formally in this essay, Boccaccio's discussion of Book IV of the *Aeneid* in his *Genealogie* (Bk. XIV, Chap. 13) identifies a poetic anachronism that might serve as a gloss on Chaucer's technique in Book II of the *Troilus*. Dido, Boccaccio notes, could not have been alive at the time Aeneas sailed from Troy to Carthage and then on to Latium. However, Vergil needed an appropriately refined and knowledgeable person to whom Aeneas could recount the story of his wanderings and "such a one above all he found in Dido."[28] Vergil also used Dido to dramatize an aspect of Aeneas' character, namely that stern sense of duty that kept him from yielding to the temptation to remain in

---

Tyti. Qui etiam et Tytus iunior dictus est. Si quis autem inde fuerit, querat, invenitur fuisse Tolosensis que civitas est Gallie. Ideoque in Gallia celeberrime docuit rethoricam. Sed postea veniens Romam ad poetriam se transtulit. Fuit enim nobili ortus prosapia; clarus ingenio et doctus aelogo [eloquio]. Cuius Iuvenalis sic meminit dicens:

"Curritur ad vocem iucundam et carmen amice
Thebaidos, letam cum fecit Statius urbem
promisitque diem. Tanta dulcedine captos
advicit ille animos tantaque libidine vulgi
auditus; sed cum fregit subsellia versu
esurit, intactam Paridi nisi vendat Agaven"
(Juvenal, *Satire VII*, 82–87)

Scripsit autem Thebaiden supra taxati imperatoris tempore. Est autem Thebais femininum patronomicum sicut Eneis et Theseis. Dictus est autem proprio nomine Statius. Papinus autem cognomine. Sursulus autem agnomine, quasi sursum canens [punctuation mine].

For a longer version of the *vita*, and the place of Statius in medieval curricula, see Paul M. Clogan, *The Medieval Achilleid of Statius* (Leyden: E. J. Brill, 1968), pp. 2–3 and 21–22. On the errors in the medieval version of Statius' biography, see Ettore Paratore, "Stazio," in the *Enciclopedia Dantesca*, IV, 419–20.

[27] See Boccaccio, *Genealogie*, Book XIV, Chap. 13.

[28] According to Osgood's note, *Boccaccio on Poetry*, trans. Charles G. Osgood (New York: Bobbs-Merrill, 1956), p. 174, Boccaccio's observation that Dido actually lived before the time of Aeneas comes from Eusebius' *Chronicon* via Petrarch, *Seniles*, 4.5.

comfortable Carthage rather than to press on and found Rome.[29] Dido's role in the *Aeneid* is certainly greater than the role of Criseyde's copy of the *Thebaid* in the *Troilus*, but they both may be viewed in terms of the same poetic theory. Chaucer uses the *Thebaid* as a (rather humorous) means of characterizing Pandarus, just as Vergil introduced Dido for the sake of characterizing Aeneas. Chaucer, and his original audience, would have recognized a glaring anachronism as such, just as Boccaccio recognized the use of a somewhat less obvious anachronism in the *Aeneid*.

III

The lapse of time between the Theban and Trojan wars was fixed, in an approximate fashion, by classical Latin literature itself, in which there are numerous references to the genealogies of the warriors at Thebes that had sons and grandsons at Troy.[30] Chaucer used this technique in the *Troilus* to underscore the propinquity of the two conflicts, and also invented a genealogy for Criseyde that plays a somewhat more complex role in the design of the poem. As I have mentioned in passing, one example of the technique appears in Book V, where Diomede, the Greek who leads Criseyde away from Troy and later becomes her lover, is said repeatedly to be the son of Tydeus. Cassandra then, in her summary of the Theban war and events leading to it, explains who Tydeus was and how he died at Thebes. Though Chaucer does not use epithets for the most part when referring to Greek or Trojan warriors, he refers to Diomede as as the son of Tydeus five times in the course of Book V (88, 803–05, 932–38, 1025, 1747), as if to make a special point of his genealogy:

> "For if my fader Tideus," he seyde,
> "Ilyved hadde, ich hadde ben or this,
> Of Calydoyne and Arge a kyng, Criseyde!
> And so hope I that I shal yit, iwis.

[29] *Genealogie*, Book XIV, Chap 13; *Boccaccio on Poetry*, pp. 68–69 and n. 32.

[30] *Aeneid* II, 261 mentions Thessandrus (the son of Polynices and Argia) and Sthenelus (the son of Capaneus) among the Greeks in the Trojan horse (and cf. the corresponding gloss in Servius' commentary). Theseus also had a son, or sons, at Troy. (See p. 111 above).

125

> But he was slayn; allas, the more harm is,
> Unhappily at Thebes al to rathe,
> Polymytes and many a man to scathe.
>
> (V, 932–38)

Diomede is referring to events in the *Thebaid* that Cassandra will soon mention again. Diomede's father Tydeus married the daughter of King Adrastus of Argos, whose name was Deiphyle. Adrastus' other daughter, Argia, married Polynices, the son of King Oedipus of Thebes. When Polynices went to war with his brother Eteocles over the throne of Thebes, Tydeus, himself an exiled prince of Calidonia, fought on the side of his brother-in-law Polynices. Thus, 'had Tydeus lived,' he would have been king of Calidonia (by birth) and of Argos (by marriage), at least in the optimistic assessment of his son Diomede. Family difficulties in Calidonia might in fact have kept him from assuming that throne.[31] Unfortunately for Diomede, Tydeus died during the siege of Thebes, 'all too soon' to be of much help to the fortunes of his son and heir. Diomede's genealogy, as described in the *Thebaid* and in the *Troilus* would appear schematically like this:

> Adrastus, king of Argos
>
> Polynices = Argia   Deiphyle = Tydeus of Calidonia
>
> Diomede

Tydeus and his father-in-law Adrastus fought with Polynices at Thebes; Diomede fought with the Greeks at Troy.

Criseyde, too, has Greek relatives in the generation that witnessed the Theban war. Chaucer elaborated on the conventional geneaolgy of Criseyde as he found it in the *Filostrato*, where her only named relations are her father Calkas and her uncle Pandarus. Chaucer grafted her, as it were, into the main genealogical tree of the *Thebaid*. He plays a bit coy with the details of Criseyde's family background, scattering the clues around his poem rather than giving them all together. This playfulness is in some contrast to his treatment of Diomede's genealogy, which is mentioned explicitly on five or six occasions in the course of one book of

---

[31] Tydeus was exiled from Calidonia under accusation of having killed his brother (*Thebaid* I, 401–02; 451 ff.; *Metamorphoses* VIII, 260–546).

the poem, and finally described *in toto* by Cassandra.[32] The scattered clues are however consistent and frequent enough to allow a simple explanation with reference to the *Thebaid*.

Following Boccaccio, and Benoit and Guido delle Colonne before him, Chaucer tells us that Criseyde is the daughter of Calkas (I, 92–99) and the niece of Pandarus, Calkas' brother (II, 76 et passim). She was apparently born in Troy (V, 956–57), and was married presumably to a Trojan, but she avoids mentioning the name of her former husband (V, 975–76). Chaucer then adds that her mother was named "Argyve" (IV, 762), by which he intends the daughter of Adrastus, whose name is spelled "Argia" in Statius' Latin, but which Chaucer anglicizes as "Argyve." Cassandra refers to Argia as "Argyve" in her summary of the *Thebaid* (V, 1509), and the name of the city of Argos, from which her name derives, also undergoes a slight change in Chaucer's Middle English, becoming "Arge" (V, 805, 934).

Chaucer also gives us other encouragement to think of Criseyde as the daughter of Argia, princess of Argos. It is recorded in the *Thebaid* that Argia possessed the beautiful jewel that Chaucer calls the "brooch of Thebes" and that Statius often refers to as the "monile Harmoniae" or the brooch of Harmonia, because it was made for Harmonia, the first queen of Thebes.[33] The brooch passed to Argia when she married the Theban prince Polynices, and she used it to bribe the wife of the seer Amphiaraus into betraying Amphiaraus' hiding place (*Thebaid* IV, 187 ff.) Amphiaraus had gone into hiding to avoid conscription into Polynices' army, but his wife, overcome by desire for the beautiful brooch, revealed his hideout and he was forced to join the siege of Thebes, where he soon died a spectacular death (*Thebaid* VII, 628 ff.). Chaucer picks up the story of the brooch more or less where Statius left off, suggesting that it passed from Argia to her daughter Criseyde (*Troilus* III, 1370–71; V, 1040, 1660 ff.).[34] There can be little doubt that Criseyde's brooch is the

---

[32] V, 1480 ff. As Root notes (p. 553), Statius and Ovid say that Meleager was Tydeus' brother, but Boccaccio (in the *Filostrato*) refers to Meleager as Diomede's 'ancestor' in general rather than as his uncle.

[33] See *Thebaid* II, 265–305; IV, 187–213; *Metamorphoses* IV, 563 ff. on the "brooch of Thebes".

[34] Apparently, Criseyde first gave the brooch to Troilus (III, 1372), and later to Diomede (V, 1040–41), though it is possible Chaucer is referring to two different brooches.

same as the "brooch of Thebes" of the *Thebaid*, for Chaucer's description of the brooch of Thebes in the "Complaint of Mars" (ll. 245–60) closely resembles his description of the jewel given by Argyve to Criseyde.[35] Having made Criseyde the daughter of Argia—a genealogical invention that is highly credible in terms of chronology, and possible in terms of what Statius tells us of Argia at the end of the *Thebaid*[36]—Chaucer is able to have a little joke late in the *Troilus* when Criseyde tells her new protector Diomede that she has heard of his noble birth (V, 979–80). Argia, according to Statius, was Diomede's aunt, and Criseyde would therefore be Diomede's cousin. Her genealogy, as Chaucer describes it, may be diagrammed like this:

Adrastus

Polynices = Argia ≡ Calkas   Deiphyle = Tydeus

Criseyde   Diomede

The genealogies of Criseyde and Diomede anticipate Cassandra's speech by fixing the Theban war in recent history. Thus, in Book III we learn that Criseyde inherited the brooch of Thebes from her mother; in Book IV the name of her mother is first mentioned; and in Book V Argia's name reappears, this time in the context of Cassandra's summary of the *Thebaid*. Diomede appears early in Book V and is referred to as the son of Tydeus four times before Cassandra explains Tydeus' part in the siege of Thebes. This situation in Book V is notably different from the first references to the *Thebaid* and the Theban war in Book II, where the significance of that book to the Trojan setting is in no way prepared beforehand. However, Chaucer could have chosen other names from the traditional cast of characters at Troy whose ancestry might recall the

[35] Troilus' situation is the same as that of Mars in Chaucer's *Mars*, who likens his loss of Venus to the loss of the brooch of Thebes (245–71). Troilus loses Criseyde, and realizes that he has lost her when he sees that Diomede possesses the brooch. Remarkably, Chaucer has Mars describe the condition of whoever possesses the brooch of Thebes and then loses it as follows: "Than had he double wo and passioun" (254), a phrase he also used to describe the course of Troilus' love for Criseyde. Furthermore, Mars' reactions to losing Venus (257–71) recall those of Troilus when he loses Criseyde.

[36] Statius implies that Creon put Argia to death (*Thebaid* XII, 461–63), but does not describe the death sentence or the execution.

Theban war,[37] and that he should go to the trouble of inventing a genealogy for Criseyde argues strongly that her Greek relatives have a further role in the design of the *Troilus*. To understand this more complex role, we must turn our attention from the Theban background of the poem to its main action.

IV

We have seen that the medieval record of ancient Greek chronology, and the concept of a succession of worldly empires that shared many features of a common archetype, suggest that the prominent allusions to Thebes in Books II and V of the *Troilus* have a particular relevance to the setting of the poem, which Chaucer exploits in his characterization of Pandarus and Cassandra. The more complex role of Criseyde's genealogy depends, in turn, on the relation between the setting of the poem and its main action. It has often been pointed out that Chaucer built a thoroughgoing analogy between the microcosm of the personal affairs of Troilus, or 'little Troy,' and the macrocosm of Troy itself.[38] Thus, Troilus falls in love with Criseyde just as his brother Paris fell in love with Helen, in a temple during a spring festival. Paris' abduction of Helen led to the Trojan war when Troy agreed to help Paris keep Helen from her husband Menelaus by force of arms; the course of Troilus' love for Criseyde mirrors the course of that war. Thus, when Troilus is most fortunate in love (Book III), the Trojan cause also enjoys good fortune; when Criseyde is exchanged for Antenor (Book IV), the effects are equally bad for Troilus and for Troy; and when Troilus is forced, in the end, to concede that Criseyde has been lost to a Greek, the nadir of his fortunes appears against the background of the fall of Troy and the loss of

---

[37] See above, n. 30, esp. Therssander (and cf. Boccaccio, *Genealogie*, p. 97), who is mentioned by Statius as well as Vergil.

[38] John P. McCall, "The Trojan Scene in Chaucer's Troilus," 264 ff. and again in his *Chaucer among the Gods* (University Park, Pa. and London: Pennsylvania State UP, 1979), p. 87 ff. For further similarities between Helen and Criseyde, see: Arn, pp. 4–8. As McCall pointed out in his article of 1962, "Chaucer's principal source told him that Troilo was afflicted by the same love that doomed all Troy to destruction" (p. 264), and he cites *Filostrato* VII, 86, in which Cassandra tells Troilo that he has "suffered from the accursed love by which we all must be undone, as we can see if we but wish" (p. 264, n. 7).

Helen to the Greeks. Since the course of Troilus' love for Criseyde recapitulates, in some degree, the events that resulted from Troy's attachment to Helen, the specter of Thebes may be brought to play against the main action of the poem as well as its setting.

I have suggested that Cassandra's role in Troilus' personal affairs parallels her traditional role in the history of the Trojan war, and that the significance of her long digression on Theban history depends in part on our recognizing the analogy between Troilus and Criseyde on the one hand and Paris/Troy and Helen on the other. This analogy is further elaborated by Criseyde's genealogy, the details of which we know before Cassandra appears in Book V.

Troilus falls in love with a woman who closely resembles Helen. Following Boccaccio, Chaucer describes her beauty in terms of Helen's (I, 99 ff. and 455 ff.); and, like Boccaccio, Chaucer describes her as having been married before the Trojan prince falls in love with her. By giving Criseyde three grown nieces, Chaucer suggests, as Boccaccio does, that Criseyde is older than Troilus, just as Helen was older than Paris.[39] By virtue of the genealogy Chaucer invented for her, Criseyde also resembles Helen in the significant details of being Greek, or, more exactly, half-Greek, as Helen is said to have been,[40] and associated with the city of Argos. Chaucer knew from the *Aeneid* that Helen was called "Argive Helen" because she was born in the Peloponnesus, an area encompassing Mycenae, Sparta, and Argos. In his gloss on line I, 650 of the *Aeneid*, Servius explains the phrase "ornatus Argivae Helenae quos illa Mycenis" as follows: "*Argivae* autem a vicinitate dixit; nam ait etiam *Mycenis*, cum Spartana fuerit, quae civitas est in Laconica."[41] A member

---

[39] Since Helen was abducted by Theseus when she was a young girl, some time before she married Menelaus, classical sources suggest that she was quite old by the time of the Trojan war. Boccaccio, with reference to Eusebius' *Chronicon* calculated her age to be thirty when she first met Paris, and went on to speculate about the nature of her charms at that age: "Et sic Helena esse potuit XXX annorum, vel circa, quando a Paride rapta est, qua etate mulieres nobiles et ingenio valentes speciosiorem formositatem suam faciunt, arte addentes, si quid forsan provectior etas subtraxerit" (*Genealogie*, p. 549).

[40] Guido delle Colonne identifies Helen's brothers as kings of Sparta, and makes light of classical myths about the role of Jove in their begetting (see IV, 1–23). Dictys Cretensis, to whom Chaucer refers in *Troilus* I, 146, has Helen describe her family in some detail. See *Ephemeridos Belli Troiani*, ed. A. Dederich (Bonn, 1837), pp. 21–23. She feels a mixed allegiance, Helen explains, because, though Greek, she is related to both Hecuba and Priam of Troy through their common ancestors Phoenix and Agenor.

[41] Ed. Rand, et al., II, pp. 275–76.

of the royal family of Sparta, Helen may be referred to as "Argive" for the proximity of her city to the region of Argos.

A brief allusion to the fall of Thebes in Book V of the *Troilus* illustrates again the analogy between Thebes and Troy on the one hand, and Troilus and Troy on the other. After Criseyde has been taken to the Greek camp, Troilus asks his 'master,' the god of love, for help in bringing the object of his desires back to Troy. The concluding stanza of his prayer involves a simile that is rather surprising in its immediate context:

> Distreyne hire herte as faste to retorne,
> As thow doost myn to longen hire to see;
> Then woot I wel that she nyl nat sojorne.
> Now, blisful lord, so cruel thow ne be
> Unto the blood of Troie, I preye the,
> As Juno was unto the blood Thebane,
> For which the folk of Thebes caughte hire bane.
>
> (V, 596–602)

The allusion is to the *ira Junonis*, or the wrath of Juno which is described in the *Thebaid* and other classical Latin works. Juno is said to be angry with the city of Thebes because her husband Jove had so many affairs with Theban women.[42] Statius gives Juno a prominent role helping the Argive forces that attack Thebes, while Bacchus, the offspring of one of Jove's affairs with a Theban woman, and Venus defend the city. The same classical sources, most importantly the *Aeneid*, present Juno as the great enemy of the city of Troy as well. Within the next few hundred lines, Cupid will indeed be cruel to Troilus, who will lose Criseyde to Diomede. What is more, Cupid will be cruel to Troilus not only as Juno was to the "blood Thebane" but as she was to the blood of Troy. The foreshadowing here of the fall of Troy by reference to the fall of Thebes is the same as that of Cassandra's speech, and the more complex ironies of this passage, like those of Cassandra's digression on Thebes, depend upon the analogy between Troilus' activities and those of Troy.

One further example of Chaucer's brief allusions to Theban history appears in Book IV, and it is no more flattering to Troilus than the

---

[42] Juno explains the causes of her wrath with Thebes in a long speech opening Seneca's *Hercules Furens*; cf. *Metamorphoses*, IV, 400 ff., and above, n. 21, for the relevant passages in the *Thebaid*.

similarities of Criseyde and Helen or the ironic implications of Troilus' prayer to Cupid. Shortly after learning that Criseyde will be traded to the Greeks for Antenor, and alternately enraged and depressed by the prospect, Troilus likens himself to Oedipus: "But ende I wol, as Edippe, in derknesse / My sorwful lif, and dyen in distresse" (IV, 300–01). As Wise and other students of Chaucer's sources for the *Troilus* have pointed out, not only the simile but much of the scene in which it appears were based on the opening scene of the *Thebaid*, in which Oedipus, already blind and enraged by the treatment he has received at the hands of fortune and his family, calls down a curse on his sons and the city of Thebes (*Thebaid* I, 46–87).[43] Statius describes Oedipus as "impius," and his internal light as "saeva dies animi," a fierce daylight of the mind that drives him to an irrational act and leads to the Theban war. Troilus, like Oedipus, curses the day nature made him (IV, 250–52); his heart is 'twisted' by rage (IV, 253–54); and he disclaims all concern for his family and state (IV, 274–78).

The limited objective of this essay has been to examine Chaucer's allusions to Theban history and to gauge something of their force in the context of those scenes where they appear. Drawing general conclusions about the role of these allusions in the larger design of the poem depends, finally, on the question of that design itself, and cannot be pursued any further here. But we may draw some tentative conclusions. Chaucer appears to be using the Theban material in much the same way through-out the poem, as a kind of recurring, satirical commentary on Pandarus and Troilus, who go about their courtly business with remarkably little concern for the momentous events that form the backdrop of their famous stage. Chaucer, in this regard, closely resembles his portrait of Cassandra, who knows about the past, suggests its relevance to the present, and, on occasion, explains it. The identity of Chaucer with Cassandra, however incomplete, suggests a possible motive for incorporating this series of allusions and extended references to Thebes, beyond

---

[43] Wise, p. 14. The simile is the subject of a short essay by Julia Ebel, "Troilus and Oedipus: The Genealogy of an Image," *ES*, 55 (1974), 15–21, who argues that Chaucer's allusion is to an Oedipus who loses physical sight but later gains the second, internal sight of wisdom. Such a regenerate Oedipus may indeed be found in classical tradition—though more notably in Greek than in Latin literature—but the many similarities between Troilus in Book IV and the Oedipus of *Thebaid* I, 46–87 indicate that Chaucer had the "impius Oedipus" of Statius in mind.

whatever satirical effect they may contribute to individual scenes. For the vision of history that placed Thebes shortly before Troy in the succession of ancient empires also identified their successors in the kingdoms of Europe founded by refugees from Troy. To use Chaucer's terms, one of the 'folk' that the 'regne' of Troy begot was the British. There is some reason to believe that Chaucer added the specter of Thebes to the background of the *Troilus* to underscore an implicit theme of the poem, namely that one fallen city may serve as a warning to another not yet fallen. As Thebes should have been to Troy, so Troy should be to England. The citizens of London, to whom Chaucer read his poem, sometimes referred to their city as "New Troy."[44]

[44] On references to London as "New Troy" in Chaucer's day, see John P. McCall and George Rudisill, "The Parliament of 1386 and Chaucer's Trojan Parliament," *JEGP*, 58 (1959), 276–88, and D. W. Robertson, Jr., *Chaucer's London* (New York: John Wiley & Sons, 1968), p. 3 et passim; "Simple Signs from Everyday Life in Chaucer," in *Signs and Symbols in Chaucer's Poetry*, ed. J. P. Hermann and J. J. Burke (University, Alabama: U of Alabama P, 1980), p. 212, n. 27.

Reviews

JUDSON BOYCE ALLEN and THERESA ANNE MORITZ, *A Distinction of Stories: The Medieval Unity of Chaucer's Fair Chain of Narratives for Canterbury*. Columbus: Ohio State University Press, 1981. Pp. xii, 258. $20.00.

The ambitions of this important book are wholly laudable, and the propositions with which it begins are sound. The authors recognize and share the desire of all readers of *The Canterbury Tales* to find some underlying unity in the work, but they show clearly how previous attempts to establish this unity have been based upon irrelevant or unhelpful assumptions. The 'geographical' method, for instance, has to invoke a type of narrative realism which Chaucer shows himself little interested in, and furthermore has to concentrate almost exclusively on the frame at the expense of the stories. Analysis which concentrates on the completed beginning and ending of the *Tales* likewise has to abandon the greater part of the work as a muddle. The evidence of the manuscripts themselves, even the best of them, is not helpful. As for the 'dramatic' principle in *The Canterbury Tales*, the authors give it short shrift: "For us Chaucer's stories are not, except trivially, speeches or dramatic monologues" (p. x). They mount an attack on the dramatic reading of the *Tales*—"Because it is so insidious, it needs especially to be put down" (p. 11) which is wholly convincing, and makes at least one reader wish to break into spontaneous applause. They have little time, either, for the sophisticated types of modern deconstructionism, which find in every poem by Chaucer a desperately subtle statement about how impossible it is to write poetry, or the similarly fashionable retreat into multiple irony—whereby the unity of the work is said to lie in its demonstration of universal disunity, and its affirmations in the denial of the possibility of affirmation. As the authors put it, with welcome trenchancy: "Irony, for the Middle Ages, is simply one of the forms of allegory, that is, not a denial of meaning but an affirmation of it" (p. 11).

What the authors propose, instead, is to try to arrive at an under-standing of the unity of *The Canterbury Tales* by taking medieval theories of tale-aggregation, as those theories may be seen in operation in commentaries on Ovid's *Metamorphoses*, and applying those to the *Tales*. The detailed study of these commentaries is promised in a forthcoming volume, but meanwhile the authors take the fourfold division of types of metamorphosis made by the commentators—natural, magical, moral, and spiritual—and use it to reconstruct Chaucer's poem as "a normative array of exempla in four groups, which exploit the literal and analogical significance of the structure of marriage in order to arrive at a definition of social order." Within the tales themselves, therefore, the reading is acknowledged to be exemplary rather than mimetic or dramatic, exem-plary, that is, of moral and other kinds of truth, though the authors claim that they are interested in the forms of narrative that allow these truths expression rather than in the truths themselves. This claim is disingenuous, and turns out to be not true.

To these original and ingenious propositions the authors bring the support of an impressive array of arguments. They point out that 'artificial' ordering of the kind they adduce is established practice in medieval writing: since narrative has no important correspondence in itself with reality, it must be manipulated into one. Characters, like-wise, are not significant in themselves, dramatically and psychological-ly, but as exempla of general truths, and the authors demonstrate this point with some remarks on the Marriage Group. Read literally, or 'dramatically,' as they point out, it is trivial, curious, merely psycholog-ical; read properly, it evokes a whole series of associations with other relationships analogous to marriage—Christ and the church, the higher and lower reason, the mind and the body, the ruler and his subjects. In this way, the particular always stands to reveal the universal, the general truth. Even the prologues and links, which some have thought to be inherently dramatic, are really part of a continuing commentary on the nature and function of narrative, a discourse on the relation between telling a story and telling the truth. If they do not seem to do so, that is because they are ironically inapt, Chaucer using them to "underscore the inadequacy of the pilgrims' expectations" (p. 53).

Everything confirms, then, that stories are—or, as the authors more guardedly put it, "poetry is 'about' "—"exempla of ethical existence" (p. 67), and the method by which they operate is not mimesis, or the causal relation of events, but analogy. Stories, and aggregations of stories, adhere by virtue of the analogical relationships that are perceived to exist between the matter of poetry and the matter of ethics. The particular manner in which these analogies are seen to operate is not important, since any mode of 'distinguishing' and ordering provides 'a normative array' if the norms are known (p. 90). The authors' innovation here, where they may seem to be straying along a familiar Robertsonian path, is to assert that such analogical modes of ordering are not necessarily confined to the eliciting of Christian, that is, Christ-centered, truth (p. 92). Analogy and typology teach how to generate relationships, but the relationships can refer to other kinds of ethical truth (provided, one is obliged to add, that they are always the same). Ovid's *Metamorphoses*, the authors explain, was understood in this way by the commentators: they saw the matter of the poem as 'changes,' they divided it into stories of different kinds of changes, and used the parallels and analogies between them to construct "a definition of the human condition in relation to man's material circumstances and his divine destiny" (p. 97). In the same way, our modern commentators identify four groups of stories in *The Canterbury Tales*, "each group exemplifying a particular kind of change and a particular kind of moral activity." These are "tales of natural changes, whose preoccupation is with the nature and exercise of human authority; tales of magic, which furnish a normative array of disorders, illusions, deceptions, and mistakes; tales of worldly moral struggle, in which merely human solutions to the problem of orderly living succeed and fail; and tales of spiritual interpretation, which furnish a normative array of human postures within which given events may be confronted, lived with, and understood" (p. 97). The first group comprises the tales of Fragment I; the second those of VIII, V, III, and VI; the third those of II, IV, and IX; the fourth those of VII and X. A chart on pp. 106–07 reveals all. *The Knight's Tale* is further used, in its four parts, as a working model of the operation of the fourfold scheme.

The authors are well aware of what they are doing: that they are using a medieval technique of reading, devised to enable edifying explanations to be offered of unpromising works, as a technique for understanding how Chaucer organized his poem. In other words, they are saying that Chaucer used a method of reading as a method of writing (p. 24). This is not a claim that can be supported by their assertion that their method of interpretation, since it corresponds to what we know of medieval theory of story-structure, is "heuristically correct" (p. 98). The commentators used Ovid in order to prove that Christian truth was universal; their technique was not a means to the understanding of literary works, but to their ideological reconstitution. It is inconceivable that such a method of reading could be used, either in composition by Chaucer or in commentary by the present authors, without a similar ideological motive. The latter explanation seems the more likely, and the conclusion follows that the authors, in doing with Chaucer what medieval commentators did with Ovid, are writing a work not of literary criticism but of moral edification. I am not sure that they would object to this diagnosis: certainly, the rhapsody on the institution of Christian marriage with which they conclude (pp. 233–41) has little to do with Chaucer's poetry, much to do with their own convictions and their desire to find in a great and serious poet an endorsement of those convictions.

There is one other argument that the authors advance in support of their interpretation, that 'it works.' "It helps to make the work clear" (p. 98). This self-confessedly pragmatic method of validating an interpretation is actually the most naked subjectivity, for all it asserts is that 'it works for me' (or 'for us,' in this case, which probably, given the excitement of collaborative enterprises, makes it rather more than less subjective). Their further defence of their method, that it places a proper value on the stories, adds another interesting gloss to 'it works': "He [Chaucer] places a higher value on story than can anyone whose categories are merely aesthetic, because he involves them directly in the real ordering of the moral universe" (p. 108). The polarized values attached to 'aesthetic' and 'real' here make it clear that 'it works' means 'it produces the right answer.' This is Augustine's explanation of the working of Christian allegory.

All one can say, equally pragmatically, of the second half of the book, in which the authors demonstrate their interpretation in a group-by-group and tale-by-tale commentary, is that it doesn't work, or at best works fitfully. There are any number of pertinent and intelligent observations on individual tales, but there is also much fanciful and, in the end, exasperating pursuit of parallels and contrasts and analogies. What of this, for instance, as an analogical association between *The Knight's Tale* and *The Miller's Tale*? "John is duped into constructing the elaborate equipment which frees Alisoun for a night with Nicholas; his *constructio* evokes, by the medieval doctrine of concordance, an analogy with the construction by Theseus of the pavilion [sic] in which the young men will contend for his ward" (p. 128). Or this 'picking up' of a detail from *The Clerk's Tale* in *The Merchant's Tale?* "Walter's proposed January–May marriage to his own daughter, which is of course pure pretense, becomes in the *Merchant's Tale* the serious basis of the narrative" (p. 195). These chapters are at times a startling record of what can happen when two intelligent people, with well-stocked minds and a limitless capacity for making associations, are let loose in a long and complex poem. One can often admire the skill with which it is done, the skill, for instance, with which the authors cover their tracks as they disappear into the forest of their reverie: "The means by which we understand what the stories mean and how to use them is the subject of the whole of this book, and we shall not, at this point, explain that. Rather, we believe that in the interpretation group Chaucer presents an array of tales suggesting an array of interpretative postures, all but one more or less wrong, and all related by the usual Chaucerian irony to the answer" (p. 212). And I particularly treasure the note affixed to a mention of Constance's two mothers-in-law (p. 185), which tells us that "Emelye's two potential mothers-in law. . . . were Antigone and Ismene" (p. 204) But these are incidental pleasures, and they provoke only momentarily the delightful suspicion that the book is a spoof. For the most part the paths of analogy, rich and bizarre as they are, lead only to the desert of platitude, as for instance when the discussion of supernatural intrusion into human affairs in 'the tales of magic,' which has been conducted with all the paraphernalia of parody, thematic echo and echoed gloss, concludes with the drawing of the lesson that such intrusions never come to good unless divinely sanctioned (p. 141). Typical of the way a new grouping will generate new things to say is the treatment of 'the moral group,' where it is found that the tales are in a kind of descending order, in terms of the rank of the participants, and then too in terms of the nature of the divine presence. "In the *Man of Law's Tale* the providentially assisting Christian God is fully and powerfully present. In the *Clerk's Tale* we have a man functioning as God, with his Godlike activity clearly underlined by allusions to Job. In the *Merchant's Tale* there are pagan gods, with real powers, working in a kind of parody of Providence to give the tale its outcome. In the *Manciple's Tale* we have a pagan god without powers, acting merely as a bachelor. In the *Shipman's Tale* there is no god at all" (p. 180). That last sentence makes the whole thing almost worthwhile.

For all its promise, therefore, the high intelligence and ingenuity which has gone into its making, and the brilliance of the opening chapters, this book goes down as an exciting failure. Like a rocket, it shoots off dramatically, explodes in a dazzling display of intellectual fireworks, and then slowly descends, growing more dim and indistinct all the time. At the end there is nothing to be seen.

DEREK PEARSALL
University of York

STEPHEN A. BARNEY, ed., *Chaucer's Troilus: Essays in Criticism*. Hamden, Connecticut: Archon Books, 1980. Pp. x, 323. $17.50.

There seems to be a need perceived for re-assessing the significance of *Troilus and Criseyde*, a kind of critical stock-taking. Alice R. Kaminsky (*Chaucer's Troilus and Criseyde and the Critics*, Ohio University Press, 1980) recently did her own sifting and the headings of her chapters— "The Historical Hypothesis," "The Psychological Approach"—indicate the partial synthesis of her results. The papers collected by Mary Salu (*Essays on Troilus and Criseyde*, D. S. Brewer, Rowman and Littlefield, 1979) are original contributions, but the approaches—textual, 'realism,' Chaucerian comedy—are often traditional enough. And now a substantial collection of seventeen essays ranges from Kittredge in 1915 to the three original contributions which close the volume. Two, C. S. Lewis, "What Chaucer Really Did to 'Il Filostrato' " and M. W. Bloomfield, "Distance and Predestination" were included in the anthology by Schoeck and Taylor (University of Notre Dame Press, 1961), but these have stood the test of time so well that they deserved reprinting yet again. Why this concentration on *Troilus*? I suppose because it is a single long poem, more manageable therefore than *The Canterbury Tales*, and furthermore because its courtliness looks back to Chaucer's early poetry and the subtlety of its characterization right forwards into the nineteenth century and beyond. So far as I know, there is as yet no Casebook; I feel sure one is in course of preparation.

In an admirably brief and modest Preface, Stephen Barney states that the essays he has chosen have been reprinted in their entirety, occasionally lightly revised by the author. A few have an Afterword which seems to me justified only where there have been important discoveries necessitating updating of the original. His consideration in providing the original pagination between slashes will be appreciated by anyone who has had to root in the periodicals stack to search for the original reference for a quotation discovered (or rediscovered) in an anthology. He has decided not to include extracts from books (with the exception of Kittredge and Empson), but his regret at the consequent exclusion of Muscatine and Payne shows something of what has been lost. His principle of selection is simply the best, the most intelligent, and the most sensitive. This is unexceptionable, of course, but his disclaimer that he did not intend to indicate variety of approach or to give a spectrum of opinion is less defensible. There is no overt Robertsonian criticism, for instance— Schoeck and Taylor included "Chaucerian Tragedy"—perhaps because once you have argued that Troilus' love for Criseyde is idolatrous there is not much more to be said, but perhaps also because so many of the disciples are such pale reflections of their master. Yet the arrangement of the essays in order of composition makes the temptation to trace changes of emphasis well-nigh unavoidable.

How simple it all seemed in 1915! Kittredge wants to persuade us to read the poem. His approach is wholly through the narrative and the characterization: this was, after all, the great psychological novel. Chaucer is still Chaucer, unencumbered by a persona which he must variously flaunt or conceal, but anyway manipulate. Mizener in 1939 is still concerned primarily with character. This would be a good essay to begin with, pragmatic and sensible yet already perceiving that Criseyde's character is essentially static. Between Kittredge and Mizener come Lewis on *Il Filostrato* (which on re-reading seemed oddly academic in its manner, quite lacking the beguiling humanity of much of *The Allegory of Love*) and Empson. Empson begins the search for *implicit* meanings, in his case puns, in an attempt to see 'a patina of subtlety" in the poem. Usually there is one natural meaning—and sometimes two possible meanings—among the welter of unlikely ones in that particular context. A later version of the same search for deliberate ambiguities is what I may call the concordance approach. The 1974 essay by John Leyerle, "The Heart and the Chain," is a good example. *Hert*, we are told, is used nearly forty times in *The Book of the Duchess*. Everyone, nowadays, is likely to agree about the deliberate pun in *hert-huntyng* at the end. But, despite Leyerle's ingenious idea of a skillful Dreamer

141

leading on an unsuspecting John of Gaunt, if the Dreamer's "I holde that this hert be goon" is meant to be a calculated ambiguity, Gaunt's immediate reply, "Y do no fors therof," is, to say the least, odd in the general context of the poem. Some of the instances of *herte* (an example of what Leyerle calls a *nucleus*) in *Troilus and Criseyde* are certainly striking (such as the exchange of hearts in Criseyde's dream about the eagle) but others (*with al myn herte, out of his herte, deere herte*) seem proverbial and hardly worth mentioning. Barbara Newman, in an essay written specially for this anthology, is more discriminating in the distinction she makes between *trouthe* and 'truth,' for concealment, 'untruth,' is inherent in courtly love. Here is a paradox which really illuminates the poem.

There is nothing included between Mizener in 1939 and Bloomfield in 1957. From now on there are no more general discussions of the poem but only of particular aspects of it, in Bloomfield's case of the apparent impotence of the Narrator in the face of the events he narrates. Yet this same Narrator continually forces his audience to view the poem from a distance, from the point of view of its end. Like God he foresees the doom of his characters: he is "the artistic correlative to the problem of predestination." But Chaucer the artist sympathizes with his characters, and in the resulting tension resides much of the poem's appeal. This is part of the preoccupation of the 1950's with techniques, in the wake of the New Criticism: how the poem *works*. By the time of one of the best-known essays included here, Donaldson's "The Ending of *Troilus*," 1963, Bloomfield's two-dimensional Narrator has become "a way of poetic life" and the tension "the emotional storm-centre" of the poem. Donaldson's sensitive criticism, written in a racy and immensely entertaining style, is at its best in showing Chaucer's uncharacteristic uncertainty of touch in the final stanzas. We see the artist in the very act of questioning accepted positions, revaluating his material. Yet, in retrospect, does this presuppose quite the degree of manipulation of the Narrator that Donaldson suggests?

Some of the subsequent essays seem to me to show signs of strain. Brenner, in 1965, has some interesting things to say about narrative structure, but they are not made more intelligible by a fairly liberal use of *dramatic, ironic, metaphor* (none of these closely defined), not to mention *ironic foreshadowings* or *linear fragmentation*. Karla Taylor, in one of the original essays, treats us to a semantic disquisition on proverbs (proverbs are clearly the new fashion: two of the final three essays deal

142

with their significance) which are part of "a matrix of language." Ambivalence is all. Although we may wince at "Chaucer too becomes a crashing oak, failing always to fix the bending reed of his poetry," these essays are far from negligible. My point is simply that the intellectual press-ups are unnecessary.

A great part of the charm of an anthology is the renewal of past pleasures and the discovery of new ones. I had missed—or else seriously undervalued—Davis Taylor's "The Terms of Love," 1976. Here is a real attempt at close stylistic criticism which, despite turning up some fairly obvious conclusions (as stylistics often does) demonstrates *how* we are brought to see Troilus' view of himself as unique in his habit of employing unqualified superlatives to describe himself, his infrequent use of proverbs with their generalizing significance, his "tendency to twist, turn and repeat before he concludes a sentence." Two essays succeed brilliantly, I think, because they focus on a limited problem or a limited section of the text. Norman Davis invokes considerable learning and a good deal of supporting evidence from outside the poem to illuminate epistolary style in *Troilus and Criseyde*. Donald Howard concentrates on the 300-odd lines from Book II in which we see Criseyde making up her mind to return Troilus' love. Two pleasant, more general, essays are John P. McCall's demonstration of how the fluctuating fortunes of Troy provide an additional dimension to the tragedy of Troilus, and Dieter Mehl's suggestion that Chaucer manipulates his material to invite his audience to ask the right sort of question about the poem. (But what *is* the right sort of question to ask about Criseyde, for example? Mehl is not really incisive enough here.) I could have done with some more essays of this latter kind, by Robert apRoberts, say (the Boethian element in the poem is rather under-represented in this collection), or Alfred David. But of course everyone will have his own candidates for the hundred best tunes. Suffice to say that Stephen Barney has done a service to Chaucer criticism by bringing together essays which both illustrate the very different responses the poem can invoke and, by placing them side by side, showing that no man has a monopoly of truth.

S. S. HUSSEY
University of Lancaster

143

ROBERT G. BENSON, *Medieval Body Language: A Study of the Use of Gesture in Chaucer's Poetry.* Anglistica XXI. Copenhagen: Rosenkilde & Bagger, 1980. Pp. 170. D. kr. 118.

Benson starts from the belief that "Chaucer's use of gesture in his best poetry is the most successful and artistically sophisticated employment of that device in English poetry before 1500" (p. 9), and is keen to see the contribution of gesture to many distinctive effects of Chaucer's poetry. After an introductory chapter, there follow three chapters, on the early poems, on some of the tales—especially *SumT*—and on *Troilus*. The last third of the book is taken up by a catalogue of gestures as discerned by Benson in Chaucer's works and quoted in full.

There are many points and insights of interest; the main failings of the study seem to me to be ones of definition and of the literary interpretation of Chaucer's use of gesture. Benson is concerned to make a very inclusive definition of gesture: he wants to see all expressive actions as gesture, rather than retaining Habicht's definition of "all physical motions or positions of the body which have a meaning but do not serve a practical purpose." Moreover, Benson does not quite seem to resolve what he thinks the literary nature of gesture may be: he makes firm distinctions between what he thinks of as conventional, stylized, and ceremonial gesture, and gesture which is dramatic, individualizing, and realistic, and contributes to characterization. Benson sensibly declares that he is not suggesting that Chaucer moved from an acceptance of stylized and traditional gesture towards a more naturalistic use, and that both conventional and realistic gestures were used when appropriate in Chaucer's later works. However, Benson's discussion does suggest that Chaucer's most successful use of gesture is in the delineation of character and realistic action. Character-development and the intrinsic appeal of colloquialism are taken as values and centres of interest in our reading against which success in use of gesture is judged. (Thus, the colloquial style and realistic, spontaneous gestures of the fabliaux are seen in association.) Gathering effectiveness in use of gesture is matched with a growing power in the use of colloquial speech and evocation of individual character in Benson's view of Chaucer's works.

In Benson's account some of the minor poems are accordingly marked by gesture which is 'decorative' rather than working for that revelation of character which he sees as its optimal literary function. Because conventional gesture tends towards generalization, even metaphorical expression, rather than individualization, it will seem static and ornamental to a reader looking for gestures which produce action or delineate character. The dream poems and *LGW* are thus disappointing for gesture, if gesture's role is seen in such terms, and although Benson has interesting points on these poems he does not acknowledge the very positive significance that can be attached to the stylized and traditional in them. However, in discussing the *Tales* Benson makes some good points on the value of calmness and stillness in tales as distinct as *SNT*, *ClT*, and *KnT*. The study concludes with a reading of some tales and *Troilus*, where most kinds of physical action and movement of the characters, although directly necessitated by the action, are considered as gesture ("The development that is evident is in the direction of what I would call organic gesture," p. 59), and sometimes the study risks becoming a synopsis of Chaucer's narratives. Not everybody will be able to follow Benson's inclusive idea of gesture here: he is examining the narratives from the viewpoint of modern 'body-language,' a less distinct and more psychological concept than traditional notions of gesture as certain acknowledged and definite physical signs, reactions, and movements.

Despite some references Benson does not include extended comparison of Chaucer's writings with their sources where known, and this might have provided a necessary way of defining the nature of Chaucer's own innovation in gesture, and the ways in which Chaucer is often very much more formal and stylized—by his own positive choice—than might have been supposed. In a text like *Troilus* there is a blend of that fluently natural action which Chaucer is especially able to create, alongside the stylized and ordered in behavior, some absorbed from the source and some added and created by Chaucer in translation (as with some interesting instances of kneeling and weeping). Benson rightly stresses how concretely Chaucer creates a sense of the body in his later poetry, and does acknowledge the interesting coexistence between the natural and the stylized in Chaucer's writing. But this is often where Chaucer's use of gesture is most distinctively challenging to modern expectations. There is the 'realism' that Benson praises, yet not because realism or the delineation of character are self-evidently valuable for their own sakes in Chaucer. There is 'realism,' but it is partial and fragmented, because other centers of interest occupy Chaucer's imagination. Through the use of traditional gesture, which is continuous from his early poetry, Chaucer can in this way see his characters at once naturalistically, yet also within a network of non-individualizing and ceremonial gesture, which endows their existences in his narratives both with the force of individuality and the strength of archetypal responses.

BARRY WINDEATT
Emmanuel College, Cambridge

CAROLINE D. ECKHARDT, ed. *Essays in the Numerical Criticism of Medieval Literature*. Lewisburg: Bucknell University Press, London: Associated University Presses, 1980. Pp. 239. $17.50.

Although the devotees of Patristic exegesis have often struck the medieval establishment as a wild band of gloomy religious zealots, they have appeared tame and sane when compared to the practitioners of numerical criticism, who too frequently have seemed to be crypto-mathematicians more at ease with slide rule and calculator than with poetry. Since the pioneer work of Vincent Hopper's *Medieval Number Symbolism* (1938) and E. R. Curtius' excursus on numerical composition in *European Literature and the Latin Middle Ages* (1948), literary criticism focusing on symbolic number and numerical structure has alienated at least as many readers as it has converted. For all the books and articles of the past generation, the need still remains for studies that explain what numerical criticism is all about and that justify its particular applications.

In its conception at least, this collection of eight essays edited by Caroline Eckhardt represents just the sort of work necessary to change the image of numerical criticism and give it legitimacy. It offers both background material and studies of specific works. It contains both numerological investigations (on the symbolic significance of number) and tectonic analyses (on varieties of numerical structure). Moreover, it cuts across national literatures and examines several important pieces of literature from the sixth to the fourteenth century: the *Consolation of Philosophy, Beowulf, Song of Roland, Nibelungenlied, Divine Comedy, Gawain and the Green Knight, Pearl*, and *Canterbury Tales*. And the volume represents the first book in English on numerical criticism since 1970, when there appeared both Alastair Fowler's *Silent Poetry*, a collection of

146

ten essays on English literature from the fourteenth to the eighteenth century, and Christopher Butler's *Number Symbolism*, a survey of numerological tradition from antiquity to the twentieth century (erroneously described by Eckhardt as a collection of critical studies, p. 231). From 1970 to 1980, the main works on numerical criticism have been in German: Ernst Hellgardt's *Zum Problem symbolbestimmter und formalästhetischer Zahlenkomposition in mittelalterlicher Literatur* (1973), on the backgrounds of numerical thought and its place in medieval German literature; and Heinz Meyer's *Die Zahlenallegorese im Mittelalter* (1975), on the symbolism of number in medieval thought, focusing on Gregory the Great, Bede, and Honorius. In terms of coverage Eckhardt's collection nicely complements these works.

Unfortunately, however, between Eckhardt's conception and the creation itself the shadow has fallen; and the offering must be described as a mixed bag. It reprints two essays—Charles Singleton's well-known and easily available study of Dante, "The Poet's Number at the Center" (1965); and Eckhardt's own "The Number of Chaucer's Pilgrims" (1975), in which, neglecting the significance of the stated number "nyne and twenty," she focuses on 33 as the final and actual number of pilgrims. It includes another essay, A. Kent Hieatt's "Numerical Structures in Verse," that is little more than a review article. Along with offering some pertinent admonitions to practitioners of numerical criticism, Hieatt is concerned mainly with reviewing Hans Käsmann's comments on a Hieatt article on *Gawain and the Green Knight* and with criticizing in turn Eleanor Bulatkin's book on the *Song of Roland*. Other essays—including Allan Metcalf's "Gawain's Number" and Thomas Elwood Hart's "Tectonic Methodology and an Application to *Beowulf*"—are not likely to win friends for numerical criticism. While one might well agree that the numbers 5 and 25 are significant in *Gawain and the Green Knight*, and that *Beowulf* might well be divided into three symmetrical parts, each of these essays not only tends to go too far in its claims of numerical significance but obfuscates more than it clarifies. A much more reasonable, and convincing, analysis is Edward G. Fichtner's "Patterns of Arithmetical Proportion in the *Nibelungenlied*," though one might object that this essay represents mainly an application of pre-existing scholarship.

The most interesting, as well as the longest, essays in the collection (each containing about fifty pages) are Russell A. Peck's general introduction, "Number as Cosmic Language," and Elaine Scarry's study of Boethius' *Consolation*, "The Well-Rounded Sphere." Peck, who has probably contributed as much to the numerological analysis of medieval texts as anyone in an English department, has written a perceptive, useful introduction to medieval number theory. Though one might regret that he offers little on number as harmony (and that he errs in identifying Boethius as the source of the redactions of Euclid followed by medieval writers of geometries), there is no denying the clarity and usefulness of his essay.

While the importance of Boethius is demonstrated further by Scarry in her occasionally provocative essay on the *Consolation*, her analysis of its structure is uneven. When focusing on the pivotal Book III, she fails to use the several important studies by Gruber, Wiltshire, and Baltes; when commenting on Boethius' use of prose, she fails to examine what he does with prose in his logical treatises; and when concerned with the total number of prose and verse sections of each book of the *Consolation*, she strangely fails to do anything at all with the total number of each, 39, a number coincidentally (?) very important in the *Nibelungenlied*, as Fichtner notes in his essay.

But the main problem with Scarry's essay—as with Metcalf's, Eckhardt's, and Hart's—is that its application of tectonic analysis seems overstated and finally unconvincing. Though Hieatt might complain in his essay of the "grumbling conservatism" of medievalists which keeps the approach "not yet highly regarded" (p. 66), in a very real sense the practitioners of numerical criticism are themselves at fault for their lack of acceptance. What I wrote in 1970 about the uses and misuses of numerical criticism may be said of these essays: "too much of the existing criticism suffers from an inability to be convincing, . . . and too often the approach seems to be more trouble than it is worth" ("Number Symbolism and Medieval Literature," *M&H*, 1 [1970], 165).

The use of number as structural principle is something that requires far more demonstration than most critics—including those in this volume—are willing to give it. And though those devoted to such analysis might think of themselves as structuralists or formalists, for many readers all of their equations, graphs, and charts must seem like much ado about nothing. If I, not at all a hostile reader, come away from many of the essays in this volume doubting and feeling that I have not really learned anything new, I can imagine how the unsympathetic

148

reader will respond. While Peck's essay should certainly be read (and Scarry's too, for all its unevenness), little else in this collection demands the attention of medievalists or their students.

EDMUND REISS
Duke University

SIGMUND EISNER, ed.; Gary Mac Eoin and Sigmund Eisner, trans. *The Kalendarium of Nicholas of Lynn*. The Chaucer Library. Athens: University of Georgia Press, 1980. Pp. xii, 248. $30.00.

Chaucer's continual fascination with the stars and heavenly motions has provided a rich lode for the scholar. Witness, for example, those subtle celestial clues in *Troilus and Criseyde* that allowed Root and Russell to date its composition. Or consider the puzzlement provided by such a simple couplet as, "the yonge sonne / Hath in the Ram his halve cours yronne," in the prologue to *The Canterbury Tales*. (We can readily check in the calendarium under review that the sun gets half way through Aries on March 27, hardly consonant with "April with his shoures soote" of the opening line.) Or, ponder what Chaucer really had in mind when in the beginning of *The Treatise on the Astrolabe* he states:

> The thirde partie shal contene diverse tables of longitudes and latitudes of sterres fixe for the Astrelabie, and tables of the declinacions of the sonne, and tables of longitudes of citees and townes; and tables as well for the governaunce of a clokke, as for to fynde the altitude meridian; and many anothir notable conclusioun after the kalenders of the reverent clerkes, Frere J. Somer and Frere N. Lenne.

Frere N. Lenne is, of course, none other than Nicholas of Lynn, whose calendar is meticulously reproduced, translated, and commented upon by Professor Eisner. Because of the *Astrolabe* we can be quite sure that Chaucer indeed used this almanac, but now that it is printed, we can all see that it does not contain longitudes and latitudes of fixed stars or of cities or towns, nor does it include solar declinations. Neither, apparently, does the almanac of John Somer, though Eisner is not quite as explicit on this point as he might be. What Nicholas of Lynn *does* have, and

149

rather uncommonly so, is a detailed table for solar altitudes and shadow lengths at Oxford, which could well be used to set a clock. And that is precisely how Chaucer uses the *Kalendarium* in at least three places in *The Canterbury Tales*—not explicitly to set a clock, but at least to establish the time by shadow length.

In good Chaucerian manner this sets more problems for the interpreter, but now, armed with a readily available almanac, we can all play the game. The first example is in the introduction to *The Man of Law's Tale*, where the host, knowing that it is the 18th of April, deduces from the observation that every shadow equals "the body erect that caused it" that it is 10 a.m. From the table (p. 87) we can readily see that at 10 a.m. and at 2 p.m. on April 18th this is so, and at no other tabulated time in all of March, April, or May. Nicholas' entry is like a wonderful footnote awaiting some supporting text, and Chaucer has indeed found a place to exploit it. But there is a problem—has Chaucer done it deliberately just to confound us? His host also "saugh wel that the brighte sonne / The ark of his artificial day hath ronne / The ferthe part, and half an houre and moore." Chaucer knows full well that the artificial day is the time between sunrise and sunset; he defines it so in the *Astrolabe*, and he can read the length for each day, so labeled, in Nicholas' *Kalendarium*. On April 18th the artificial day is 14^h19^m, and a quarter part of that is 3^h35^m, or 8:25 a.m. Matters would be much simpler if Chaucer had said a third part of the arc, which would be 4^h47^m, or 9:37 a.m., and with about half-an-hour more, it would be at least approximately 10 a.m. With the *Kalendarium* now conveniently available, it can be left as a problem for the reader!

The second example, from *The Nun's Priest's Tale*, is, happily, entirely straightforward: Chauntecleer, not your ordinary cock, crows precisely at nine a.m., knowing "prime" has arrived because the sun is at 41° and more, and because the sun is in Taurus at 21° and somewhat more. Both details match Nicholas' *Kalendarium* for the stated date, May 3rd.

The third example, in Eisner's words, "swirls with difficulties." At the beginning of *The Parson's Tale*, Chaucer again uses a shadow length to determine the time; with that, actually, there is no problem, and it can be worked out against the *Kalendarium*, but, alas, this leads to a date of April 17th, a day earlier than the first example. I am inclined to follow John North, who suggests that Chaucer simply had in mind an April pilgrimage, and that we should not ask for complete consistency of detail. The other problem is that Chaucer says, "Therwith the moones exaltacioun, / I meene Libra, alwey gan ascende," whereas Nicholas' *Tabula ad inveniendum dignitates planetarum in signis* clearly shows that the moon's exaltation is in Taurus, not Libra, and this is not a point of ambiguity in the astrological tradition. The obvious solution is to concede that Chaucer sometimes made mistakes.

In the prologue to the *Kalendarium*, Nicholas states that he is preparing the calendar in 1386, and eclipses are illustrated from 1387 to 1462; hence it must have been quite new when Chaucer used it for his tales. Fifteen manuscript copies are known, and at least four of them could have been seen by Chaucer. Eisner has selected a virtually complete copy at the Bodleian as his principal source document. The numerical tables are handsomely typeset, with the translations of the headings found in the introduction. The two pages of prologue and the twenty pages of canons have the English translation and lists of variants on facing pages.

Except for the eclipses, the *Kalendarium* is in fact a perpetual calendar independent of year. This means that it does not contain any planetary positions, which would change from year to year, but because of the moon's 19-year rhythm (the Metonic cycle), it is possible to provide a scheme for calculating its positions and phases; consequently it is also possible to find for any arbitrary year the dates of movable feasts dependent on the moon, such as Easter. In his introduction Professor Eisner shows how this may be done through the use of the golden number and dominical letter, and he uses these devices from the *Kalendarium* in a sample Easter calculation for 1394, which falls on April 19th. For good measure he also shows us how to calculate the position of the moon on December 17th, 1975 [sic]: with the moon in Gemini, it would have been an unpropitious time for bloodletting from the shoulders, arms, or hands. In other words, there is more to Nicholas' opuscula than just shadow lengths. Now that the *Kalendarium* is conveniently available, perhaps other, more subtle examples of Chaucer's use of this reference will be discovered.

OWEN GINGERICH
Harvard-Smithsonian Center for Astrophysics
Cambridge, Massachusetts

JOSEPH GIBALDI, *Approaches to Teaching Chaucer's* Canterbury Tales. Modern Language Association: Approaches to teaching masterpieces of world literature 1. New York: Modern Language Association, 1980. Pp. xvi, 175. Paper $6.50. Cloth $13.50.

This book is the first in a series of works designed to present a number of viewpoints on the teaching of great works of literature. Except for Shakespeare, Chaucer is the author whom undergraduates not majoring in literature are most likely to encounter, and it is fitting that the series begin with approaches to *The Canterbury Tales*. As the inaugural volume, this book sets an admirable standard by which subsequent titles may be evaluated.

The plan of the book is useful: Part One, Materials; Part Two, Approaches; a list of participants in a survey on teaching Chaucer; a list of works cited; and an index of names and titles. The list of materials includes texts, anthologies, dual language editions, translations, background materials, critical studies, etc. These are not merely mentioned, but are briefly (and fairly) evaluated by Professor Gibaldi, who has synthesized the opinions and comments of the respondents in the survey. Over one hundred teachers participated, and opinions expressed are based on classroom experience. Any reader considering texts for adoption—whether the complete works, a book of selections, an anthology, or even a translation—will benefit from the comments included. Thus it is with ancillary materials: what various teachers expect their students to read, study, or have available constitutes a formidable list, but one which all of us appreciate. Most of the titles are still in print, and many of the best articles in journals have appeared in the anthologies of criticism mentioned in the bibliography.

Part Two deals with "Approaches," and its five parts consider the presentation of Chaucer in various modes. First is John Fisher's "The Student as Reader of Chaucer," (and Fisher means 'reader aloud' and so emphasizes the oral performance approach to the poet). Other modes of presentation in this part of the book are the overview of the Chaucer course; specific approaches—rhetorical, linguistic, Boethian, cultural—used in the whole course; Chaucer in the survey course; Chaucer in the thematic course. The authors of these fifteen essays include the well-known and the less-known, but the essays of all are rooted in classroom experience. Some of the articles append course syllabi, but no one included example examination questions (those gave me the most trouble in my first years of teaching). This part of the book raises a few questions which remain after the book is closed. Part One is generally factual, a listing of materials. But Part Two is frankly subjective in its approach, and each reader of the book has for implicit comparison his or her own approach to Chaucer.

What will the teacher of Chaucer think, after making these comparisons? Reactions will range from incredulity (do people really cover that much—or that little—in a limited number of classes?) to an appreciation of the warmth and affection for the subject which some of these teachers display. The Preface expresses the hope that teachers might want to put the book into the hands of their students. But the student is too often seen as a problem in these essays: his lack of background, his ignorance of language, of tradition, of serious purpose—these overshadow the student as a human being. Chaucer's tone in *The Astrolabe* is benevolent, and apparently inimitable. If I were asked to recommend to a new teacher of Chaucer only one essay in this collection, it would be Donald Howard's "The Idea of a Chaucer Course." It is, as Howard mentions, somewhat crochety, but it deals with the students we have now, in the 1980's. It is a practicable approach filled with good advice.

Having read the book, one inevitably wonders about the usefulness at this time of a pedagogical approach to Chaucer. Who will adopt many (or any) of the ideas presented? Why wasn't such a book available in the 1960's when colleges were being established, Chaucer courses being added, and students going on to graduate school? The appearance of the book now may seem too late; but it will be helpful to teachers developing thematic courses (Susan Schibanoff's "The Crooked Rib: Women in Medieval Literature" is an excellent model); it will be helpful for survivors in an English department who step in for a departed colleague. Yet even for those who have taught Chaucer for many years to classes of various sizes and varying degrees of preparation, the book has something to offer. We are reminded that the Chaucer each of us introduces to a class is not the whole man; that although our immediate aim might be to present a medieval worldview, or to generate an interest in Middle English, or to deal with the problems of medieval rhetoric and poetic, Chaucer is greater than the total of these and other things. He can make our students better people. Our job is to help.

GERALD L. EVANS
Marietta College

153

RICHARD FIRTH GREEN, *Poets and Princepleasers: Literature and the English Court in the Late Middle Ages*. Toronto and Buffalo: University of Toronto Press, 1980. Pp. xii, 253. $20.00.

The study of literature has until comparatively recently been characterized by a lamentable disinclination to consider it in its social and historical context. There are some good reasons for the deficiency: the texts which are either most significant as historical documents or most characteristic of the society within which they were generated are, as a rule, not those with the most to offer to a critical intelligence primarily concerned with poetic excellence, and it is more immediately rewarding to select for study those texts which conform to our idea of what poetic excellence is rather than attempt to define or justify that idea by a comparison of such texts with the great mass of seemingly mediocre literature of the period. The dangers of an unhistorical approach to literature hardly need emphasizing: at best an undirected aestheticism devoid of intellectual rigor, at worst the exaltation of subjective impression to the status of a theory of interpretation whereby the author is denied effective control over his meaning and the reader is effectively invited to recompose each text afresh for himself. Creative misinterpretation of this kind, besides being enjoyable, is arguably a legitimate use of literature; even if it were not, it is in practice an inevitable element in the historical development of a literary tradition, and as such needs to be taken into account. But as an end in itself it hardly amounts to criticism; small wonder, then, that there should have developed a vogue for more or less mechanistic theories of criticism aspiring to the condition of science. The dangers of such approaches should be equally clear: that criticism tends to reduce itself to a series of decisions as to what to ignore (in the limiting case everything) in order to arrive at a predetermined answer. A compromise between rampant empiricism and rampant theory is perhaps in order.

As a starting-point for a sensible balance the Middle Ages have much to recommend them. One would hope to define as far as possible those conditions which determine the form and content of a work so as to isolate the element of autonomous response on the author's part in the understanding of which, together with a counterpoised sense of communal values, resides most of such social function as the reading of literature may be supposed to have. That this cannot be done in a mechanical way, since each text in its entirety is itself an historical document, is evident, and one could as legitimately follow the reverse procedure of attempting to abstract from as wide as possible a range of texts those elements which are evidently common to the literature of the period, and thus a suitable basis for historical generalization. But, whether it is the literary critic who is making use of the findings of the historian or the reverse, the Middle Ages are well suited to the enterprise, for the material, if dauntingly extensive, is not unmanageably so, and the cultural gap, through wide enough to necessitate a conscious adjustment of perspective is arguably not so unbridgeable as to threaten total incomprehension.

Among earlier attempts to set medieval literature in its social and political context one might cite V. J. Scattergood's *Politics and Poetry in the Fifteenth Century* (1971) and Charles Muscatine's *Poetry and Crisis in the Age of Chaucer* (1972). The first of these uses the whole range of political poetry in the widest sense to illustrate contemporary historical processes and attitudes; the latter attempts to identify the various responses to a particular set of historical circumstances of the three fourteenth-century authors who best conform to our conception of literary excellence. Dr. Green's readable and illuminating study of the English court and the literary culture associated with it is perhaps more historical in its emphasis than either in its attempt to provide a comprehensive view of aristocratic literary taste in England at the end of the Middle Ages. The impression the reader receives of such taste differs considerably from that generally canvassed in university English departments, based as it is on what is called 'courtly' literature. The difference is in part a result of the concentration of historical evidence in the fifteenth rather than the more immediately alluring fourteenth century, but it is also an important part of Dr. Green's thesis that polite romance and love-poetry represent only a subsidiary element in late medieval court culture and that didactic and historical matter were much more to contemporary taste and a much more likely object of such desultory patronage as was available. We have, in effect, been conditioned in our view of late medieval literature by our modern preconceptions of what is interesting or valuable in it: the error of subjective reading, so to speak, on a grand scale.

Three chapters are devoted to a definition and description of the court audience and three to the literature produced for it. The first is taken up with the development of the royal *familia*, the second with the *camera regis* which developed towards the end of the Middle Ages as an inner elite within the *familia* and afforded a center for the social and cultural life of the court. The third chapter, "A Lettered Court," is concerned with the education of the members of this elite, the rise of literacy among its members, especially in the fifteenth century, and the consequent development of an environment favorable to the cultivation of literature. The evaluation of these chapters must be left to the professional historian; there is, however, nothing in them which appears intrinsically improbable in the light of what we know of the literature. In the fourth chapter Dr. Green shows how the rapid decline of professional minstrels as a source of literary entertainment left the way clear for a new class of amateur poets associated with the court, whose compositions were bound up with the polite social rituals observed there, especially the 'game of love,' and conditioned as to tone and manner, in the case of the aristocratic amateur, by a sense of participation in those rituals, or else, as the case of Chaucer illustrates, by a deliberate manipulation of the tensions incident to a poet who was in but not of aristocratic society. The ability to compose verse was merely one social accomplishment among many, as the portrait of Chaucer's Squire, so gleefully parodied in the sketch of Absolon in *The Miller's Tale*, implies. It is suggested that no great prestige—though presumably more than the Miller would allow—was attached to such compositions. Chaucer, at least in his 'courtly' vein, remains a figure on his own, and has yet to be explained away in sociological terms.

In so far as literature was actively patronized at court at all, the preference, to judge from the evidence of book-lists, was for didactic works, and these form the subject of the fifth chapter. The main categories here are those of the history or chronicle and the mirror for princes; Boethius and the *de casibus* tradition form another important group, and, not altogether predictably, Vegetius *de re militari* yields a number of versions. Dr. Green suggests that the instructive value of all these was widely taken for granted, and it seems that many of them were commissioned. The poet's function in such cases was for the most part that of a compiler or translator, and the popularity of such literature may well have contributed to the prestige attached to translation rather than freer modes of composition, to the extent that Chaucer could be praised by Deschamps as "grant translateur." It is further suggested that Chaucer's reference to "Lollius" in the *Troilus* represents in fact a serious attempt to pass that poem off as a translation of an authoritative, if totally obscure, historical work, the name of Boccaccio being insufficiently familiar at the time to carry appropriate authority. Dr. Green's remarks on the figure of Chaucer within *The Canterbury Tales* deserve quotation:

> It is perhaps not over-fanciful to see in the two tales which Chaucer assigns to himself within the Canterbury framework an expression of two contrasting aspects of the court author's role: his position as court entertainer, successor to generations of professional minstrels, is belittled in the self-mockery of *Sir Thopas*, but as the adviser to kings the author of *Melibee* writes essentially without irony.

It is evidently time for us to put on a brave face and look at *Melibee* afresh.

The last important function of the poet, considered in the final chapter, is that of propagandist and apologist. Here, if anywhere, one would expect to find professional poets kept on the strength. Yet even here, Dr. Green suggests poets may at times have written out of personal conviction—Gower's support of Bolingbroke's usurpation is put forward as an instance— rather than to order, and such commissions as there were seem to have been for the most part desultory. Lydgate, for a time after 1425, appears to represent the nearest approach to an official propagandist, and his case, whether one considers circumstances or results, well illustrates the author's comment that "in general the lot of English court authors in the late middle ages was not a happy one." It becomes evident from Dr. Green's investigations that, though literature was produced at court in considerable bulk, and though the product was widely appreciated and the authors to some extent rewarded, patronage was unsystematic and the professional status of poets at best tenuous. In particular, any idea we may have had of the English court at any time as a nest of singing birds must be regarded as entirely exploded.

Dr. Green's thesis is compellingly argued, and, though lovers of medieval literature who have recreated the Middle Ages in their own image may find its conclusions at first sight dispiriting, it should, by encouraging a reconsideration of much neglected fifteenth-century literature, eventually refresh our understanding of the period. Not every detail, of course, is beyond contention. I doubt, for example, whether the amorous hyperbole of courtly poetry ever became part of a common

157

code of polite behavior, for, if it did, the comic exaggeration of the first book of the *Troilus* would be no more than Chaucer's private joke at the expense of his audience, whereas it seems to me that they are being encouraged to share the fun. More seriously, the frequency with which the nature of the evidence necessitates extrapolation from the French or Burgundian courts to the English raises the question of how far it is possible to define a literary culture associated with the English court as such in this period. Except in the reign of Edward IV the English court seems to have existed at a somewhat lower level of opulence, to say nothing of sophistication, than its Continental counterparts; the whole idea of a distinctive English court culture at the end of the Middle Ages may well prove to be chimerical. What Dr. Green has in fact given us is a study of the aristocratic culture of the time, to some extent curtailed in its scope by the accident of association with the king's retinue; but for that limitation it could have been extended to cover the great works of provincial fifteenth-century aristocratic literature, from the solid competence of the *Destruction of Troy* to the flawed splendors of the *Morte Arthure* and, above all, the *Wars of Alexander*. This would in turn have done much to diminish the modern critic's sense of alienation in the face of the literary tastes documented in the fifth chapter.

Nor am I convinced that Dr. Green has altogether refuted the arguments for an increasing middle-class element in fifteenth-century English literary culture. It will certainly not do merely to say that "if we accept Peter Laslett's definition of a class as 'a number of people banded together in the exercise of collective power, political and economic,' then we must recognize that the aristocrat, the country gentleman and the city merchant all belonged to one and the same class," since the factor conditioning taste is likely to be not so much the objective structure of power relationships as the subjective perception of social position. That city merchants, country gentlemen, and aristocrats were aware of an overriding community of interest remains to be demonstrated, and without such an awareness it is hard to see how these groups could be said to be banded together. As long as we use the word 'class' indiscriminately in its objective and subjective applications as though they referred to the same phenomenon, we shall, I fear, continue to get into this kind of confusion. For a sharp instance of class consciousness in the fourteenth century, even if an objectively muddled one, we need look no further than *Wynnere and Wastoure*. Dr. Green is reasonable in claiming that "it is inherently improbable that the city merchant would aspire to cultural models essentially different from those of his superiors"; yet a fair number of the medieval English romances seem to me to represent the aspiration rather than the achievement, while the cynicism of a text such as Thomas Chestre's *Sir Launfal* may well draw attention to the gap between the two.

Further, the fifteenth century, which we are accustomed to see, at least south of the Tweed, as a literary desert, embraces the copying of most of the surviving manuscripts of *Piers Plowman* and of *The Canterbury Tales*; the compilation of a number of manuscript miscellanies, of which the Cambridge manuscript numbered Ff 2.38 is most notable; the most important revisions of the York and Wakefield mystery cycles, and the compilation and at least partial composition of the *Ludus Coventriae*. By no stretch of the imagination could all the activity involved be fitted into Dr. Green's categories. As such material is excluded from his brief, he cannot be criticized for not discussing it; but it is claimed, whether by the author or the publisher is not clear, that the study "demonstrates the overwhelming cultural dominance of the aristocracy in this period," and this claim must be modified in the light of the other evidence.

NICHOLAS JACOBS
Jesus College, Oxford

N. R. HAVELY, ed. and trans., *Chaucer's Boccaccio: Sources of Troilus and the Knight's and Franklin's Tales*. Totowa, New Jersey: Rowman & Littlefield, 1980. Pp. 225. $31.50.

This volume offers a complete translation of Boccaccio's *Il Filostrato*, excerpts from *Il Teseida*, and excerpts from *Il Filocolo*. It deliberately does not include works which Chaucer 'might' have known, such as the *Decameron* and the *De Casibus*. There are three appendices. The first traces the story of Troilus and the other central characters from Homer up to Boccaccio; the second and third provide translated excerpts from Benoit de Sainte-Maure's *Roman de Troie* and Guido de Columnis' *Historia Destructionis Troiae*. The Introduction emphasizes the Neapolitan setting for Boccaccio's writings, particularly Angevin court life under King Robert of Sicily (1309–43), but also the influence of classical models, and of Dante. Chaucer may have learned Italian from native speakers or from English travellers (both were to be found in the London mercantile community and at court); his first touch with Italy itself came with diplomatic duties in Genoa, Florence, and Milan. Havely also notes the great interest in Boccaccio's early romances and Latin works at the French court. Chaucer might have benefited from that interest, and probably had a French version of *Il Filostrato* in hand when he wrote the *Troilus*. But Chaucer must have received *Il Teseida* directly from the Italian and used it in writing his earlier works. Whether or not his copy of the *Teseida* contained Boccaccio's *chiose* or glosses to the poem will continue to be disputed.

Why Chaucer never mentions Boccaccio's name is a question which has troubled many readers, particularly since he does mention Dante and Petrarch (but not Statius). Chaucer may have been unaware of authorship in certain cases, but since he did spend time in Florence, his silence invites further explanation. Havely's suggestion that Chaucer saw Dante and Petrarch reverentially as 'auctors,' but regarded Boccaccio as an equal does not quite resolve the matter, given the enormous literary indebtedness to Boccaccio in *The Knight's Tale* and the *Troilus*. Chaucer probably saw Gower as more of an equal, and of course he mentions him.

The translation of the *Filostrato* is accurate, clear, and serviceable. It will help readers to follow the original, and it will give students who have no Italian access to its contents. The prose of earlier translations had been strained to repackage poetic lines, but Havely's rendering flows naturally, still giving a sense of how complex Boccaccio's syntax can be. And this translation is free of the creaky archaisms of earlier ones.

About a quarter of the *Teseida* has been translated here, along with selected *chiose*. Most of what has been omitted from the *Teseida* is epic paraphernalia and introductory sonnets, so that our attention, like Chaucer's, can center on the romantic elements. The omissions are judiciously chosen, but several passages about Palemone and Arcita might well have been included, because they sharpen our awareness of what was done in the English version. I am thinking of *Teseida* V, 45–54, where Arcita tries to talk Palemone out of fighting; I also think that the scene in which Teseo comes upon Palemone and Arcita (V, 64–85) should have been translated, because Chaucer's handling of it is remarkably different.

This is a book which should be on reserve shelves for undergraduate and graduate Chaucer students. It is one experienced scholars will probably want to keep handy. More than any other Chaucerian "sources," the *Filostrato* and the *Teseida* provide the opportunity to watch Chaucer make and shape, and this, if it can be done as part of the comparative study of style rather than a mechanical survey of contents, is good exercise for any humanist. I don't think that we should bless ourselves and hope to ward off the intentional fallacy, when we have evidence of this sort before us. We can believe that Chaucer was working on *The Knight's Tale* and the *Troilus* within a few years of one another, and we can see their similar thematic content. Are some of the changes Chaucer made in each work analogous, coming perhaps from the same radical part of his poetic vision? The resemblances of characterization and homiletic ideas among Palamon and Arcite and Troilus are obvious, but perhaps more should be said about Pandarus, Theseus, and the theme of human creation. One is a king, the other is nearly a bawd, but each is obsessed with a design which fails.

My one reservation about this book has to do with the contents of the Introduction. Less might have been said about contemporary doings at court, which are marginally relevant to Boccaccio's writings. Havely might have said more about Boccaccio's art of narrative poetry, for that is what a clear prose translation usually has to let evaporate.

THOMAS A. VAN
University of Louisville

DONALD R. HOWARD, *Writers and Pilgrims: Medieval Pilgrimage Narratives and Their Posterity*. Berkeley and London: University of California Press, 1980. Pp. x, 133. $10.95.

Bananas figure prominently in narratives of the Jerusalem pilgrimage: "an elongated fruit, called the apple of paradise, having a wonderful taste, and soft, so that it melts easily in the mouth," so exclaims Wilhelm von Boldensele, a German Black Friar and wide-eyed tourist travelling to Palestine in 1332. Long apples of paradise, John Mandeville calls them repeating Wilhelm's nomination but adding a somewhat imaginative comment about cross-sections, both lengthwise and crosswise: "though ye cut them in never so many gobbets or parts overthwart or endlong, evermore ye shall find in the midst the figure of the holy cross of Our Lord Jesus." This curious detail, part fact, part cruciform fiction (lengthwise?), informs one of the central ideas in Donald Howard's new book.

The book aims to resuscitate interest in a genre immensely popular in the Middle Ages (over 500 surviving instances from 1100 to 1500) and only recently fallen into the shadow of obscurity. After an introduction, the second chapter offers a brief overview of the genre and a taxonomy: log, guidebook, and narration. It is with the last that Howard concerns himself primarily, and then only with the best: seven writers of the fourteenth and fifteenth centuries are dealt with in approximately one page each, with ten pages given finally to the pre-eminent Felix Fabri. The third chapter is devoted to Mandeville's *Travels*, which brings to fruition for the first time, says Howard, the literary tendencies potential in earlier examples of the genre, namely, that they were written to teach and to entertain; that they provided a vicarious experience; that they depended upon the author's keen observation and acute memory of his experience; that in the fifteenth century at least, authors begin to tell about themselves and their fellow pilgrims, and from a multiplicity of viewpoints; that finally, travel compels comparison of one's venue with one's own land, planting the seeds of irony and satire. All these tendencies burgeon in Mandeville, who unlike his predecessors constructs his travels out of others' books, merely pretending to have gone on the journeys himself. Some critics have seen this as regrettable or fraudulent. Howard sees it as medieval, the *Travels* as an encyclopedic *summa* of travel lore. Mandeville's pretense, or stance as Howard prefers to call it, of an eyewitness observer *de facto* brings into being a device that points forward to Chaucer: the device of the fictional narrator.

Although the book ends with a chapter which is briskly concerned with the posterity mentioned in the subtitle, and which proposes that pilgrimage narratives helped shape prose fiction, it is the penultimate Chapter Four that seems the raison d'être of the whole. The subject is Chaucer, and Howard contemplates the implications of considering *The Canterbury Tales* as a development of the genre of pilgrimage narration. Students of the *Tales* have benefited from several other recent studies of pilgrimage itself, particularly the historical studies of Jonathan Sumption and Donald Hall; Christian Zacher's book on the association of *curiositas* with pilgrimage, which, he shows, was thought of as a degenerating institution by the fourteenth century; and Victor and Edith Turner's anthropological study of *Image and Pilgrimage in Christian Culture*, whose relevance to Chaucer was recently suggested by John C. Hirsh (*MÆ*, 49 [1980], 158–60). But Donald Howard's book is what none of these others are: a genre study.

As one might expect, *The Canterbury Tales* at first glance appears to depart more strikingly than it conforms to exemplars of the genre. Pilgrim authors usually report, whereas Chaucer writes fiction; they write with straightforward objectivity, Chaucer with ironic self-awareness; their subjects are the sights and sounds of pilgrimage, Chaucer's the pilgrims and their tales; they write prose, Chaucer verse; and so forth. But Mandeville allows Howard to argue that *The Canterbury Tales* merely extends the literary tendencies of the pilgrim authors. Thus Mandeville's *Travels*, constructed out of older pilgrimage narratives, based therefore upon books and not upon observation, told by a fictional narrator who claims to report the truth, anticipates the more nimble-footed narrative stance and bookish fictions of the Canterbury pilgrimage. Howard's most perceptive and fruitful points, however, involve the relationship of travel to literature. Because travel is exploration of the strange, the new, or the alien, writings about it offer a form of vicarious experience, which can invite several kinds of participation and activity from the reader. The simplest pilgrimage narratives offer only the sharing of the experience itself. In more complex narratives, like Mandeville's, the reader is invited or forced to compare the alien with what he knows and is. In such a rounding upon oneself and one's own world lie the roots of irony and satire, Howard suggests. Chaucer exploits these potentialities even further by constructing a narrator whose judgment about what he sees as he travels is blatantly unreliable, and who thereby forces the reader to distance his own judgments from the daft observer by whom the pilgrimage is being reported. Thus, says Howard, "Chaucer had inherited from the tradition of travel and pilgrimage writings a form that had evolved naturally—one that invited vicarious participation and personal reaction from the reader, an open-ended form that allowed the reader to believe or doubt as he saw fit, to be fascinated or repelled, skeptically 'distanced' or imaginatively involved" (p. 100). There may be, says Howard, a random or chance quality about our reactions, they may be contradictory or inconsistent, but the variety is what Chaucer intends. What is important is that our reactions, varying according to our frames of mind, be part of the experience of reading.[1] And so, bananas: "What is interesting and amazing in such books [of pilgrimage and travel] must be in conflict with what is unimpeachably factual—the bananas pilgrims described are credible enough, but the crucifix they saw in a banana cut crosswise (and lengthwise too) is what makes good reading"; "medieval pilgrims in the Holy Land doubtless 'really saw' a crucifix at the center of a banana cut crosswise—and was that any more outlandish or less real than what *we* see in a banana?" (pp. 101, 10). Not the banana but the idea of the banana: "the truth of a poem . . . must be in our idea of it" (p. 102).

There are things to complain about in this book. Some will find its impact diminished by familiarity; the reading of Mandeville, a generous portion of what is said about Chaucer, the theory of the Three Medievalisms all have appeared in print before. There is also an odd disproportion between the book's ambition and its size. "This large, forgotten body of writings has something to reveal about the rise of fiction, of satire, of the novel; about the context of medieval literature not just in its own day but in later eras; and about the context of English literature up until about the time of Pound" (p. 5)—that is a long row to hoe in 127 pages, even for a critic of Howard's talent. The brevity is particularly painful in Chapter 2, which is the "aerial view of a forgotten genre" promised earlier. Though one is told that the best of the pilgrimage narratives (as opposed to logs or guidebooks) deserve to be treated as literature, only one (by Felix Fabri) is discussed for more than a page and a half. Except for the occasional aficionado of banana lore, I imagine few will rush out after this chapter to read through the thirteen volumes of pilgrimage narratives printed by the Palestine Pilgrims Text Society or long regret that the texts, the genre, and the Society itself passed into oblivion in the 1890's.

Howard's work deserves credit certainly as the first study of a neglected medieval genre, but its greater significance lies in his attempt to locate the genre of *The Canterbury Tales*. The genres of its tales have been much studied, its own genre largely ignored. In linking the *Tales* generically with pilgrimage narrative, Howard is furthering arguments put forth in *The Idea of the Canterbury Tales*, where he had proposed that

[1] See Howard's comments on *inventio* and tidings in "Chaucer's Idea of an Idea," *E&S*, 29 (1976), 39–55.

Chaucer would never have intended to show a return journey on the Canterbury pilgrimage, and that therefore the *Tales* is substantially finished. The literary idea of pilgrimage in the Middle Ages, as distinct from the real experience, did not involve a return journey; pilgrimage was conceived and written about as a one-way journey to a destination. No pilgrimage narrative written before the late fifteenth century recounts the return. Consequently Howard can claim here that Chaucer's idea of *The Canterbury Tales* is in one of its facets an idea of genre. One may cavil at the inclusiveness of Howard's generic category, which appears to define genre by subject matter; some may dispute the propriety of joining non-fictional pilgrimage narratives with fictional stories, of remembered sights and marvels in the Holy Land with remembered tales told on the road to Canterbury; those with even modest anxieties about influence may prefer more evidence that Chaucer had read any pilgrimage narratives besides Mandeville's. But even dissenters must agree that Howard's book does Chaucer studies a service by focusing attention on the genre of *The Canterbury Tales*, and by opening a debate that should provide us with new generic measures of Chaucer's achievement.

PENN R. SZITTYA
Georgetown University

ANTHONY JENKINS, ed., *The Isle of Ladies or The Isle of Pleasaunce*. Garland Medieval Texts, Number 2. New York and London: Garland Publishing, Inc., 1980. Pp. 193. $20.00.

This book contains a new edition of the text of *The Isle of Ladies* (about 70 pages), together with an introduction, notes, and glossary. It is most welcome to have a new edition of this poem: the only other 'modern' text was produced by Jane B. Scherzer in 1903, and is not available in some major libraries. Professor Jenkins has made a new transcription of the poem from the earliest manuscript (Longleat 256), and has provided variant readings from B.L. Addit. 10303 and Speght's *Chaucer* of 1598. If he had done no more than this he would have deserved our gratitude: the poem badly needs more discussion and Professor Jenkins has now given us the necessary starting point. I have not been able to check the

165

accuracy of his transcription, but a check on the variants from Speght revealed no mistakes.

The poem is a love-allegory, and a curious one. The sixteenth-century editors called it *Chaucer's Dream*, and Speght maintained that it described the courtship of John of Gaunt and Blanche of Lancaster. Critics for the last hundred years have spent their energies on trying to find another couple at a later date who would fit the circumstances described in the poem, or with trying to isolate other features which would provide us with clues to the date and provenance of the work. It survives only in late and somewhat corrupt copies, and any linguistic clues to its date are obscured by the process of transmission.

Professor Jenkins tackles all these problems in his edition. He takes his text from the oldest manuscript, emends it sparingly, provides substantive variants from the other witnesses, and adds a lengthy introduction and some notes. His main interest, however, is in the literary merits and context of the work: the bulk of the introduction and many of the notes discuss the poet's style and felicities of expression, and the poem's place in the development of late medieval allegory. But it is very hard to keep such questions separate from the problems of text and date, and some of Professor Jenkins's discussions reveal the difficulty. For instance, page 15 of the introduction is devoted to the poet's use of pronouns: Professor Jenkins argues that a "distinct clue" to the date of the poem lies in his handling of the second person pronouns. The poet of *The Isle of Ladies* preserves the distinction between the second person singular and plural very carefully—but then the same distinction is observed in *The Court of Sapience, Morte Darthur*, and *The Pastime of Pleasure*. He argues, in addition, that the poet carefully distinguishes between the nominative and accusative forms of these pronouns (ye/you and thou/thee)—a distinction that is not observed in the printed text of Hawes. This does not seem to be a very precise clue to the poem's date, even as it stands, but it is not in any case observed in the setting up of the text. Professor Jenkins does not give the variant forms of the pronouns from the other witnesses in the apparatus, and he does not emend or annotate those lines which do not agree with his statements in the introduction. For instance, the poet writes, "And of th' enditinge take the no hede / Ne of the termes, so God you sped" (lines 67–68)—where, if the editor's arguments on page 15 are correct, *the* must be a misreading for *ye*—a very common manuscript error. Similarly, *you* in line 42 ought to be *ye* (as it is in Speght, but this is not recorded in the apparatus), and also in lines 179, 1623, besides the lines listed on page 15. Professor Jenkins does not use this 'rule' as a basis of emendation, but he does go on to make a literary point about the effectiveness of the poet's shift to the singular pronoun. This occurs in only three cases: the knight's address to death, the God of Love's speech to the knight, and the poet's words to his own heart. But here Professor Jenkins omits to note that it was quite usual to address death in the singular (there are many examples in *MED*), and it would be very odd to address one's own heart in the polite plural, so that is is only the third example which can be used to show that the poet "furthers the drama" by this particular usage, and even there it could be argued that speaking to a lady requires the polite plural (in a very polite poem), rather than that the poet is making a skillful distinction between the God of Love and his liegeman on one hand, and the God of Love and the Lady who is not yet his servant on the other.

In fact, the handling of this point illustrates Professor Jenkins' method, merits, and defects throughout. It is certainly not a defect to be sparing in emendations, but if he is unwilling to alter his copytext, he ought at least to provide footnotes to passages which seem to require emendation. For example, *brother* (line 418) is nonsensical, but the note attempts only to rationalize it: " 'our fellow' or 'comrade.' The scribe of H felt uneasy with the seeming contradiction of *suster/brother* and changed these words to *as truest.*" This criticism of H does nothing to help a modern reader: if the editor was not prepared to suggest the emendation to *bother* (genitive of *both*, see *MED: bothe*), the note should have discussed the real difficulty of the passage, rather than glossing it away. Similarly in line 2170 the Longleat MS. reading, "For ther was ladye, no creature" seems to require the emendation to *nas* (Speght), but Professor Jenkins both lets Longleat stand and gives no note. And in line 2208 *his* should surely be *her*, since the poet has been addressing his lady for the previous 20 lines, there is no male referent anywhere in the vicinity, and both of the other witnesses read *her*. Professor Jenkins' note, "i.e. the God of Love's, and by implication, the Christian God's," seems a willful misreading in an attempt to make a literary point: it supports the attempt, made elsewhere in the edition, to match the religious language of love in the poem to Christianity.

The notes are a bit thin throughout. *MED* and *OED* are cited in the key to abbreviations, but they do not seem to have been used very thoroughly in the preparation of the notes. For instance, *fesaunce* (line 354) is not "a playful nonce-word for 'pheasants' " but a normal form, listed as such in *MED*. The long note on *sleeves* (line 1195), gives some information on medieval sleeves, and then, rather obscurely, suggests that this might help in dating the poem since sleeves in the later fifteenth century "often had a vertical slash generally laced across," and concludes by adding, "See *gowne, dublet and shirte*, line 1719." This seems wholly unhelpful: *OED* had quotations showing that things could be kept in sleeves at any period from 1400 until 1529, and it gives quotations about doublets from 1400. Why are we directed to see line 1719 at all? There is no note there that makes things plain. No notes are provided to "after castles" (parts of ships? line 709), or "closed letters" (line 2000), and the simile "beaten as blue as new dyed cloth" (line 1709–10) is not illuminated by a completely irrelevant and erroneous note.

Professor Jenkins' main interest is in the literary place of the poem; the bulk of his introduction is devoted to a discussion of its possible milieu and literary merits. The nature of the poem has suggested to more than one critic that it is a *roman à clef*, but it now seems impossible to find out to what occasion it refers. Professor Jenkins is sensibly agnostic about the whole question of the identities of the participants. But to attempt to chronicle the poem's excellences is a harder task, and the description of the poet as "unbookish in the extreme," with "little appreciation of the purely visual," together with his "unmetaphorical turn of mind," "concrete simplicity," "single-minded and unliterary style," "characteristic economy of detail," "lack of verbal fireworks," and "unsophistication," rather betray the argument, or at least reveal the slightly defensive tone in which it is cast. But Professor Jenkins is also anxious to place the poem in a key position in the development of fifteenth-century allegory, and this, I think, is a theme which really deserves an article to itself, rather than a dozen pages in the introduction. Professor Jenkins is forced to simplify and generalize too much. It is not possible to argue so simply that there is a straight development from Chaucer's use of the dream-allegory as a "resolution of problems" to the lyrics of the early sixteenth century. It is true that Skelton wrote an allegory with a dreamer called Drede, but this is to ignore more peaceful poems such as *The Pastime of Pleasure*, which may well be later than *The Isle of Ladies*, or the serene *Court of Sapience*, which may be earlier. The 'breakdown' of medieval allegory seems to be more complex, influenced as much by personal style as by inexorable trend. It is very useful indeed to have a new edition of *The Isle of Ladies*, but it is not really necessary to make inflated claims for its literary importance.

E. Ruth Harvey
University of Toronto

Terry Jones, *Chaucer's Knight: The Portrait of a Medieval Mercenary*. Baton Rouge: Louisiana State University Press, 1980. Pp. xiv, 319. $20.00.

This book by the very talented and admirably humane English satirist Terry Jones falls into two main parts, a detailed study of the Knight in Chaucer's General Prologue and a commentary on *The Knight's Tale*. It concludes with a brief chapter on *The Monk's Tale* and the Knight's interruption, and an appendix on the meaning of 'chivalrie,' 'trouthe,' 'honour,' 'freedom,' and 'curteisie.' The argument is that, "In the *Prologue* he [Chaucer] describes a typical mercenary of his day, whose career has been one of bloodshed and oppression. . . . In *The Knight's Tale*, he presents a chivalric romance, seen through the eyes of a mercenary captain, which consequently turns into a hymn of tyranny—just as the mercenaries themselves had become the mainstay of the modern tyrant. In *The Monk's Tale*, he (apparently both Chaucer and Monk) 'quits' the Knight's authoritarian and materialistic view of the world by illustrating the debasement of modern chivalry and by asserting the right of the people to bring down tyrants. At the same time the Monk asserts the Boethian view of the folly of seeking human happiness in worldly power and glory" (p. 222).

Dissatisfied with conventional academic commentaries on the Knight in the General Prologue, Jones tries to recover the nuances that the description would have communicated to his "first audience" (p. xi). He concentrates on late medieval military campaigns against non-Christian

169

peoples; 'crusading' against Christians; tournaments and 'lists'; ideas concerning the status, duties, and appropriate dress of a knight; and especially he works on late medieval discussions and depictions of the professional soldiers, the European, Christian mercenaries, forerunners of wealthy companies and militarists in our own 'free' world currently making grotesque profits out of trade in weapons of mass slaughter, and even now preparing to initiate a nuclear holocaust in Europe with the appalling new American 'counter-force' or 'first strike' strategy. Jones has collected materials on late medieval culture and society which should be of real interest to readers of Chaucer and his contemporaries. He establishes that it is wrong "to assume that all Chaucer's contemporaries shared the unbounded enthusiasm of modern commentators for knights who went off to kill Arabs, Turks, and Lithuanians in the name of Christ" (p. 35: to his evidence one should add the fine, late thirteenth-century tract by the friar William of Tripoli, *De statu saracenorum*). 'Crusading' had become a topic for debate, on which Chaucer's friend Gower had strong views, and there is no a priori or historical reason to assume Chaucer must have shared in a violent, militaristic crusading ideology which was such a horrible betrayal of the pacifism of the New Testament and the early Christian churches (consult Roland Bainton, *Christian attitudes toward war and peace*, London: Hodder & Stoughton, 1961). Jones also illustrates how the competing popes' readiness "to preach crusades against their fellow-Christians was one of the scandals of the age" (p. 39). Having done this, he uses modern historians and late medieval chroniclers and poets to establish both the realities of the campaigns in which Chaucer tells us the Knight performed and a range of late medieval assessments of them. Contrary to received academic wisdom, Jones shows that some of the campaigns Chaucer names were infamous and much criticized by contemporaries (e.g., pp. 42–49, 68–73); some were recorded by chroniclers as "lawless pillaging raids" of Christian mercenaries and brigands against Christians (pp. 55–59); while through some Chaucer unequivocally presents the Knight in the service of 'heathen' fighting 'heathen' (pp. 64–67, 86–88). Jones concludes that through the long list of carefully selected campaigns Chaucer discloses "the Knight's career has not been that of a responsible member of the knightly class, nor even of a dedicated militant Christian but of a self-serving itinerant mercenary," one whose "career is a catalogue of

bloodthirsty massacres" (pp. 100, 114). For Jones, Chaucer is a satirist
defending a fading "feudal" order allegedly based on loyalty and personal
"social relationships" against "the general erosion of social values"
represented by the "mercenary ethic" which is, allegedly, "the corruption of a social relationship" Chaucer unequivocally and uncritically
admires (pp. 11–13, 18, 24, 30, 163, et passim).

I say 'allegedly' because Jones has extraordinarily little evidence to
flesh out his highly generalized commonplaces about this present but
fading "feudal" age, and quite ignores Chaucer's own family background
and its rise to prosperity, more through energetic participation in the
world of urban markets and trade than by the Court; he constantly
underplays the fact that mercenaries (and thus the ethos they reflect) had
already become, in his own words, the "backbone" of fourteenth-century
militarism (pp. 13–14). Indeed, in the collection of advice offered to
Pope Gregory in 1274 (over a hundred years before *The Canterbury Tales*)
were recommendations that the Church should collect more money to
employ mercenaries to go on crusades in the Holy Land, a practice
already customary: the fourteenth-century crusade theorist, Marino
Sanudo, observed that modern war called for professional skills which
could only be found in professional soldiers, mercenaries who could be
hired, and, as Palmer A. Throop noted, "he advised the Church to offer
crusade indulgences for money only. This money would go to pay skilled
mercenaries" (*Criticism of the Crusade*, Amsterdam: Swets & Zeitlinger,
1940, pp. 101–03, and 170). Fourteenth-century war, as H. J. Hewitt's
excellent study of *The Organisation of War under Edward III* makes plain,
fully manifested what Jones calls the "mercenary ethic"; his work would
have benefited by looking closely at the actual career of Chaucer's friend
Clanvowe, and considering the apparent contradictions between the
writing and the life of this 'lollard knight.' In my opinion, Jones should
not have simply *assumed* that Chaucer's own position is unequivocally
hostile to those forces in his world which were responsible for the
"general erosion" of what Jones all too vaguely calls "feudal relationships" (pp. 12–13). One could argue that Chaucer's life and great
literary achievements actually depend on such forces. Perhaps Jones's
reluctance even to acknowledge the importance of such social and
ideological forces to Chaucer's own perspectives accounts for the very
confused and superficial treatment of the poet's relation to lollardy:
Jones treats the Parson and his so-called 'tale' as manifesting a lollardy as

disruptive of the old social order which Chaucer allegedly cherishes as the "shabby," badly dressed mercenary; yet he also uses Chaucer's friendship with the 'lollard knights' as justification for assuming that Chaucer would have shared the critical attitudes to traditional and aristocratic funerals of the 'old' order which their wills display, and so would have automatically condemned the traditional "conspicuous waste" at the pagan magnate's funeral in *The Knight's Tale* (pp. 25–27, 135, 159–61, 281).

Nevertheless the first part of the book at least sets orthodox medievalists problems which they must take seriously. They must now abandon their repetitive, pious chorus about the Knight as "champion of the Church, the righteous . . . the compassionate protector of the weak" who only (!) fought "against the heathens" (quotation from orthodox authorities on p. 1), campaigns representing "a grand review of Christian heroism" (R. E. Kaske, *ELH*, 24 [1957], 256, not quoted by Jones). And now they must undertake genuine research on the issues Jones has rightly raised. I for one will draw the information in the first part of the book to the attention of those whom I teach in courses on medieval literature and culture.

I will not, however, be doing the same for the second part, the 75-page essay on *The Knight's Tale*. Jones introduces this part by stating the one idea according to which he believes the total structure and all particulars of the poem are organized: "the *Tale* is a dramatic reflection of the narrator," a narrator who has "no courtly background, no education" and who is a bloodthirsty murderer of civilians (pp. 114, 122, 125, 145). His whole reading thus rests on a major and quite unexamined, undefended, and indeed indefensible assumption: that tales in *The Canterbury Tales* are designed as 'reflection' of the fictional teller's state of consciousness and daily practices. Such an a priori assumption necessarily deafens its proponents to the way Chaucer develops different 'voices' within tales formally attributed to one pilgrim and is, fortunately for us, not interested in 'reflecting,' consistently, the intellectual, psychological, moral, and cultural limitations of the pilgrim-tellers as they appear in the General Prologue. It is curious that Jones offers no comment on the story of "the love of Palamon and Arcite" (*LGW*, Prologue (F), 420) which preceded the conception of the Knight and *The Canterbury Tales*, nor on the available evidence for Chaucer's modes of composition in *The Canterbury Tales*. Such issues do not engage him, however, and when he comes to write about *The Monk's Tale* he fits it into his scheme simply by changing his assumptions, still without any discussion or defence. Now the fictional teller, so memorably described in the General Prologue is quite ignored, and the perspectives and style of the tale unquestioningly identified with the great self-reflexive poetic satirist, Chaucer himself (Chapter 5). Begging issues that are so *fundamental* to his interpretation is disastrous.

A second major assumption shapes the reading of *The Knight's Tale*, one I have already mentioned in relation to the first part of the book. Jones assumes (most of the time) that the poet Chaucer writes from a perspective identical to the one represented by the most uncritical admiration of courtly ideals and idealized courtly life embodied in the most conventional kind of 'chivalric romance.' All deviations from what one might expect to find in 'a chivalrous romance' (e.g., p. 186, but passim) are immediately attributed to the perversions of the teller, that sinister mercenary, allegedly uncourtly and uneducated but someone whose impoverished, vicious consciousness and life Chaucer wishes to 'reflect' at considerable length. With this assumption Jones inevitably fails to see that *The Knight's Tale* is, among other things, a profoundly critical exploration of many aspects of courtly culture, including its literary forms (Jones's 'chivalric romance,' for example), its erotic forms, its forms of aggression (individual and collective), the decisive political dimensions of its aesthetic and sexual practices, and its leaders' highly partial, self-interested uses of metaphysics and theology (something Chaucer would be familiar enough with at the courts of Gaunt and Richard II). I have attempted to substantiate and justify these comments in my own recent book, *Chaucer, Langland and the Creative Imagination* (Routledge & Kegan Paul, 1980), and however these may be received, Jones's own approach rests on a sentimentalized version of fourteenth-century courts and their cultural and social practices—it is characteristic that he should collapse a dialectical, collusive relationship between late medieval courts and what he calls 'mercenary' life into a simple one of antithesis and antagonism.

So when the poem departs from its Italian source to show the friendship of Palamon and Arcite turning into mortal war between two aggressive egotists consumed with sexual desire, frustration, and pride, Jones claims that because their lust is presented as a battle, and because "Venus is the sower of discord not harmony," we are being shown the warped mind of the uneducated teller-murderer contaminating all the beautiful things he touches (pp. 147–51). This is typical of the way Jones dissolves Chaucer's marvellous explorations of psychic and ethical realities underlying the order and reconciliations sought in courtly forms and ideals, his examination of the destructive machismo underlying the male-controlled conventions of courtly eros, his understanding that 'coercion' of women in (and outside) marriage was *not* the case only among mercenaries and in "the tavern and the dark alleys of the town," but a central reality of courtly and aristocratic life (cf. E. Power, *Medieval Women*, and Aers, *Chaucer, Langland*, Chapters 5–7). So it is not altogether surprising that the writer's comments on *The Parliament of Fowls* ignore the elements of satiric subversion directed at the courtly birds and their courtly idiom (pp. 147, 150, 169, 170—on p. 170 Jones or his mercenary printer conjures up a 'Goose in *The House of Fame*'). It is also not surprising that the approach encourages some desperate attempts to discredit the narrator in every detail—even the skillful and appropriate use of alliteration in describing the violence of the tournament is claimed to exemplify the unskilled hand of the uneducated murderer and we are to find a "mocking effect" in the passage (what we are to find in the astonishing range of voices, and in syntactic, imagistic, and rhythmical skills through the rest of the text Jones does not venture to suggest). This claim is supposedly supported by the famous comment of the Parson "I am a Southren man, / I kan nat geeste rum, ram, ruf by lettre." It is odd that the absurdity of this suggestion is missed by Jones, for the Parson contemptuously rejects *poetic fictions* altogether, and so is hardly the appropriate figure to appeal to as the unequivocal representative of the theories of literary decorum held by our greatest medieval poet and maker of fictions!

One final irony I must record. Jones gives welcome attention to *The Tale of Melibeus* as "a pacifist tract" worked up by Chaucer with full engagement (pp. 2, 144–45). Yet the effect of his approach to *The Knight's Tale* is to obscure its powerful critique of all militarism and glorification of war, a critique superbly embodied in the writing about the temple of Mars. For, once more, Jones reads the magnificent writing here as the depraved product of the uneducated mercenary murderer Jones finds in the Knight/teller. He asserts that the horror Chaucer conjures up is a *perverted* vision which distorts what the poet Chaucer wanted us to think of as the "splendour of the battlefield." Nothing could be more mistaken. Chaucer's poetry evokes the human reality of war, brilliantly fusing officially sanctioned, 'legitimate' violence with individualistic acts of 'illicit' barbarism and plunder, decisively unveiling the repulsive defences and glorification of war which still plague our culture—we deform other humans in our language and imagination before we slaughter them. Anyone wanting a sensitive literary and ethical commentary on Chaucer's writing here and at the death of Arcite, with discussion of its relation to the source, should turn to the commentary written nearly twenty years ago by that outstanding medievalist whose tragically early death all who have tried to learn from her and her work now mourn, Elizabeth Salter, *Chaucer: The Knight's Tale and The Clerk's Tale* (London: Arnold, 1962). In discussing Theseus' abuse of Boethius and his 'tyranny' Jones rightly uses both her work and R. Neuse's shrewd essay ("The Knight: The First Mover in Chaucer's Human Comedy," *UTQ*, 31 [1962], 299–315). But, again, even with these guides, his interpretive framework inevitably transforms Chaucer's profound critique into one directed at "military despotism in northern Italy" reflected in the allegedly incompetent, uneducated, and murderous narrator—a sad reduction and displacement of the imaginative and intellectual power of the poem.

DAVID AERS
University of East Anglia

TRAUGOTT LAWLER, *The One and the Many in the Canterbury Tales.* Hamden, Connecticut: Archon Books, 1980. Pp. 209. $17.50.

In ordinary English the phrase 'the one and the many' suggests strictly philosophical usage, especially the problem discussed by Plato in the *Sophist* (244B–245E), in a particularly difficult passage, if I remember my old undergraduate days aright. Boethius deals with an aspect of the problem of wholeness, unity, and parts in the *De Consolatione* (III, prose 10), and here Chaucer would have come upon a simpler application in Philosophia's demonstration that 'perfect goodness and perfect unity' are identical, together with the identity of God and "blisfulnesse," as Chaucer translates: " . . . alle thise thinges ben al o thyng."

175

The literary critic who lifts this phraseology from its philosophical context does so at his own peril, whether it be the simple application of Boethius or the more complicated problem posed by Plato's discussion of Parmenides' "one being." Professor Lawler states in his 'Introduction':

> The subject of this book is the subject which these brief passages illustrate: the complementary relationship in the *Canterbury Tales* between unity and diversity, oneness and multiplicity—between the one and the many. I shall argue that this relationship is the most pervasive issue in the poem, and its major unifying force (p. 15).

Now, there is something troubling in this assertion. Either it is self-evidently true, if the work of art achieves the perfection of form we associate with a skillfully constructed complex narrative, or it is 'true' but almost certainly destructive of the form and meaning of the work of art if a "relationship" ('the one and the many') is an "issue" in the poem, "the most pervasive issue." "Unifying force" is the result of successful formal construction, not the object of its being created. 'Unity' is abstractable from a complex narrative by the act of literary analysis; it should not be either the specific subject matter of formal creation or partake of the 'meaning' or the 'argument' of the work. An aesthetic tautology cannot be a poem, or at least I am not aware of having ever read one.

The "all pervasive issue" becomes an "issue" in *The Canterbury Tales* because the author of this study has seen fit to put it there. "I have tried to provide an organizing rubric for certain related phenomena in the *Canterbury Tales*, not a key to Chaucer's mind" (p. 15). Exactly. As "an organizing rubric," a peg, for Professor Lawler to hang his various interpretations of some tales upon, 'the one and the many' admirably serves its purpose. Sometimes the original philosophical phrase seems capable of trivialization. For example, on p. 48 we are told: "Another one-and-many aspect of the professional tales is the issue of privacy—('pryvetee')—versus exposure." The author has lost me here. I simply do not understand how this "issue" constitutes a "one-and-many aspect." He explains what he means, but I do not understand the explanation, just as I do not understand his linguistic legerdemain when he tries to make *The Knight's Tale* (I, 2533) illustrate his thesis:

In all these cases, the diversity is eventually resolved into, or contrasted with, some unity—though that unity is itself usually in some way precarious, threatened, or incomplete. The passage in the Knight's Tale is followed immediately by a particularly grand appearance of Theseus, alone, 'at a wyndow set / Arrayed right as he were a god in trone', who silences the crowd with the help of a herald who cries "Oo"—his very cry means "one" (p. 14).

But his very cry does not mean 'one.' The herald calls for silence by calling out 'ho!', meaning 'cease.' You can either put it in quotation marks (Robinson, Bennett) or treat it as an attributive noun (Skeat). It cannot represent the ME numeral 'oo,' 'oon,' with or without nasal bar.

> Chaucer's treatment of sex and marriage suggests that we are one where we would prefer to be many—all men are alike, all women are alike, all marriages are alike—and divided where we would prefer to be unified—in marriage. Marriage is a thrust toward unity that still leaves us mired in multiplicity. If the pilgrims, or the reader, or Chaucer, are to find a source of genuine unity, they must look elsewhere.

Does he mean that all marriages are unalike, like Tolstoy's unhappy marriages? I cannot see the force of the argument as applied to real marriages, imagined marriages, or to the treatment of marriage in Chaucer's poem. In Chapter IV ('Experience and Authority') he begins: "Authority is related to experience as one to many. Authority codifies the general experience of men, and treats it in a unified and unifying way, without allowing for individual exceptions." A long footnote to the first sentence quoted takes us over a miscellaneous collection of Chaucerians—Justman, Robertson, Howard, Muscatine, Elbow, Hoffman, and Payne. But nowhere do I find mention of Curtius, Auerbach, Paré, J. A. W. Bennett, and Arendt, scholars who have most fully illuminated the meanings of *auctoritas* in Classical Antiquity and the Middle Ages. Professor Lawler's definition of authority's relation to experience seems to this writer a private and special application. Authority 'perceives' experience 'as one'? I suppose an authoritative injunction might perform this purpose—of leaving us no other sensible choices, if the verb is jussive or imperative. Professor Lawler quotes 'Cato' in *The Miller's Tale* (I, 3228) in support of his argument, where the grammatical force is just that. But that is the force of the verb, a consequence of grammar, not a property of 'authority,' at least as I understand the concept.

The author writes well on the Parson's prose style (pp. 56–57) and he later shows his ability to provide an interesting interpretation of *The Parson's Tale* (pp. 159–72), though I do not agree with it. I do not think he has satisfactorily explained what he (and others) have mistakenly come to call 'Chaucer's Retraction.' He has read Dr. Sayce's article in *Medium Ævum*, but I cannot imagine that he has seen the implications of her argument. Finally, I must protest, the dust-jacket's 'blurb' (normally supplied by the author) should not contain a 'puff' of the book in advance of its publication, critical reception, and evaluation. I am shocked that such a lapse of taste should have been permitted by the publisher, the author, or the 'authority' cited.

JOHN NORTON-SMITH
The University, Dundee

ROBERT A. PETERS, *Chaucer's Language*. Western Washington University. Occasional Monographs I. Bellingham, Washington, *Journal of English Linguistics*, July 1980. Pp. xvi, 125. Paper $4.00.

The problem of teaching Chaucer's language to undergraduates who have small grammar and less history of the language is gradually being resolved. The recent Oxford Glossary, for example, by striking a balance between the shortcut glossaries of the major editions and the labyrinthine standard dictionaries of ME, manages to be both simple and complete. Now Robert Peters has provided a short 'out-of-class' text which describes Chaucer's language in a traditional grammar for the "average student of English literature." It tries to strike a balance between the technical ME grammars and the standard generalizations by which the major editors hope to bring the student to an approximation of Chaucer's sounds and forms. In some respects, then, this monograph is a kind of snapshot taken from Peters' own *Linguistic History of English* (1968), presenting only the portions which apply to Chaucer and eschewing any particular theory or "artificially created system." Unfortunately, students may find it too simple, in style at least; and teachers may think it incomplete. Nonetheless, this conservative description of Chaucer's language will provide a partial solution to the problem.

For many students the linguistic descriptions will surely be as dull as sand; for teachers, the manner of organizing the chapters, the confusing type-setting of the headings, and the lack of an index or even a detailed table of contents will make reference to the book quite difficult. You may find it helpful, as I finally did, to read the book inductively, that is, by gathering independent items from the brief, often single-sentence paragraphs, making your own cross-references, and drawing your own conclusions. Expect footnotes to appear in the text under the frequent heading NOTE. The book has the segmented style, but not the ready access, of a glossary. Thus, the Introduction (8 pp.) has the following segments: two plates preceding the heading (one an outline of the branches of Indo-European, and the other a map of the dialect areas of ME), then a question-and-answer dialogue with the student about the purpose of the book, a list of major differences between Chaucer's and MnE, a warning about manuscript and editorial variations, a paragraph on the Germanic origin of English, a list of its periods and dates, a list of the dialects of ME and therein an identification of Chaucer's London speech, and then four pages on the Norman influence. The order here is intelligible enough, but the transitions and ligatures normally found in textbook prose are often omitted.

Chapter 2, "Vocabulary" (4 pp.), provides paragraph-lists of sample loanwords from various languages. Students could easily be encouraged to make their own list from the etymologies in the Oxford Glossary, but Peters leaves it to the teacher to provide exercises and otherwise to activate the student's curiosity. A useful addition to this chapter might be a listing, perhaps according to frequency, of archaic or confusing words and of words bearing 'dangerous' senses (along the lines of Barney's *Word-Hoard* for students of Anglo-Saxon). In spite of the narrow scope of linguistic description which Peters has chosen, it still seems a shame that this chapter does not expand far enough into semantics even to mention standard tools for vocabulary study such as Tatlock, Ross, or Elliott.

The bulk of the enchiridion is devoted to phonology (49 pp. plus 9 of transcriptions) and expands the materials available in more readable form in Kökeritz' *Guide to Chaucer's Pronunciation* (13 pp. plus 13 of transcriptions). We want our students to hear Chaucer when they read. In a valuable essay "An approach to Teaching Chaucer's Language," in Joseph Gibaldi, *Approaches to Teaching Chaucer's* Canterbury Tales (New York: MLA, 1980), pp. 105–09, Thomas Ross has recommended that student transcriptions be combined with listening to expert recordings. Peters gives the student more detail for making transcriptions and for integrating them with the metrical environment than does Kökeritz; but unfortunately he stops short of adding the metrical features to his transcriptions. Part of the reason for the greater length of Peters' treatment is the generous spacing allowed for his lists, and part is his willingness to insert a lengthy section on Chaucer's spelling. For some peculiar reason this section has numbered sub-sections. It turns out to be a catchall for sundry material, mostly historical, including a brief handling of the vowel shift which is buried in the first of two sub-sections numbered 8. It would be an improvement, following the organization of Fisiak's *Short Grammar*, to begin with a chapter on graphemics.

The chapter on morphology (35 pp.) is a valuable conflation of the relevant chapters in Peters' history of the language and Fisiak's fine work. Organized according to word-classes, the chapter covers the rudiments of derivation and inflection, with a few paradigms of pronouns and verbs. The matter of strong and irregular verbs is skimmed, and word-formation is confined to suffixation. On the other hand, the sections on adverbs and function words are singularly helpful, clarifying the functions of some of the most frequently encountered words, for which students seldom think to consult a glossary. This chapter is also marred by extraneous paragraphs and ends with a page of afterthoughts on strong verbs and metathesis. In a book with such a sparse sense of reference and discourse, untimely repetition is bound to stick out; but like Chaucer in the *Astrolabe*, perhaps "it semith better to writen unto a child twyes a god sentence, than he forgete it onys."

The final chapter on syntax (25 pp.) covers the ordering of Chaucer's words into phrases, clauses, and sentences. It is a syntax of the surface: no rules, no system, only partial lists of patterns of words. The chapter goes beyond Baugh's excellent description of noteworthy usages in *Chaucer's Major Poetry*. However, here, as elsewhere throughout Peters' book, only the students who make comparisons to their own MnE will discern the 'irregular' or puzzling ME constructions. If the material of this chapter were combined with discussion of the constraints of prosody and the colors of rhetoric, following the design of Dillon's *Language Processing and the Reading of Literature*, the student could profit considerably.

The failure of this book, by design, to integrate phonology, morphology, and syntax with semantics, prosody, and discourse analysis is disappointing to one whose definition of language goes beyond the sentence. However, it is important to remember that whenever we present the language *or* the literature of Chaucer in isolation from the other, we run the risk of selling Chaucer short. Until we have a complete handbook for undergraduate readers of Chaucer we are safe to trust Peters' assumption in *Chaucer's Language* that the teacher and the poetry itself can supply the necessary vitality and integration.

WALTER S. PHELAN
Rollins College

D. W. ROBERTSON, JR., *Essays in Medieval Culture*. Princeton. Princeton University Press, 1980. Pp. xx, 404. Paper $12.95. Cloth $35.00.

D. W. Robertson, Jr. occupies so conspicuous a place among medieval scholars, and his widely ranging publications have become so influential, that this handsome, admirably edited and indexed selection from his papers published between 1941 and 1977 will be welcomed by all to whom medieval literature is of consequence. *Essays in Medieval Culture* is a collection of capital importance. Most of the familiar articles are here, and it is useful to have in one book such permanently valuable papers as "Historical Criticism" (1950), "The Doctrine of Charity in Medieval Literary Gardens" (1951), "Some Medieval Literary Terminology, with Special Reference to Chrétien de Troyes," (1951), and "The Historical Setting of Chaucer's *Book of the Duchess*" (1965). One will perhaps regret the absence of Robertson's ground-breaking study of *Troilus and Criseyde*, "Chaucerian Tragedy,"[1] and his equally innovative

---

[1] *ELH*, 19 (1952), 1–37.

"The Subject of the *De Amore* of Andreas Capellanus";[2] but inasmuch as the substance of both these papers may be found largely intact in *A Preface to Chaucer* (Princeton, 1962), we may forgive their omission here in order, presumably, to leave room for less accessible work. Together, the twenty-four essays in this volume touch on the principal subjects which have occupied Robertson over the years: medieval literary theory and practice, and their relation to religious culture; literary iconography; the poetry and drama of medieval England and France; attitudes towards love in later medieval texts. There are, besides, papers on method in literary studies, Mannyng, medieval preaching, and Latin lyrics by Jean de Savoie and from the *Carmina Burana*, along with glances at Leonardo, Shakespeare, Sidney, and Pope. Each essay is preceded by a note in which the author comments on his work, sometimes amplifying or modifying it in details and citing recent scholarship. In a partially autobiographical Introduction, Mr. Robertson gives us an interesting account of the genesis of some of his ideas and methods: an appropriate, if all too brief, summing-up, for the publication of these *Essays* in 1980 coincided with his retirement from the Murray professorship at Princeton. In the same discreetly celebratory spirit, the volume ends with a list of his publications, which includes several papers then "in press": a fact which allows us to hope that this distinguished bibliography will receive yet further augmentation in the years ahead.

Ever since the appearance three decades ago of "Historical Criticism" and (with Bernard Huppé) of *Piers Plowman and Scriptural Tradition* (Princeton, 1951), Robertson has been widely regarded as the leading proponent of patristic, or allegorical, criticism; and as he proceeded to develop and apply his critical procedures in the succession of papers and books which followed—especially *A Preface to Chaucer*—his work has gradually become a powerful force in medieval studies, and generated much fruitful discussion. Even his unsympathetic critics have generally acknowledged the force of his ideas and the value of his writings.[3] His

---

[2] *MP*, 50 (1953), 145–61.

[3] An exception, however, and a striking example of the emotional responses which Robertson's work has sometimes called forth, is F. L. Utley's embarrassingly choleric "Robertsonianism Redivivus," *Romance Philology*, 19 (1965), 250–60. Cf. A Leigh DeNeef, "Robertson and the Critics," *ChauR*, 2 (1968), 205–34.

work continues to be a significant influence, as any survey of recent scholarship will reveal, and most practicing Chaucerians (among others) have been touched by it, some profoundly. In 1973, William Provost noted: "Robertson has had enormous influence on the study and criticism of Chaucer and on the question of love in Chaucer."[4] Only last year there appeared a collection of essays on symbolism in Chaucer's works which declares that it was "inspired by the work of D. W. Robertson, Jr., whose *Preface to Chaucer* has exerted tremendous influence in medieval studies and given rise to the current work in literary iconography."[5] Elsewhere in the same volume, the editors assess Robertson's role in Chaucer studies thus: "D. W. Robertson, Jr. has, in recent years, been at the center of the most fruitful critical work on Chaucer. Many scholars, whether favorably or unfavorably impressed by the so-called allegorical criticism, have found themselves confronting new aspects of Chaucer's poetry and modifying long-held critical positions after the intellectually invigorating experience of first looking into Robertson's Chaucer."[6]

Robertson's scholarly *oeuvre*, though copious and diverse, has been strikingly consistent in its development, as the reader will be reminded if he turns to *Essays in Medieval Culture* for a sampling of work published in the two decades since the *Preface* suddenly had Chaucerians chattering (sometimes grumpily) of charity and cupidity, allegory and iconography, St. Augustine and Boethius, the Vatican Mythographers and Alexander Neckam and (of course) the *Glossa Ordinaria*. For instance, "Some Observations on Method in Literary Studies" (1969) and "The Allegorist and the Aesthetician" (one of two hitherto unpublished lectures in the volume) amplify and extend certain ideas previously developed in "Historical Criticism," and may usefully be read in conjunction with a re-reading of the earlier paper. Robertson, as we would expect, remains wedded to the informed and sympathetic reconstruction of the past, through extensive use of primary materials, as the best way to

---

[4] Jerome Mitchell and William Provost, eds., *Chaucer the Love Poet* (Athens: U of Georgia P, 1973), p. 6.

[5] John P. Hermann and John J. Burke, Jr., eds., *Signs and Symbols in Chaucer's Poetry* (University, Alabama: U of Alabama P, 1981), rear cover.

[6] *Signs and Symbols in Chaucer's Poetry*, p. 1. See also Roy R. Barkley, *A Study of the Historical Method of D. W. Robertson, Jr.* (University of Texas thesis, 1974).

appreciate older literature; and he is no less insistent now than a generation ago that use of post-medieval systems of analysis is likely to distort such efforts of reconstruction, and should be sedulously avoided by the medievalist. His more recent approach to this latter issue, however, is less categorical and more disposed to qualification:

> In general, new categories should not be imposed on the past. Freudian psychology, for example, represents a series of generalizations based on the effects of a kind of social structure that developed during the course of the later nineteenth century. The relevant social conditions together with certain concomitant attitudes toward sex did not exist in the eighteenth century, and are now rapidly disappearing. Hence efforts to analyze earlier cultural phenomena in Freudian terms inevitably lead to false conclusions. This is not to say that Freudian psychology is or was "wrong," but simply that its truths have a date and locale attached to them. To put this in another way, Freudian psychology is part of a "universe of discourse" with a nexus of relationships to other elements in that "universe." To insert it into an earlier universe of discourse where no such nexus exists is to create absurdities. That is, Freudian "complexes" have about as much place in discussions of Shakespeare as have carburetors or semi-conductors. It cannot be emphasized too urgently that any age in the past can be understood only when we analyze it in so far as is possible in its own terms. If we can begin to understand those terms in their own context, we can begin to understand the age, but if we impose our own terms on it, we might as well be studying ourselves rather than the past (p. 80).

"Some Observations on Method in Literary Studies," from which this paragraph is taken, is Robertson's ripest discussion of the difficulty in understanding early literature, owing to the shifting shapes of language, "human nature," and culture generally. How is the student of medieval literature to cope with this complex problem? Robertson urges the approach of stylistic history, citing as models the work in art history of Heinrich Wölfflin and his successors.

The same issues are taken up with a more facetious pen in the entertaining dialogue-lecture, "The Allegorist and the Aesthetician." These papers show Robertson in his most speculative vein, exhibiting an impressive command of modern thought, including the literature of art history. More than ever, he sees the Middle Ages as painfully elusive, and our most cherished critical vocabularies—even words like "art" and "humanities"—as expressions of a quite different, later culture, and therefore of only limited use in describing medieval poems. Still, the vastly challenging task of trying to penetrate to the particularities of the medieval past, learning to speak a few syllables of its language and perceive a few glimpses of its landscape, is well worth the trouble, and in fact may be for us a kind of moral imperative:

> The specious and easy "relevance" achieved by positing "universal humanity" and then imposing our own prejudices on the past is not merely detrimental to understanding. It will soon become absurd in the light of a growing awareness of the complexity of historical processes. Finally, it is barely possible that the recognition of valid realities established by earlier generations may lead us at least one small step away from that rancid solipsistic pit into which the major tendencies of post-romantic thought have thrust us (p. 82).

Another, more exclusively literary product of "post-romantic thought" which continues to elicit Robertson's scorn—to him a deplorable example of a post-medieval idea misapplied—is, as everyone knows, courtly love (or "courtly love": the inverted commas speak pages). In "The Concept of Courtly Love as an Impediment to the Understanding of Medieval Texts" (1968), Robertson takes up the matter once more, with *The Book of the Duchess* and *Troilus* as his chief texts. In a detailed and witty analysis, he recapitulates and augments his earlier assertions that Chaucer conceived such figures as the Black Knight and Troilus with irony rather than as embodiments of acceptable chivalric or courtly behavior. What is new in this paper, however, is an enlarged concern with social and political data. The following account of a tiny episode in *Troilus* will serve as an example, one of many:

> Medieval men had a strong sense of social hierarchy. Disturbances in society were thought of as violations of that hierarchy, and failures to maintain the integrity demanded by one's estate or degree were thought to be productive of social chaos. Chaucer plays amusingly on this theme in Book 3. At the opening, in the house of Deiphebus, Criseyde approaches Troilus as he lies in bed feigning sickness with a request for "lordship" and protection. But what she receives is a promise from Troilus that he will be under her "yerde." The phrase *sub virga*, which this

promise reflects, was conventionally used to describe the condition of children, or, occasionally, wives. Although this inversion is amusing on the surface, the implications for "New Troy" are hardly comic. We can see an analogy to this situation in the punishment for "common brawlers" decreed in the City of London by John of Northampton. A convicted "brawler" was to be led through the City with minstrelsy, holding a distaff with tow on it in his hand and placed in the "thews" or stocks designed especially for women, the implication being that his unruliness deprived him of the worth proper to the masculine estate. The predicament of the "brawler" as he holds his distaff is amusing, but the implications of his presence are nevertheless serious. To call Troilus' desire to be under Criseyde's "yard" a manifestation of "courtly love" is a little like saying, quite seriously, that the distaff in the hand of the brawler is a sign of the irrepressible medieval reverence for women (p. 270).[7]

In most of his best work since the *Preface*, Robertson has in fact turned from the patristic and iconographical analyses which had occupied much of his attention till that time, and in which he made such signal contributions, to the materials of the social historian, the forms and details not only of religious but also of 'secular' life, social and economic and political. The object, however, has obviously remained the same: to recreate the *milieux* of medieval literature, for the sake of understanding and appreciating that literature. The four Chaucerian papers among the *Essays*, all written since 1965, exemplify this shift of focus. In "The Historical Setting of Chaucer's *Book of the Duchess*," as in the piece on "courtly love" discussed previously, Robertson draws mainly on historiographical materials in order to relate poem to occasion, modern reader to fourteenth-century listener, and so to give an historical complement to the iconographical analysis of the work which he had presented in previous publications.[8] The poem is a formal commemorative piece, a public gesture; neither John of Gaunt nor Chaucer himself, nor even the Duchess Blanche, is directly represented in it. The 'characters' are not mimetic representations of real persons at all, but rather personifications of certain attitudes, feelings, or attributes which were relevant to the

---

[7] See also D. W. Robertson, Jr., *Chaucer's London* (New York, 1968), p. 103.

[8] *A Preface to Chaucer* (Princeton: Princeton UP, 1962), pp. 463–66; *Fruyt and Chaf* (Princeton: Princeton UP, 1963), Chap. II.

public mourning for the real Duchess Blanche. This is, one notices, an application of the theory which Robertson had advanced previously with respect to medieval literary characterization;[9] and even those who would nevertheless prefer to put the matter differently are likely to be shaken out of any lingering critical complacency by the wealth of cogent documentation which Robertson brings to bear. So, too, in "Chaucer's Franklin and his Tale" (1974), and, even more, in "Some Disputed Chaucerian Terminology" (1977), the activities of the Franklin, Sergeant of the Law, Reeve, and Yeoman are significantly clarified by Robertson's fresh investigations of their social contexts.

One of the noteworthy features of this collection, quite clearly, is its diversity, which justifies the book's title at the same time that it reminds us of the unusual scope of Mr. Robertson's achievement as a scholar and critic. Very few American medievalists have made sustained contributions of prime importance in both Middle English and Old French studies; yet today one is hardly likely to approach, say, Chaucer, the *Roman de la Rose*, Andreas Capellanus, Chrétien de Troyes, or Langland without wishing to take serious account of his work. In the first two of these areas (at least) his findings and methods of allegorical analysis have been extended by students and other younger scholars into fruitful and even dominant schools of criticism, while not a few older scholars, including some of those scarcely hospitable to his approach, continue to reflect his influence in their own work. Similarly, his mastery of Latin literature, classical and medieval, and especially of the patristic materials of the medieval church, has long enabled him to escape the tyranny of the vernacular, a malady from which few of us, alas, are so fully exempt. Many papers in the present collection are distinguished by his latinity, and two or three—notably "Two Poems from the *Carmina Burana*" (1976)—are substantial expressions of it. St. Augustine's *De Doctrina Christiana* (New York, 1958) made accessible to literary students a crucial text of the patristic tradition which he has so often invoked, and which has been a cornerstone of his critical procedure.

Moreover, as we have already noted, the emphasis of Robertson's work has in recent years turned to the detailed study of the social and cultural *milieux* of Chaucer and other medieval authors, and thus to historiog-

[9] *A Preface to Chaucer*, pp. 248–57, et passim.

raphical materials. Besides several important papers, two volumes have
come thus far from this phase of his scholarship: *Chaucer's London* (New
York, 1968) and *Abelard and Heloise* (New York, 1972).[10] Here, too, as
in his concern with iconography and *Kunstgeschichte*, Robertson reveals
his indifference to narrow departmental boundaries, and the remarkable
breadth of his scholarly competence.

Mr. Robertson is, in fact, as these *Essays in Medieval Culture* amply
attest, a cross-disciplinary medievalist who, starting from a firm foundation in the classics and in general culture, ranges in his work over much
of medieval literature, art, and history. Nor, indeed, does he confine
himself strictly to the Middle Ages: readers of *A Preface to Chaucer* will
recall that he is nearly as likely to refer them to a text of Goethe, Blake,
or Shakespeare as to a passage in Petrarch or John of Salisbury. One of the
most provocative papers in the present collection is a previously unpublished lecture entitled "A Medievalist Looks at *Hamlet*," which, with
Robertson's familiar mixture of detailed historicism and relentless icon-
oclasm, supports the theory that Hamlet's melancholy is really *accidia*. A
prefatory note to this paper embraces several of his most characteristic
positions, and may be quoted here in part:

> The attitude adopted here was first formed many years ago and is in part a
> reaction against popular views of *Hamlet* that seek to make the protagon-
> ist admirable, in spite of the fact that he is an obvious moral weakling and
> an unrepentant felon, or to make him sympathetically "understandable"
> as an innocent adolescent in search of "identity." Shakespeare would have
> been completely unable to understand the latter view, since it reflects a
> peculiarly modern problem; the former would have been grossly repug-
> nant to his sensibilities and inconsistent with attitudes toward tragedy
> current in his time. It is unfortunate that the morality of Shakespeare's
> tragedies has often been misunderstood since the shortsighted and histor-
> ically inaccurate observations of Dr. Johnson, and today we suffer also
> from a reaction against nineteenth-century literalism and hypocrisy that
> makes it difficult for us to understand, much less to sympathize with, the
> moral principles embraced, often with surprising enthusiasm, by our
> medieval and Renaissance ancestors in Western Europe. These were

[10] See also two papers published after the *Essays*: " 'And For My Land Thus Hastow
Mordred Me?': Land Tenure, the Cloth Industry, and the Wife of Bath," *ChauR*, 14
(1980), 403–20; and "Simple Signs from Everyday Life in Chaucer," in *Signs and Symbols
in Chaucer's Poetry*, pp. 12–26.

188

frequently classical in origin, although transformed by attitudes that were then thought to be distinctively Christian. Above all, we should be aware of the fact that such principles were then practical, not merely theoretical, and necessary to the preservation of a reasonably liveable social environment, however they may differ from views about human nature and society fashionable today (p. 312).

But the qualities of Robertson's work which most decisively remind us of such European-trained humanist scholars as Curtius, Panofsky, and Auerbach are an abiding concern with the theoretical bases of literary interpretation, a certain elusive ideal of civilization, and a fundamental philosophical and moral seriousness which sets his best pages apart from the pedantic reflexiveness of most academic writing, even of a high order of competence. Like Marianne Moore, Robertson seems often to be reminding us that "there are things that are important beyond all this fiddle." Such seriousness, which a few have mistaken for solemnity—a distinction which Robertson has been at some pains to clarify with respect to the Middle Ages themselves—is discernible throughout his work, in large ways and small. He will thus say, in passing, of a book which he admires very greatly: "The fortunes of *The Consolation of Philosophy* in the modern world roughly parallel the fortunes of a rigorous belief in Divine Providence" (p. 332). Or of Chaucer: "In our own society, although a few poets like Mr. Eliot continue to emphasize the value of love in Christian terms, the urgent need for a love that is neither lust nor avarice has now become the affair of psychologists and sociologists. So far as Chaucer is concerned, we may as well recognize the fact that he was a Christian poet."[11] With his manifest conviction that great poetry addresses the mind and nourishes the life of the spirit, and with his ill-concealed contempt for shoddiness, levelling, novelty, pretension, egotism, self-indulgence, the merely sensational, and all forms of "sentimentality" (his *bête noire*), Robertson would appear to be the least fashionable of scholars. That he has become, and remains, as these *Essays in Medieval Culture* impressively remind us, one of the most influential, will seem to some a reason for reflection and satisfaction.

MAXWELL LURIA
Temple University

[11] *A Preface to Chaucer*, p. 503.

THEODOR WOLPERS, *Bürgerliches bei Chaucer*. Abdruck aus: *Über Bürger, Stadt und städtische Literatur im Spätmittelalter*, Abhandlungen der Akad. d. Wiss., Phil.-Hist. Kl., 3. Folge, Nr. 121, Göttingen: Vandenhoeck & Ruprecht, 1980. Pp. 73. DM 12.

It has often been remarked that Chaucer is a philosophical and psychological realist with a deep knowledge of the contingencies of human life and the weaknesses of human nature. Proceeding from this judgment, interpretations of the poet's attitude to the world and to mankind have been subsumed under 'umbrella' concepts which express the totality and comprehensiveness of Chaucer's view and portrayal of life. It is, therefore, all the more surprising that, for about the last thirty years, Chaucer has been almost exclusively associated with the courtly tradition and with courtly taste; surprising, too, that even the mere notion of 'bourgeois' characteristics having colored the courtly elements in his poetry has been dismissed as misleading.

Wolpers' thesis offers a contradiction to the premises and tenor of previous research. He analyses suprapersonal formalizations in Chaucer's work which can be traced back to the imaginative cast of mind and habits of thought of the late-medieval burgher. In doing so, concepts such as 'bourgeois' and 'realistic' are not employed ahistorically, or typologically, but are derived from the concrete working-world of the London citizen in the late fourteenth century. Wolpers does not regard the category of 'bourgeois' simply as the antithesis of 'courtly,' or as an aspect of contemporary style; rather, his investigations lead him to an examination of the special ethos and ethics of class distinction and the consequent forms of 'bourgeois' conduct. He proceeds from the assumption that Chaucer, as a servant of the king, and a citizen of London, was conversant with the modes of behavior which were typical of the culture and social structure of his time, and which he employed in his literary portrayals. The result of this approach is a new and more discriminating evaluation of late-medieval English realism, and also a definition of the specific character of this literature, which is marked by a more open and interpenetrated concept of society—in contrast to the more rigid and stratified class system on the Continent. Wolpers implies that the distinguishing mark of Chaucer's attitude is an appreciation of the English 'burgher' and his autonomy. He regards Chaucer's fabliaux no longer as counterparts or negative distortions of courtly literature, but as specifically structured narratives, which, not least through their own set of values, are quite independent and self-contained, with the result that the logical and realistic development of the plot contributes indirectly to the characterization.

Wolpers illustrates his thesis with an analysis of six texts taken from the General Prologue of *The Canterbury Tales*, the *Tales* themselves, and *Troilus and Criseyde*. In addition to Chaucer's obvious esteem of everything courtly, Wolpers notes above all the feeling of pride in the importance, worth, and abilities of the 'burgher.' Far from being portrayed as a homogeneous social group, or even a class, the 'bourgeois' are seen as being hierarchically structured. Wolpers conjectures that there was in London (as, similarly, in Italian cities) a gradation which ranged from the urban aristocracy of the patrician families down to the 'unincorporated' laborers. Corresponding to this hierarchy is the increasingly marked differentiation of the basic activities in particular trades and professions, with their implications of a correspondingly graded social prestige. Chaucer's pilgrims are not only chosen according to the criteria of exemplary representation; they are, in addition, masters of their particular fields, and prove themselves such by means of complicated plot structures.

In this new organizational principal of logically structured, clear-cut, and comprehensibly interwoven action, Wolpers sees what is really innovative in Chaucer's conception of plot. Chaucer is one of the first to discover the aesthetics of the work-process, but he is less concerned with the final product of craftmanship than with the dynamics of involvement and execution. He is above all interested in an adequate and realistic portrayal of typical ways of life; and mercantile attitudes and methods color his work in the process—credit and debit, and the careful balancing of accounts. The analogy between Chaucer's methods of arrangement and 'bourgeois' work-procedures is particularly interesting and well-documented; it is made quite clear that these function as a basic principle of Chaucer's technique of disposition and arrangement.

The dangers of what are fundamentally very sound and useful methods of criticism become apparent in the chapter on Chaucer's *Troilus and Criseyde*. In Pandarus' hard-headed plans, calculations, and machinations, Wolpers sees "bourgeois ways of thinking." Even if Pandarus' plotting reminds us of the Merchant, old Januarius, or the master-builder in Geoffrey de Vinsauf's *Poetria Nova*, we would hesitate to term it 'bourgeois.' The reason for this probably lies in the fact that 'bourgeois' (in contrast to English 'middle class,' etc.), at least in German, conjures up associations of particular social structures and oppositions which really cannot be transferred to Troy. The forms of thinking and planning peculiar to Pandarus can only be categorically defined in relation to Troilus. Perhaps it may even be further objected that what Wolpers terms 'bourgeois' is, all things considered, the beginning strain of a new empirically oriented epistemological approach to the facts of this world.

Such reservations, however, do not detract from the heuristic value of this novel interpretation. Wolpers expressly emphasizes that his results do not negate, or even qualify, the findings of other research on such aspects of Chaucer's writing as originality, humor, tolerance, and 'popular-naive' realism. In the light of the present plurality of interpretational approaches to Chaucer, it must be acknowledged that Wolpers succeeds in demonstrating that what he would term 'bourgeois' attitudes have contributed far more crucially and discriminatingly to Chaucer's view of the world and conception of poetry than previously recognized.

KARL HEINZ GÖLLER
Universität Regensburg

An Annotated Chaucer Bibliography
1980

Compiled by John H. Fisher
University of Tennessee

With the assistance of:

Robert apRoberts, *California State University, Northridge*; Thomas W. Ross, *Colorado College*; Edmund Reiss, David G. Allen, *Duke University*; Daniel J. Ransom, *Indiana State University*; Shinsuke Ando, *Keio University, Japan*; Beverly Taylor, *University of North Carolina, Chapel Hill*; David W. Hiscoe, *University of North Carolina, Greensboro*; Nan Arbuckle, J. Lane Goodall, Lynne Hunt Levy, *University of Oklahoma*; Stanley Hauer, *University of Southern Mississippi*; Laurita Alexis, Marsha Barrett, Kristen Benson, Charles Reese, *University of Tennessee, Knoxville*; James Wimsatt, Rebecca Beale, *University of Texas, Austin*; Lorrayne Y. Baird, Rosemarie Barbour, *Youngstown State University.*

This bibliography continues those published since 1975 in previous volumes of *Studies in the Age of Chaucer*. Bibliographical information up to 1975 may be found in Eleanor P. Hammond, *Chaucer: A Bibliographical Manual* (1908; rpt. New York: Peter Smith, 1933); D. D. Griffith, *Bibliography of Chaucer 1908–1953*, Seattle: U of Washington P, 1955; W. R. Crawford, *Bibliography of Chaucer 1954–63*, Seattle: U of Washington P, 1967; Lorrayne Y. Baird, *Bibliography of Chaucer 1964–73*, Boston: G. K. Hall, 1977; and J. H. Fisher, selected bibliography to 1974, full 1975–79 in *The Complete Poetry and Prose of Geoffrey Chaucer*, New York: Holt, Rinehart and Winston, 1982.

The annotations are based upon listings in the 1980 *MLA International Bibliography*, with additions. Additions and corrections should be sent to Lorrayne Y. Baird, Department of English, Youngstown State University, Youngstown, Ohio 44555. Authors' own annotations (75 words for articles; 150 words for books) are invited. Preferably they should be sent on 5 × 8 index cards, and comply with the form of *SAC*'s published entries. For a list of abbreviations for Chaucer's works, see p. 249. We will search the major journals for reviews published in any given year. However, authors are urged to send us citations to reviews which might otherwise be overlooked.

Classifications

Bibliographies and Reports   1–4
Manuscripts and Editions   5–7
Background and General Criticism   8–14
Chaucer's Influence   15–24
Lexicon and Onomastic   25–30
Audience   31–33
Rhetoric, Narrative Technique   34–37
Themes and Images   38–46
Teaching Chaucer   47–49
Canterbury Tales, General   50–58
CT—General Prologue   59
CT—The Knight and His Tale   60–64
CT—The Miller and His Tale   65–70
CT—The Reeve and His Tale   71–72
CT—The Man of Law and His Tale   73–75
CT—The Wife of Bath and Her Tale   76–81
CT—The Friar and His Tale   82–84
CT—The Summoner and His Tale   85–86
CT—The Clerk and His Tale   87–88
CT—The Merchant and His Tale   89–91
CT—The Squire and His Tale
CT—The Franklin and His Tale   92–94
CT—The Pardoner and His Tale   95–98
CT—The Shipman and His Tale
CT—The Prioress and Her Tale   99–101
CT—The Tale of Sir Thopas*
CT—The Monk and His Tale   102
CT—The Nun's Priest and His Tale   103–06
CT—The Second Nun and Her Tale   107–08
CT—The Canon's Yeoman and His Tale
CT—The Manciple and His Tale   109–11
CT—The Parson and His Tale 112–13
Troilus and Criseyde, General   114
TC—Prosody, Text   115–16

TC—Literary Relations   117–22
TC—Themes of Love, Fortune, Religion   123–28
TC—Narrative Technique   129–32
TC—Characterization   133–34
TC—Criseyde   135–38
TC—Troilus   139–41a
TC—Pandarus   142–44
Book of the Duchess   145–48
Parliament of Fowls   149–54
House of Fame   155–56
Legend of Good Women   157–60
ABC   161–62
Former Age   163–64
Truth   165
Romaunt of the Rose
Boece
Book Reviews   166–89

Journal Abbreviations

AN&Q	*American Notes and Queries*
ChauR	*Chaucer Review*
CJItS	*Canadian Journal of Italian Studies*
DAI	*Dissertation Abstracts International*
ELN	*English Language Notes*
ES	*English Studies*
Expl	*Explicator*
JEGP	*Journal of English and Germanic Philology*
JMRS	*Journal of Medieval and Renaissance Studies*
L&H	*Literature and History*
LitR	*Literary Review*
MHLS	*Mid-Hudson Language Studies*
MÆ	*Medium Ævum*
MLQ	*Modern Language Quarterly*
MP	*Modern Philology*
NM	*Neuphilologische Mitteilungen*
N&Q	*Notes and Queries*
OL	*Orbis Litterarum*
PQ	*Philological Quarterly*
PMLA	*Publications of the Modern Language Association*
RES	*Review of English Studies*
RMSt	*Reading Medieval Studies*
RUS	*Rice University Studies*
SN	*Studia Neophilologica*
SSF	*Studies in Short Fiction*
SAC	*Studies in the Age of Chaucer*
TLS	*London Times Literary Supplement*
USF Language Quarterly	*The University of South Florida Language Quarterly*
YWES	*Year's Work in English Studies*

Bibliographical Citations
and Annotations

Bibliographies and Reports

1. Bazire, Joyce, and David Mills. "Middle English: Chaucer." *YWES* 58(1977):107–23.

2. Fisher, John H., et al. "An Annotated Chaucer Bibliography, 1977–1978." *SAC* 2(1980):221 85.

3. Ikegami, Tadahiro. " 'Parliament' of Chaucerians." *Eigo Seinen* 125(1979):214–17.

Report on the First International Congress of the New Chaucer Society. (In Japanese.)

4. Kirby, Thomas A. "Chaucer Research, 1979: Report No. 40." *ChauR* 15(1980):63–84.

Manuscripts and Editions

5. Brown, Emerson, Jr. "Thoughts on the Variorum Chaucer." *Chaucer Newsletter* 2,i(1980):4–6.

A variorum editor should record "fully and impartially, the history of what people have *thought* that his author wrote and meant." And he "should not 'editorialize' at all."

6. ———. "Thoughts on Editing Chaucer: The 'Electronic-Information Revolution' and a Proposal for the Future." *Chaucer Newsletter* 2,ii(1980)2–3.

Explains how computer technology could allow continual updating of and access to information pertinent to a variorum edition.

7.   Owen, Charles A., Jr. "A Note on the Ink in Some Chaucer Manuscripts." *Chaucer Newsletter* 2,ii(1980):14.

Variations in the ink color of MSS. Ellesmere and Hengwrt have yet to be accurately described and may provide information concerning the order in which the parts of the mss were written.

Background and General Criticism

8.   Ikegami, Tadahiro. "Chaucer and His Age." In *Introduction to English Literature—Society and Literature*. Ed. Bishu Saito. Tokyo: Shuppan Pub. Co., 1978, pp. 57–66. (In Japanese.)

9.   Kern, Edith. *The Absolute Comic*. Bloomington: Indiana UP, 1980.

Mikhail Bakhtin's study of the grotesquerie of medieval folk festivals encourages us to view certain Chaucerian characters in the carnivalesque spirit of absolute comedy: moral offenders such as Alysoun escape unscathed; Nicholas is punished only by accident; the trickster, Daun John, goes scot-free; May is not censured for deceit.

10.   Knight, Stephen. "Chaucer and the Sociology of Literature." *SAC* 2(1980):15–51.

Modern sociological theories of criticism are applied to Chaucer's major works—*BD, HF, PF, TC,* and *CT*. In particular Pierre Macherey's ideological analysis is applied to structure and mimesis in Chaucer, and Jacques Lacan's theories on subjectivity to characterization.

11.   Mann, Jill. "Now Read on: Medieval Literature." *Encounter* (1980): 60–64. [Rev. art.]

Recent critics of Chaucer—Terry Jones, David Aers, and others—are conventional in their desire to moralize medieval literature. The trend of contemporary criticism of *FranT, TC,* and *KnT*, as examples, is to isolate from the story

198

tableaux serving as subjects for moral reflection. The open-endedness of the narrative procedure carries its own moral significance, however, and the moralizing of tableaux is to be resisted at the point where narrative loses its sense as a story.

12. Ridley, Florence H. "Chaucerian Criticism: The Significance of Varying Perspectives." *NM* 81(1980):131–41.

Chaucer's enduring appeal derives from his poetry's visuality, its presentation of unchanging human behavior, its deliberate ambiguity. The broad ranges of psychological criticism are viable as long as they are understood as imaginative constructs of the critics and not the poet.

13. Rogers, William E. "The Raven and the Writing Desk: The Theoretical Limits of Patristic Criticism." *ChauR* 14(1980):260–77.

A theoretical objection to patristic criticism is that it is guilty of question-begging because it assumes that a work is intended to promote *caritas*. It is not the assumption of coherence that produces the fallacy but the assumption of a particular kind of coherence.

14. Shippey, T. A. "Catching Up: English Literature 1: From Alcuin to Chaucer." *TLS* Nov. 30, 1979, pp. 73–74.

Medieval scholarship and criticism suffers from reading texts without contexts, allowing modern perspectives to influence the interpretation of medieval writers, and careless translation.

See also: 16 41 78 89 114

Chaucer's Influence

15. Bowden, Betsy. "The Artistic and Interpretive Context of Blake's 'Canterbury Pilgrims.' " *Blake* 13(1980):164–90.

In his paintings of the Canterbury pilgrims, Blake shows the influence of previous illustrations for and commentary upon *CT*, but goes beyond the artistic and textual tradition to set the group of pilgrims in his own Blakean

199

cosmos, pairing characters against each other as opposites—e.g., Parson and Pardoner—to produce both visual and spiritual symmetry in a complex system of binary relationships.

16. Donaldson, E. Talbot. "Chaucer in the Twentieth Century." *SAC*, 2(1980):7–13.

In this first presidential address to the New Chaucer Society Professor Donaldson wittily summarizes the 20th-century conflict of opinions regarding Chaucer's work to conclude that Chaucer is partly to blame for the confusion. Like all great poets Chaucer reveals mysteries but does not solve them.

17. Gugelberger, Georg. "Zum Mittelaltereinfluss in der modernen Dichtung: Ezra Pounds Chaucerbild." *OL* 35(1980):220–34.

In *ABC of Reading* Pound praises Chaucer above Shakespeare and Dante, and in his *Cantos* he makes important use of Chaucer's works, the short poems especially. Chaucer provides a setting-off point for understanding Pound's ideas about poetry and his manner of composition.

18. Hardman, C. B. "Eloquence and Morality in the Old Poet and the New: Chaucer and Spenser." *RMSt* 6(1980):20–30.

Though Chaucer's reputation in the 16th century depended partly on works wrongly attributed to him, he was thought of as a proto-Puritan thinker, a model of eloquence, a love poet. Thus Spenser found it advantageous in the *Shepheardes Calendar* to see himself as descendant of "the olde famous Poete Chaucer," imitating him (or Chaucerian apocrypha) in the eclogues of November, December, May, June, and July; and by paying homage to him in the concluding eclogues, which echo *TC*.

19. Ikegami, Tadahiro. "Chaucer's Influence." In *Introduction to English Literature—Society and Literature*. Ed. Bishu Saito. Tokyo: Shuppan Pub. Co., 1978, pp. 68–72. (In Japanese.)

20. Mack, Maynard. "Pope's Copy of Chaucer." In *Evidence in Literary Scholarship*. Eds. René Wellek and Alvaro Ribeiro. Oxford: Clarendon Press, 1979, pp. 105–21.

Pope's copy of Chaucer, with his own youthful annotations, still survives. And though his marking of the text shows careful perusal of it (especially *Rom*), these early annotations are ultimately not very revealing of Pope's maturer feelings about Chaucer.

21.   Olsen, Alexandra Hennessey. "Chaucer and the Eighteenth Century: the Wife of Bath and Moll Flanders." *Chaucer Newsletter* 1,ii(1979):13–15.

Notes broad similarities between the Wife of Bath and Moll Flanders and concludes that Moll is an 18th-century analogue of Alison.

22.   Rowland, Beryl. "Dryden Refurbishes Chaucer's Barnyard." *Archiv* 217(1980):349–54.

The Augustans were the last English poets to possess enough confidence in their own idiom to attempt to make Chaucer their contemporary. Dryden's modernization of Chaucer was intended to achieve verisimilitude for his 17th-century audience. It would surprise him to know that his transformations would require elucidation for 20th-century readers.

23.   Scattergood, V. J. "A Caxton Prologue and Chaucer." *Chaucer Newsletter* 2,i(1980):14–13.

In his prologue to his edition (1484) of *CT*, Caxton apparently borrows some of Chaucer's phrases to describe Chaucer's poems.

24.   Turner, Robert K. "*The Two Noble Kinsmen* and Speght's Chaucer." *N&Q* 27(1980):175–76.

The detail in *The Two Noble Kinsmen* IV.ii.103–05, where the blond prince's locks are said to be "hard-haired" and "curled," suggest that Shakespeare and Fletcher used Speght's 1602 edition of Chaucer when they based their play on *KnT*. In that edition Speght misprints Chaucer's line "His crispe heer lyk rynges was yronne" (2165) as "His crispe haire like rings was of yron," clearly the source for the curious image in the play.

Lexicon and Onomastic

25. Caluwé-Dor, Juliette de. "Le Diable dans les *Contes de Cantorbéry:* Contribution a l'étude sémantique du terme *devil.*" In *Le Diable au Moyen Age: Doctrine, problèmes moraux, représentations* (Sénéfiance 6). Pubs. de CUER MA, U de Provence, 1979.

In English literary tradition before Chaucer the concept of the devil has great vitality. But in *CT*, only in *SumT* and *ParsT* does the term *devil* have its traditional force; for the most part one finds a transition away from the medieval idea.

26. DeWeever, Jacqueline. "Chaucerian Onomastics: The Formation of Personal Names in Chaucer's Works." *Names* 28(1980): 1–31.

Chaucer uses 636 proper names (excluding about 300 additional topographical and geographical names). They fall into four categories: astrological, Biblical, classical, and mythological. Names from Lat. and Gk. appear in the oblique case (e.g., *Ysidis*, gen. sing. of *Isis*). Names may show metathesis. There is inconsistency of spelling, e.g., i/y, e/i. Names may be contracted for metrical reasons. The spelling may be determined by pronunciation.

27. Ikegami, Yoshihiko. "The Semological Structure of the English Verbs of Motion: Old and Middle English." *Key-Word Studies in* Beowulf *and Chaucer* 1(1980):67–104. (In English.)

The article, which follows essentially the same theoretical line of approach as the same author's *Semological Structure of the English Verbs of Motion* (Tokyo, 1970; originally a Yale University dissertation), presents a description of the meanings of verbs of motion in Old and Middle English. The Middle English data is limited to Chaucer's usage.

28. Ross, Thomas W. "ME 'meving.' " *Chaucer Newsletter* 2,ii(1980):11.

Shows that *MED*'s definition of "mevyng" is correct, and that the word is not a scribal error for "menyng" but exists in its own right.

29. Takamiya, Toshiyuki. "Chaucer's *Sad* and its Related Words." *Key-Word Studies in* Beowulf *and Chaucer* 1(1980):59–65. (In English.)

202

An examination of Chaucer's use of *sad* in his works and the manuscript reading in *Rom* A211 makes it clear that he probably did not bear in mind the modern meaning of 'sorrowful' or 'mourning'.

30. Terasawa, Yoshio. " 'Daunger': Specimen of Chaucer Lexicon." *Key-Word Studies in* Beowulf *and* Chaucer 1(1980):17–22. (In English.)

The article analyses and describes a Chaucerian key-word 'daunger' and its derivative 'daungerous' in respect of etymology, semantic development, frequency of occurrence, form, riming structure, grammatical and semantic collocation, association, and senses. In line 514 of *WBT*, Chaucer ingeniously makes a pun on 'daungerous' (difficile, aloof: dangerous), where there might be an additional pun on 'love-daunger', the only occurrence of which seems to be found in *Pearl* (l. 11).

See also: 56a 65 92 109 120 134

Audience

31. Reiss, Edmund. "Chaucer and His Audience." *ChauR* 14(1980):390–402.

Chaucer's audience influenced his using familiar material and subjects to convey his points. Their ability to evaluate and judge must have figured in his manipulation of truth and seeming in the stories. We must use their intended presence in responding to his work.

32. Saito, Isamu. "A Gateway to Chaucer." *The Rising Generation* 127(1980):66–68.

Examination of the oral clichés of some of Chaucer's works on the assumption that, in 14th-century England, tales or romances were usually recited orally.

33. Strohm, Paul. "Chaucer's Audience." *L&H* 5(1977):26–41.

Special individuals of the lesser gentry—knights, esquires, and women of equivalent rank closely connected with the court, in such professional positions

STUDIES IN THE AGE OF CHAUCER

as the Chancery, secretaryships, and legal work—found their complicated life-experiences embodied in Chaucer's poetry of juxtaposition, with its polarities, disruption of hierarchies, and assertion of the relativity of traditional values.

Rhetoric, Narrative Technique

34. Andersen, Wallis May. "Rhetoric and Poetics in the *Canterbury Tales*: The Knight, the Squire, and the Franklin." *DAI* 41(1980):239A.

The ways these three pilgrims use four rhetorical devices—*occupatio, brevitas, digressio*, and *descriptio*—reveals their personalities. The Knight's self-conscious narrative stance shows his pretensions: his insensitivity in his use of rhetorical techniques reveals that he is not nearly as wise and high-minded a person as his *GP* portrait suggests. The Squire's rhetorical errors are generally an intensification of his father's and show him to be a trivial, rather silly person. *FranT* is rhetorically superior to *KnT* and *SqT*. The Franklin's utilitarian use of rhetorical techniques provides an indirect critique of the Squire's, and to some degree the Knight's, social and rhetorical pretensions.

35. Graham, Paul Trees. "The Meaning of Structure in Chaucerian Narrative." *DAI* 40(1980):5045A.

The categorical proposition, or sentence, is offered as a global model for narrative structure. The sentence structure, which makes meaning by suggesting the significant similarities between what might have been and what is actually said, takes the topos as its place for drawing the story into line with tradition and for drawing out the important differences between tradition and a particular performance. In *KnT*, the oppositions which threaten perpetual violence and despair are reduced in the paradigmatic perspective to opposites in alternation rather than in tension. In *NPT*, the mechanical intelligence of a beast-like man is the theme and the basis, in part, of its humor. In *BD*, the difference between memory and present fact is thematic and the auditor is forced to face grief directly.

36. Morgan, Mary Valentina. "The Shaping of Experience: A Study of Rhetorical Methods and Structure in Narrative Works by Chaucer, Fielding, and Dickens." *DAI* 41(1980):2126A.

Rhetoric functions to shape the content of the narrative in a particular way and is successful when it enables the reader to actively participate in constructing the fictional world. Chaucer, Fielding, and Dickens call attention to their narrative strategies and examine the tools of narrative art as their stories are told. Chaucer's *MLT* and *MkT* fail dramatically as stories—they challenge the reader's expectation of compatibility of subject matter and the narrator's treatment of that matter, demanding to be read and understood on quite different grounds.

37.   Runde, Joseph. "Magic and Meaning: The Poetics of Romance." *DAI* 41(1980):2128A.

An examination of some works commonly classified as romances—*WBT, Sir Gawain and the Green Knight, The Tale of King Arthur, The Tempest, The Winter's Tale*, and *As You Like It*—yields a definition of "romance." It is the magician who defines romance and his magic—his deep understanding of nature—that defines the development of the plot. Through the magician, the hero can overcome the obstacles that lie before him at the outset of the plot; and, through the intervention of the magician, the audience can come to hope in a benign providence rather than a cruel, inexorable fate.

See also: 56a

Themes and Images

38.   Ando, Shinsuke. "Chaucer's Conception of Nature." *Key-Words in Beowulf and Chaucer* 1(1980):49–57. (In English.)

Chaucer's Nature, when the term is explicitly used, is an *idée fixe* essentially based on the orthodox medieval conception. The writer, however, examines the interest and attitude with which Chaucer represented the various aspects of humanity, and recognizes in him a certain embryo of what may be termed modern Naturalism.

39.   Andreas, James R. "Festive Liminality in Chaucerian Comedy." *Chaucer Newsletter* 1,i(1979):3–6.

Reviews, by way of the anthropological studies of Turner and van Gennep, the effects of pilgrimage on the social behavior of the pilgrims in *CT*. Pilgrimage removes them from the center of normative social behavior: it homogenizes social rank, blurs sexual distinctions between male and female, and combines religion and comedy.

40. Hilary, Christine Ryan. "The 'Confessio' Tradition From Augustine to Chaucer." *DAI* 41(1980):242A.

The religious *confessio*-tradition includes three modes: *confessio peccati*, *confessio fidei*, and *confessio laudis*. *Confessio fidei*, which implies a self-testimony, provides the dominant mode for the secular literary *confessio* tradition, which parallels but does not derive directly from the devotional *confessio*-tradition. All literary confessions include self-witnessing speakers who also witness a philosophy of life shared by a general community, and who derive fictional credibility from the philosophical notion of entelechy, whereby they seem to share the desire to reproduce themselves with words. The literary *confessio*-tradition can thus include such disparate confessors as Augustine and the Wife of Bath because they share a form of utterance that shows their mode of characterization to be identical.

41. Hira, Toshinori, "A Love 'Par Amour,' Conventionalized and Satirized, in Chaucer." *Bulletin of the Faculty of Liberal Arts, Nagasaki University* (Humanities) 20(1980):69–81. (In English.)

A study of the change and development in Chaucer's conception of love. The subject is discussed in terms of Chaucer's biography and his times.

42. Kelly, Henry Ansgar. "The Genoese Saint Valentine and Chaucer's Third of May." *Chaucer Newsletter* 1,ii(1979):6–10.

Argues that Chaucer's St. Valentine is a Genoese saint whose feast was May 2, and not the Valentine of February 14. Thus the appropriateness of spring imagery.

43. Klene, Jean, C.S.C. "Chaucer's Contribution to a Popular Topos: The World Upside-Down." *Viator* 11(1979):321–34.

Chaucer defines the 'up-so-doun' world using three devices: dramatized "impossibilia" (the rhetorical expression of a passionate conviction believed to be an impossibility), role reversal (involving a triumph of the weaker over the stronger), and explicit statements (suggesting man's perverse judgments and actions). Parody provides the structural similarity of the three devices.

44.   Loftin, Alice. "Landscapes of Love and Poetry: Chaucerian Dream Allegory in England through the Renaissance." *Chaucer Newsletter* 1,i(1979):17.

Argues that Chaucer was famous in the 15th and 16th centuries not as a love poet but as a visionary poet, a dreamer of dream allegories, and as such influenced Lydgate (*Temple of Glas*), Skelton (*Garland of Laurel*), Cowley (*Dreame of Elysium*), Douglas, Dunbar, Green, and Breton.

45.   MacCurdy, Marian Mesrobian. "The Polarization of the Feminine in Arthurian and Troubadour Literature." *DAI* 41(1980):2596A.

The image of woman is the focal point for the controversy regarding the good or evil nature of the physical world. Early Christian and Gnostic writings, selected troubadour lyrics, *Gawain and the Green Knight*, Malory's *Le Morte d'Arthur*, and Chaucer's *TC* demonstrate the polarization of images of the feminine: she is either positively portrayed as a spiritual guide, the source of all worth, or as the demonic temptress who can cause the ruin of entire civilizations. Most of the images that are linked to the physical are negative, and most that help man raise himself out of the physical are positive.

46.   Schuman, Samuel. "Man, Magician, Poet, God—An Image in Medieval, Renaissance, and Modern Literature." *Cithara* 19(1980):40-54.

The magical pageant of the Briton clerk (*FranT*) is imitated in Shakespeare's masque of Ceres (*The Tempest*); Humbert Humbert (*Lolita*) is an analogue of Prospero. The image of the magician in each work points to the activity of the creative artist as illusionist, and leads to a theological esthetic. The notion of the artist and artistic process implies the analogue of the divine creator.

See also: 51 53 69 71 75 76 78 83 84 104 127 129 136 145

Teaching Chaucer

47.   Spraycar, Rudy S. "The Prologue to the 'General Prologue': Chaucer's Statement about Nature in the Opening Lines of the 'Canterbury Tales.' " *NM* 81(1980):142–49.

The spring opening of *GP* may reflect Alain de Lille's concepts in *De Planctu Naturae*, indicating the connection between nature's amorous regeneration and man's need for spiritual renewal.

48.   Owen, Charles A., Jr. "Undergraduate and Graduate Courses: New Patterns." *Chaucer Newsletter* 2,ii(1980):7–10.

Provides a broad outline for an undergraduate course in Chaucer and a complete syllabus for a graduate course, the latter based on the author's conception of the development of *CT*.

49.   Weissman, Hope Phyllis. "One Way to End a Chaucer Course." *Chaucer Newsletter* 2,ii(1980):3–7.

Suggests that after studying in *CT* the relationship of different poetic styles to different social or cultural classes, one might examine the visual art of the Limbourgs' Calendar in the *Tres Riches Heures*. The stylistic iconographies of the poet and the painters provide fruitful comparisons and contrasts.

See also: 68

Canterbury Tales—General

50.   Crisp, Delmas Swinfield, Jr. "Internal Evidence of Formulaic Diction in *The Canterbury Tales*." *DAI* 40(1980):5450A.

Though *CT* was neither orally prepared nor heavily alliterative, traces of both traditions are present in the work. The oral tradition almost certainly influenced Chaucer's work more predominantly. The evidence of formulaic diction in *CT* is strong; and it is shown that Chaucer relied on formulaic diction to the same degree at both the beginning and end of his writing career.

51. Heffernan, Carol Falvo. "The Use of Simile in Dante's *Divine Comedy* and Chaucer's *Canterbury Tales*." *CJItS* 3(1980):72–80.

John Speirs' claim that both poets use similes to promote "distinct visualization" in the service of allegory and realism is borne out by *The Divine Comedy* but not *CT*. Dante's similes produce visual accent, serving as ancillary devices within a highly controlled allegorical system, but the simile for Chaucer is a crucial structural device, helping to illustrate character, shape theme, and create irony.

52. Higgs, Elton D. " 'What Man Artow?' Harry Bailly and the 'Elvyssh' Chaucer." *MHLS* 2(1979):28–43.

The tension between Harry Bailly's governance over the pilgrims and the tolerance and permissiveness of Chaucer's fictional narrative voice is implied in three link passages: between *KnT* and *MilT*, in the Prologue to *MLT*, and in the Prologue to *ParsT*. The 'knitting up' of *ParsT* and *Ret* brings the varied human experience represented by the pilgrims' tales, as well as the limited perceptions of the Host, Chaucer the Pilgrim, and Chaucer the author, under divine governance.

53. Justman, Stewart. "Literal and Symbolic in the *Canterbury Tales*." *ChauR* 14(1980):199–214.

There are in *CT* examples of the late medieval attack on the symbolic attitude. The literal use of the Song of Songs in *MerT*, and the Wife of Bath's scriptural interpretation, are respectively examples of the mockery and parody of analogical thought.

54. Leicester, H. Marshall, Jr. "The Art of Impersonation: A General Prologue to the *Canterbury Tales*." *PMLA* 95(1980):8–22.

Readers have over-emphasized the persona of the narrator(s) in *CT*, making the tales themselves but an appendage to the frame. But in fact there are many internal contradictions in such a 'dramatic' reading of the poem. The tales are insistently 'textual,' i.e., written things, and the only voice is that *of* (not *in*) the text itself. *CT* is an extended attempt to see from the manifold points of view of others, and hence one might speak not of 'Chaucer the maker' but of 'Chaucer the poem.'

55.   McGrady, Donald. "Were Sercambi's *Novelle* Known from the Middle Ages On? (Notes on Chaucer, Sacchetti, *Cent Nouvelles nouvelles*. Pauli, Timodeda, Zayas)." *Italica* 57(1980):3–18.

Scholars need to reassess the extent of Sercambi's literary influence. A survey of some analogues of the framework and tales of his *Novelle* prove conclusively that his work was imitated in Italy, Spain, France, and Germany. Parallels in *ShT* and in the framing devices of *CT* point to Chaucer's indebtedness.

56.   Middleton, Anne. "Chaucer's 'New Men' and the Good of Literature in the *Canterbury Tales*." *Literature and Society*. Ed. Edward W. Said (Selected Papers from the English Institute, NS 3[1978]). Baltimore: Johns Hopkins, 1980, pp. 15–56.

Chaucer's pilgrims agree that "the pleasure and the use of literature are one thing," that the utility of literature lies not only in the kernel of its theme but in the felicities of its style and the pleasure of its audience as well. In this view, Chaucer anticipates the "new men" of the Renaissance. "Enditing" was to Chaucer a courtly, affirmative art, not a transcendental one.

56a.   Salmon, Vivian. "The Representation of Colloquial Speech in *The Canterbury Tales*." In *Style and Text: Studies Presented to Nils Erik Enkvist*. Ed. H. G. Ringbom. Stockholm: Skriptor, 1975, pp. 263–77.

Evaluation of the characteristics of genuine, spontaneous conversation supports the conclusion that *CT* provides realistic evidence of English speech in the late fourteenth century. Chaucerian conversation is affected by the need of speech to reflect character, the interrelationship of its participants and the attitudes of the participants to one another and to the situation.

57.   Shikii, Kumiko. "A Religious Approach to *The Canterbury Tales*." *Sella* (March 10, 1980):28–32.

CT is basically religious in spite of its various secular elements. The religious connotation depends rather on Chaucer's Catholic view of life than on the outward signs. All the characters and their tales, both sacred and secular, are equally important to present an ideal image of human society.

58.   Stugrin, Michael. "Ricardian Poetics and Late Medieval Cultural Pluriformity: The Significance of Pathos in the *Canterbury Tales*." *ChauR* 15(1981):155–67.

The pathetic tales must been seen in connection with the Ricardian emphasis on emotionalism and the commonality of Christ's human nature and man's. The aim of the pathetic voice is not to make any sweeping statement of human experience but to provide one possible response to it.

See also: 7   10   39

CT—General Prologue

59.   Sklute, Larry. "Catalogue Form and Catalogue Style in the General Prologue of the *Canterbury Tales*." *SN* 52(1980):35–46.

Chaucer builds his descriptions of the pilgrims according to the traditional catalogue plan of the accumulation of details. But he breaks with tradition in drawing details of a portrait from differing angles, thereby surprising his reader and expanding the reader's customary expectations. The pilgrims are in a 'middle state' between the typical and the mimetic.

See also: 15   33   47

CT—The Knight and His Tale

60.   Anderson, David. "The Legendary History of Thebes in Boccaccio's *Teseida* and Chaucer's *Knight's Tale*." *DAI* 40(1980):4585A.

The complex and suggestive analogies between the *Teseida* and Statius' *Thebaid* forces a re-evaluation of the question "What did Chaucer do to the *Teseida*?" in light of what Boccaccio had already done to the *Thebaid*. The *Teseida* is modeled on the epic form as it was understood by his age: an historical account which introduces fabulous elements in order to underscore the lessons of that history. The 'romance' in the *Teseida* reinterprets the theme and main action of the *Thebaid* according to how the lessons of Theban history were interpreted in the Middle Ages. The fate of the analogies between Boccaccio's and Statius' work in

211

the hands of Chaucer further shows that late medieval authors used Theban history to reflect the basic tenets of medieval historical thought.

61. Hanning, Robert W. " 'The Struggle between Noble Design and Chaos': The Literary Tradition of Chaucer's Knight's Tale." *LitR* 23(1980):519–41.

Statius celebrates the triumph of Theseus' righteous wrath as an agent of civilization and order over murderous rage and chaos; Boccaccio celebrates the triumph of the courtly code variously applied. As teller of the Theban tale, Chaucer's Knight presents the conflict from the perspective of medieval chivalry. Though Saturn exercises ultimate control, a precarious mundane control over raw violence is represented by the tournament, especially in the image of horses chewing golden bridles.

62. Hoeber, Daniel R. "Chaucer's Friday Knight." *Chaucer Newsletter* 2,i(1980):8–10.

Disputes Lowes' interpretation of *KnT* 1534–39. The sudden changes of mood, of Arcite, and of Chauntecleer (on a Friday) in *NPT*, the meaning of "gere" (a wild or changeful mood), and the first Adam's fall on the sixth day all suggest that Friday is not different from other days but that it is a day of dramatic changes.

63. McCobb, Lillian M. "The English *Partonope of Blois*, Its French Sources, and Chaucer's *Knight's Tale*." *ChauR* 11(1977):369–72.

Analysis of the conclusion of the English *Partonope* and its French source's conclusion suggests the English as a later work done under the influence of Chaucer's tale. The author may have followed a copy of Chaucer's work.

64. Nelson, Joseph Edward. "Chaucer's *Knight's Tale*: A Vision of a Secular Ideal of Chivalry." *DAI* 41(1980):242A.

Unlike the knight of the chivalric theorists, who is ideally a force for justice and stability, the knight of the courtly romance is a solitary figure whose primary concern is self-fulfillment without regard to the community at large. As a courtly poet, Chaucer wrote for an audience which knew and appreciated both the notions of courtly love and the values inherent in the code of chivalry. *KnT*, then, especially in the person of Theseus as its chivalric protagonist, posits a vision of a viable secular order based on chivalric values. *KnT* represents Chaucer's mature reflections on a secular order and is ultimately optimistic in its conclusion.

See also: 11   34   35

CT—The Miller and His Tale

65.   Cooper, Geoffrey. " 'Sely John' in the 'Legende' of the *Miller's Tale*." *JEGP* 79(1980):1–12.

Sely (from OE *gesaelig*) originally meant 'happy, fortunate,' and hence 'blessed by God, pious, holy.' Later, however, the word took on connotations of 'pitiful' and 'silly, rustic,' while still retaining its earlier meaning in different contexts. Chaucer uses *sely* in all these various senses in his poems, and its ambiguous use in *MilT* as an epithet for John the carpenter is rich in irony and multivalence of meaning (recalling the similar device of the tag "hende" Nicholas).

66.   Dane, Joseph A. "The Mechanics of Comedy in Chaucer's *Miller's Tale*." *ChauR* 14(1980):215–24.

Chaucer achieves maximum concentration on the moment of dénouement by organizing his characters into two parallel and static triadic sets. When the characters are in their triadic configurations, no action takes place. The resolution of tension by action takes place when the characters are in dyadic relationships.

67.   Goodall, Peter. "The *Reeve's Tale*, *Le Meunier et les ii Clers* and the *Miller's Tale*." *Parergon* 27(1980):13–16.

Chaucer's improvements result from adapting source to the framework of *CT*—giving the tale to the highly individualized Reeve, whose emphasis upon "quitting" the Miller requires that Symkin become the strongest character in the tale. The most successful changes occur in the fight scene, where Chaucer expedites the action by involving the second clerk and the wife.

68. Milosh, Joseph E., Jr. "Reason and Mysticism in Fantasy and Science Fiction." In *Young Adult Literature: Background and Criticism*. Eds. Millicent Lenz and Ramona M. Mahood. Chicago: American Library Association, 1980, pp. 433–40.

John, the cuckolded carpenter in *MilT*, delights in a simple faith which makes star-gazing unnecessary. The *NPT* revolves around the problem of translating intuitive knowledge into action. In both modern and medieval images of the universe, searching is essentially the same. Using historical backgrounds to give young readers perspective, teachers can nourish this quest.

69. Nitzsche, Jane C. "Herbal Imagery in Chaucer's *Miller's Tale.*" *Chaucer Newsletter* 2,i(1980):6–8.

Licorice, according to medieval herbals, quenched thirst (thus allowing Nicholas to stay in his room for a long time?). Cetewale, as zedoary, dispels gas (Nicholas' fart?). It is also an aphrodisiac and the *nardus* of Canticles, a symbol of the Lord's passion. Commentaries on Nardus encourage us to see Nicholas as a parody of Christ the Lover.

70. Revard, Carter. "The Tow on Absalom's Distaff and the Punishment of Lechers in Medieval London." *ELN* 17(1980):168–70.

MilT's reference to Absalom's "having moore tow on his distaf " (I, 3774) adds another significance to its long recognized proverbial one when we realize that carrying a distaff with tow on it to the pillory was statutory punishment in Chaucer's London for persons guilty of crimes of sex and violence.

See also: 9

CT—The Reeve and His Tale

71. Brown, Peter. "The Confinement of Symkyn: The Function of Space in the *Reeve's Tale.*" *ChauR* 14(1980):225–36.

The conception of the action of *RvT* in three dimensions is designed to provide more than narrative realism. By reducing the miller's area of influence, Chaucer represents metaphorically his being cut down to size by the students.

214

72.   Heffernan, Carol Falvo. "A Reconsideration of the Cask Figure in the *Reeve's Prologue.*" *ChauR* 15(1980):37–43.

The cask figure combines religious and sexual symbols in the reference to wine and baptism and to the phallic spout. These connect to the tale with the fear of impotence and the careless oaths, suggesting that the Reeve misses the hidden religious solution to old age in his own words.

CT—The Man of Law and His Tale

73.   Clark, Susan L., and Julian N. Wasserman. "Constance as Romance and Folk Heroine in Chaucer's *Man of Law's Tale.*" *RUS* 64(1978):13–24.

Constance is that rarity, a romance *heroine*, who, like the more familiar hero, learns through trials and difficulties. The tale is thus perhaps one of those narratives that marks the transition from matriarchy to patriarchy in European culture. The tale is a romance but it still bears the marks of its Märchen roots, especially in the mechanism of female initiation. The events portray a "continual representation of a dying matriarchy unable to generate new queens, which yields to the male principle."

74.   Roddy, Kevin. "Mythic Sequence in the *Man of Law's Tale.*" *JMRS* 10(1980):1–22.

Problems of tone—comic versus tragic—make the reader of *MLT* uneasy. There is also the problem of the weakness of the "literal narrative and the heavy-handed intrusions of the author." One can discern meaningful form, however, if one observes that the four supernatural interventions in the tale correspond to the first four (of five) stages in the "archetypal process of salvation." Constance's prayer establishes a "continuity between the mythic past and the experiential present." Christ appears as her champion, reflecting the 'ransom' theory of salvation. Constance is in turn the Christian soul; the Virgin, "a *propugnatrix* in a world made damnable by women"; and mankind. Chaucer modifies Trivet to underscore this mythic pattern. The narrative, thus understood, fits the narrator, who reflects the moral fervor of the English middle class in the fourteenth century.

75.   Sleeth, Charles. "Astrology as a Bone of Contention between the Man of Law and the Franklin." *Chaucer Newsletter* 1,i(1979):20–21.

In *GP* the Franklin and the Man of Law are presented as companions, but they have antithetical views on astrology: the Man of Law insists on its value, the Franklin condemns it as "supersticious cursednesse."

See also: 36   158

CT—The Wife of Bath and Her Tale

76.   Palmer, Barbara D. " 'To Speke of Wo that Is in Mariage': The Marital Arts in Medieval Literature." In *Human Sexuality in the Middle Ages and Renaissance*. Ed. Douglas Radcliffe-Umstead. U of Pittsburgh: Center for Medieval and Renaissance Studies, 1978, pp. 3–14.

Evidence about medieval marital relationships appears in *auctoritee*—Church and civil records—and in *experience* reflected in literature. Legal and penitential documents depict an astounding range of sources of marital conflict, especially sexual transgressions. Medieval literature, from lyrics such as the *chansons de mal mariée*, to *CT*, to *Piers the Plowman* and the drama cycles, generally focuses on infidelity and shrewishness as two principal sources of marital discord.

77.   Reisner, M. E. "New Light on Judoc the Obscure." *Chaucer Newsletter* 1,i(1979):19–20.

Adduces reports that St. Joce's relics were brought to Winchester (Hyde Abbey) in 901. The abbot of Hyde lived next to the real Tabard Inn and Chaucer may have introduced St. Joce into *WBP* as a bit of local lore.

78.   Robertson, D. W., Jr. " 'And For My Land Thus Hastow Mordred Me?': Land Tenure, the Cloth Industry, and the Wife of Bath." *ChauR* 14(1980):403–20.

Land tenure laws and cloth industry figures suggest that the Wife was a bondswoman with holdings in the industry acquired from her first husband and used to attract four more and to finance expensive pilgrimages. A bondswoman character is also supported by the fleshly nature.

79.   Schulenburg, Jane Tibbetts. "Clio's European Daughters: Myopic Modes of Perception." In *The Prism of Sex: Essays in the Sociology of Knowledge*.

Eds. Julia A. Sherman and Evelyn Torton Beck. Madison: U of Wisconsin P, 1979, pp. 33–53.

One of the best and earliest observations of the basic distortion of history with regard to women and their roles is made by the Wife of Bath (III, 688–96). Christine de Pisan makes a comparable but more elaborate statement of the mistreatment of women by clerical historians.

80. Weissman, Hope Phyllis. "Why Chaucer's Wife Is from Bath." *ChauR* 15(1980):11–36.

Literary tradition and iconography connect "bath" to prostitution, also suggested by the Wife's living outside the former patriarchal city. These symbolize her prostitution in marriage, thwarting the system, her enrichment, and ultimately her own martyred age.

81. ———. "The Pardoner's Vernicle, the Wife's Coverchiefs, and Saint Paul." *Chaucer Newsletter* 1,ii(1979).10–12.

The headwear of the Wife of Bath and of the Pardoner, in light of 1 Cor. 11:3–12, links the two pilgrims symbolically, both rejecting their proper sex roles and thus simultaneously flouting Paul's distinction between male and female and literalizing his invitation to transcend sex differences.

See also: 21 37 43 53 137 158

CT—The Friar and His Tale

82. Besserman, Lawrence. "Chaucer and the Pope of Double Worstede." *Chaucer Newslatter* 1,i(1979):15–16.

Argues that *GP* 259–62, 642–43, and *TC* II, 36–37 are allusions to the Great Schism: the Friar like a pope in his "*double* worstede"; the pope like a popinjay (of two voices?), and the proverb that more than one way leads to Rome.

83. Hassan-Yusuff, Z. Dolly. " 'Wynne thy cost': Commercial and Feudal Imagery in the *Friar's Tale*." *Chaucer Newsletter* I,ii(1979):15–18.

By using the language of feudal economics Chaucer equates the summoner with the devil.

84.   Zellefrow, W. Ken. "Chaucer's View of Robin Hood." *Chaucer Newsletter* 1,i(1979):12–15.

Traces broad similarities between *FrT* and the Robin Hood ballads to suggest that Chaucer knew early forms of the ballads and adapted them for comic effect.

See also: 43

CT—The Summoner and His Tale

85.   Crowther, J. D. W. "The *Summoner's Tale*: 1955–69." *Chaucer Newsletter* 2,i(1980):12–13.

The Friar, who does not want Thomas to divide his money among several confessors, argues that likewise an ill man should not divide his among several physicians. He thus materializes the penitential injuction not to divide one's confession among several confessors (see *ParsT* 1006).

86.   Wentersdorf, Karl P. "The Motif of Exorcism in the Summoner's Tale." *SSF* 17(1980):249–54.

Scatological jests, such as dividing Thomas' "yifte," are derived from classical sources and adapted to Christian theology. Thirteenth- and fourteenth-century manuscripts frequently show defecation or breaking of wind to drive away the devil. The squire's grotesque solution to the "departynge" of the gift hints at avarice among mendicants and parodies the Pentecostal distribution of the Holy Spirit, which they believed themselves heir to. Probably derived from iconographic depictions of the twelve winds, the motif was not objectionable to aristocratic audiences, for whom, indeed, it was designed.

See also: 43

CT—The Clerk and His Tale

87. Hardman, Phillipa. "Chaucer's Tyrants of Lombardy." *RES* 122(1980):172–78.

Chaucer's contemporaries were familiar with his "tyraunts of Lumbardye" (*LGW*, G. 353), notorious for their cruelty. The Lombard setting of *ClT* suggests proverbial Lombard tyranny for Walter, an imperfect mixture of tyranny and pity, for he rues Griselda's suffering. *MerT*, a parody of *ClT*, emphasizes lust, for which Lombard tyrants were also notorious, as well as avarice, another of their vices.

88. Middleton, Anne. "The Clerk and His Tale: Some Literary Contexts." *SAC* 2(1980):121–50.

Examines medieval redactions of Boccaccio's Griselda story to suggest that Chaucer retells it in order to raise literary questions analogous to moral ones. The Clerk combines Petrarch's affective purpose and high style with the exemplary force and plain style of the French versions in an attempt to create a tale with the "best sentence and moost solace."

CT—The Merchant and His Tale

89. Cahn, Kenneth S. "Chaucer's Merchants and the Foreign Exchange: An Introduction to Medieval Finance." *SAC* 2(1980):81–119.

Demonstrates that the Merchant engages neither in usury nor in illegal speculation. Selling "sheeldes" (imaginary coins "of accounts" employed in Flanders) is simply a means of *borrowing* English sterling through foreign exchange. The Merchant is a borrower ("he was in dette"), not a lender. As such, the odds against his making a profit from the exchange were enormous.

90. Kossick, S. G. "Geoffrey Chaucer's The Merchant's Tale." *Unisa English Studies* 18(1979).3–14.

A reading of *MerT*.

91. Schleusener, Jay. "The Conduct of the *Merchant's Tale.*" *ChauR* 14(1980):237–50.

The Merchant's language snares the reader into displaying his own bad taste. It accomplishes this by making May a sympathetic character and by allowing him to belong to a select group which sees through the deceptions of the tale. However, the reader's good sense eventually sets him free.

See also: 9   53   87

CT—The Squire and His Tale

See: 34

CT—The Franklin and His Tale

92. Fujimoto, Masashi. "A Reading of Chaucer's 'The Franklin's Tale.'" *The Bulletin of Faculty of Literature of Tokai University* 32(1980):123–42.

Chaucer's view of *gentilesse* sharply contrasts with that of the teller of *FranT*. High comedy develops in the course of the Franklin's performance.

93. Rosenberg, Bruce A. "The Bari Widow and the *Franklin's Tale.*" *ChauR* 14(1980):344–52.

Among the oral-tradition analogues for *FranT* is the story of the Bari Widow, similar to it in ways that Boccaccio's is not. Analysis of Chaucer's adept use of it and other oral-tradition stories demonstrates the mastery of his creation.

94. Watanabe, Ikuo. "*The Franklin's Tale*—A Narrative." *Tenri Daigaku Gakuho* 132(1981):91–109.

FranT develops on the level of the narrator's own self-contentment, and it seems that it is he who most enjoys the tale.

See also: 11   34   46   75

CT—The Pardoner and His Tale

95.   Coletti, Theresa. "The Pardoner's Vernicle and the Image of Man in the *Pardoner's Tale.*" *Chaucer Newsletter* 1,i(1979):10–12.

The vernicle, an image of Christ, reminds us that man is made in God's image, and emphasizes the Pardoner's perversion of that image, both morally and spiritually. Yet it also provides hope that the Pardoner may reform himself.

96.   Jungman, Robert E. "The Pardoner's 'Confession' and St. Augustine's *De Doctrina Christiana.*" *Chaucer Newsletter* 1,i(1979):16–17.

Cites *De Doctrina*, IV, xxvii, 59 as a source or gloss at least on the Pardoner's 'confession': Augustine notes that the wicked may preach what is right and good.

97.   McAlpine, Monica E. "The Pardoner's Homosexuality and How It Matters." *PMLA* 95(1980):8–22.

In Chaucer's famous line "I trowe he were a geldyng or a mare" the word *mare* is best glossed 'homosexual,' and the description of the Pardoner fits all three medieval confusions with homosexuality: effeminacy, eunuchy, and hermaphroditism. In his tale the Pardoner alludes to a fleshly unpardonable sin (379–80), which may be his own. He is a pardoner who cannot himself (he feels) be pardoned. His relics, therefore, entice others away from true contrition and are, like his body to himself, a source of sin.

98.   McKenna, Conán. "The Irish Analogues to Chaucer's *Pardoner's Tale.*" *Béaloideas* 45–47(1977–79):63–77.

Common characters and incidents in *PardT* and three Irish versions of Aarne-Thompson folktale Type 763 may indicate cross-fertilization between folklore and medieval literature. Most arguments favor an oral source for the *PardT*. The episode of the old man giving directions and the chemist scene are exclusive features of *PardT*.

See also: 81

CT—Shipman's Tale

See: 55

CT—The Prioress and Her Tale

99.   Collette, Carolyn P. "Sense and Sensibility in the *Prioress's Tale.*" *ChauR* 15(1981):138–50.

The Prioress' preoccupation with emotion and the diminutive reflects the 14th century's concern for a particularized and emotional style in the arts. Though her tale seems odd and inconsistent, it has a consistent sensibility which uses the particular to produce not types but emotional responses.

100.   Hamel, Mary. "And now for Something Different: The Relationship between the *Prioress's Tale* and the *Rime of Sir Thopas.*" *ChauR* 14(1980:251–59.

Th contains a covert similarity to *PrT*. If, by means of the lily, the elf-queen is identified with the Virgin Mary, the structure of *Th* may be seen to parody that of *PrT*. Both protagonists have gemlike chastity, are born "in fer contree," and are devoted to an immortal woman.

101.   Jacobs, Edward Craney. "Further Biblical Allusions for Chaucer's Prioress." *ChauR* 15(1981):151–54.

Madame Eglentyne's "Amor vincit omnia" where we would expect "Caritas vincit omnia," is used for ironic effect. Since Paul defines *caritas* as the "bond of perfection," Chaucer's use of the motto to bind together the Prioress' rich beads is another element of parody.

CT–The Tale of Sir Thopas

See: 100

CT—The Monk and His Tale

102. Shikii, Kumiko. "Chaucer's Anti-clericalism as Seen in the Monk." *The Fleur-de-lis Review* (December 25, 1980):25–54.

Chaucer's Monk is by no means an ideal clergyman. He is one of the best targets of Chaucer's satire. He shows the degenerating states of the Church and the religious orders, to remind the readers of the need of renovation from within.

CT—The Nun's Priest and His Tale

103. Correale, Robert M. " 'Nun's Priest's Tale,' VII, 3444–46." *Expl* 39(1980):43–45.

NPT's "my lord" (VII, 3445), generally taken as referring to a bishop or archbishop (by J. H. Fisher to Jesus or God) may refer to St. Paul, thus resembling the conclusion of a homily for the Feast of the Conversion of St. Paul in the 15th-century priest's handbook *Mirk's Festial*, EETS ES 96(1905):p. 56.

104. Crépin, André. " 'Sustres and paramours': Sexe et domination dans les *Contes de Canterbury*." *Caliban* 17(1980):3–21.

NPT illustrates the alternation of sexual dominance in *CT*. The priest among his nuns is like Chanticleer, "paragon des phallocrates," among his wives. But neither maintains dominance. Moreover, in *NPT*, as in *CT* as a whole, questions of sexual domination are ultimately transcended.

105. Crider, Richard. "Daniel in the 'Nun's Priest's Tale.' " *AN&Q* 18(1979):18–19.

Chauntecleer's citation of Daniel (VII, 3128–29), frequently taken to refer to Daniel 7, more pertinently refers to Daniel 4 where Nebuchadnezzar relates a dream similar to Chauntecleer's and to the dreams Chauntecleer cites. This dream and its aftermath show a fall from greatness and then a reversal like that in *NPT*.

106. Wentersdorf, Karl P. "*Heigh Ymaginacioun* in Chaucer's Nun's Priest's Tale." *SN* 52(1980):31–34.

Line VII 3217—"By heigh ymaginacioun forncast"—means not that the fox's attack was predestined, or foretold in the cock's dream, but that the fox had carefully planned his act of high treason against the royal Chaunticleer.

See also: 36   62   68

CT—The Second Nun and Her Tale

107.   Johnston, Mark E. "The Resonance of the *Second Nun's Tale*." *MHLS* 3(1980):25–38.

The artistic purpose of *SNT* is clarified by examining the tale in the thematic and dramatic context of *CT*. The saint's legend of Cecilia broadens the themes of the Marriage Group, contrasting secular with spiritual union; together with *CYT*, it also reveals opposing viewpoints on the evil consequences of man's search for truth and value in the world; and it thus contributes to the moral texture of *CT*.

108.   Reames, Sherry L. "The Cecilia Legend as Chaucer Inherited It and Retold It: the Disappearance of an Augustinian Ideal." *Speculum*, 55(1980):38–57.

The eldest version of the Cecilia story is the *Passio S. Caeciliae*, extant mss of which date from the eighth century. Its central meaning involves an ideal of perfection close to Augustine's teachings. Chaucer translates the version of the story from the *Legenda aurea* up to about line 344, where he changes his source to the longer *Passio*—which, instead of translating, he abridges. Jacobus had emphasized supernatural power at the expense of human understanding and choice. Chaucer goes even further than Jacobus in eliminating material from the *Passio* that affirmed the value of human nature and earthly experience. The tale thus loses its Augustinian perspective and assumes an increasing theological pessimism. Perhaps Chaucer, like Jacobus, but unlike Augustine, visualized grace as abolishing nature, not raising and perfecting it.

CT—The Canon's Yeoman and His Tale

See: 107   111

CT—The Manciple and His Tale

109. Brown, Emerson, Jr. "Word Play in the Prologue to the *Manciple's Tale*, 98: 'T'acord and love and many a wrong apese.' " *Chaucer Newsletter* 2,ii(1980):11–12.

Argues for a pun on nonce-word "ape-ease." The Cook has drunk "wyn ape." If appease (ad pacem) is merely ape-ease, then clearly wine is no real remedy for the pilgrims' dis-ease ("whan that they were seke").

110. Fulk, R. D. "Reinterpreting the Manciple's Tale." *JEGP* 78(1979):485–93.

MancT—a warning to the Cook with whom the Manciple quarrels—supports three main themes: the insignificance of social rank (ll. 105–270), the danger inherent in anger (271–91), and the foolishness of a wanton tongue (292–362).

111. Marshall, David F. "A Note on Chaucer's *Manciple's Tale* 105–10." *Chaucer Newsletter* 1,i(1979):17–18.

Links the python slain by Apollo with an alchemic symbol and argues that *MancT* is thematically related to *CYT*.

CT—The Parson and His Tale

112. Correale, Robert M. "The Source of the Quotation from 'Crisostom' in 'The Parson's Tale.' " *N&Q* 27(1980):101–02.

The Parson's quotation from St. John Chrysostom (X, 109–10) is translated from St. Raymund of Pennaforte's *Summa Casuum Poenitentiae*. Its ultimate source, however, is a Latin homily (not in the modern editions of the fathers), the *Sermo de Poenitentia*, attributed to Chrysostom.

113. Luengo, Anthony E. "Synthesis and Orthodoxy in Chaucer's *Parson's Tale*: An analysis of the concordance of different authoritative *sententiae* according to the principles of the medieval *artes praedicandi*." *Revue de l'Université d'Ottawa* 50(1980):223–32.

Chaucer's treatment of *sententiae* in *ParsT* is best understood in terms of the schema provided by Thomas Walleys in his 14th-century *De modo componendi sermones*. The Parson adopts many of Walleys' 14 methods of linking *sententiae* to control logically the 160 biblical and patristic quotations and paraphrases used in his sermon, and to oppose the misleading use of *sententiae* by pilgrims like the Wife and Pardoner.

Troilus and Criseyde—General

114. Kaminsky, Alice R. *Chaucer's* Troilus and Criseyde *and the Critics*. Athens, Ohio: Ohio UP, 1980.

A sophisticated evaluation of some 500 items of *TC* criticism considered under the headings Historical, Philosophical, Formalistic, and Psychological. In addition to illuminating the poem, the book provides a trenchant critique of modern critical theory and practice.

See also: 10   11   18   45   82

TC—Prosody, Text

115. Stokes, Myra. "Recurring Rhymes in *Troilus and Criseyde*." *SN* 52(1980):287–97.

The repeated rhymes *trouthe/routhe, serve/disserve*, and *mente/entente* accentuate the poem's development. The first two pairs underscore the perversion of *fin amours*. Troilus asks for his lady's *routhe* in exchange for his *trouthe*, but her *untrouthe* causes him *routhe*. He ideally deserves better for his service. Repetition of *mente/entente* illustrates the disharmony between conscious and unconscious motives.

116. Windeatt, Barry. "The Text of the *Troilus*." In *Chaucer Studies III: Essays on Troilus and Criseyde*. Ed. Mary Salu. Cambridge: Brewer, 1979, pp. 1–22.

Root's contention that his alpha, beta, and gamma classifications represent stages of Chaucer's revision of *TC* is untenable. The ms evidence must be judged for itself, not in comparison with other 'revision' problems such as those in Gower and Langland, nor should the evidence be forced into a mold based on preconceptions of ms relationships. The major difference among *TC* mss (Troilus' song, the 'predestination' soliloquy in Book IV, and Troilus' ascent) when seen in context show that from the start Chaucer conceived of his long poem with these passages included.

TC—Literary Relations

117.   Ainsworth, Jeanette Therese. "The Welsh *Troelus A Cresyd*: Toward a Better Understanding." *DAI* 40(1980):4015A–16A.

The dramatic Welsh work written in Shakespeare's time is a unique and important contribution to the Troilus-Cressida tradition. The author eliminates any elements of plot, theme, or character from his sources (Chaucer's *TC* and Henryson's *Testament of Cresseid*) which might undercut his more tragic, moral, and philosophical focus. Characters are less complex than their English counterparts. Calcas is the author's original contribution. Unlike 16th-century portrayals of her as a shameless harlot, Cresyd is a tragic heroine, a victim of love and war, and a personification of all individuals trapped by circumstances they are too weak to control.

118.   Dulick, Michael George. "*La Celestina* and Chaucer's *Troilus*: A Comparative Study." *DAI* 40(1980):5852A.

Chaucer and Rojas shared common sources and concerns, and their works are most alike in their use of sophisticated dialogue, but Rojas' vision is more destructive. Troilus and Calisto are both 'courtly' lovers, but Calisto is a debased version of Chaucer's hero. Whereas the ambiguities in Criseyde's character create a *chiaroscuro*, in Melibea's they become antitheses; and while Chaucer forgives Criseyde's infidelity, Rojas allows us to suspect the worst of Melibea. The go-betweens in each succumb to the fates they arrange, but unlike Pandarus, who incarnates a valid pragmatism, Celestina demonstrates the very negation of meaning. The authorial voices, Parmeno and Pleberio, pay more dearly for the lovers' passion than their counterpart in *TC*, who merely feels a "doble sorwe."

119.   Mieszkowski, Gretchen. "R. K. Gordon and the *Troilus and Criseyde* Story." *ChauR* 15(1981):127–37.

227

Gordon's translation of *Le Roman de Troie* distorts Benoît by omitting important passages. The most critical omission is one of a moralizing nature which emphasizes the fickleness of Criseyde and all women. Gordon must have been influenced by the gentle interpretation of Criseyde current in his time.

120. Olmert, Michael. "Troilus in *Piers Plowman*: A Contemporary View of Chaucer's *Troilus and Criseyde*." *Chaucer Newsletter* 2,ii(1980):13–14.

The verb *troiledest* ("deceived"; *Piers Plowman*, C, xxi, 321), a *hapax legomenon* introduced in 1393 when *TC* was at its most popular, may be a reference to the treachery recorded in Chaucer's poem. Langland uses it to refer to Satan's temptation of Adam and Eve.

121. Taylor, Ann M. "A Scriptural Echo in the Trojan Parliament of *Troilus and Criseyde*." *Nottingham Medieval Studies* 24(1980):51–56.

Chaucer's presentation of a Trojan parliament unanimously resolving, despite the reasonable objections of Hector, to exchange an innocent Criseyde for a wicked Antenor (*TC* IV, 141–217), makes allusions to the trial of Christ before Pilate; Chaucer's sources do not. In *TC* the biblical echoes serve to characterize the depth of Troilus' sorrow, and may also indirectly criticize Troilus' immoderate love for Criseyde.

122. Wimsatt, James I. "Realism in *Troilus and Criseyde* and the *Roman de la Rose*." In *Chaucer Studies III: Essays on Troilus and Criseyde*. Ed. Mary Salu. Cambridge: Brewer, 1979, pp. 43–56.

Two major sources of the realism in *TC* are the Platonic cosmic fables (e.g., the *Boece*) and the arts of love or handbooks for lovers, particularly the *Pamphilus*. The fables would seem far removed from realism; however, their writers' concern with human generation makes them useful to the *TC* poet in his endeavor to create realism. The *Roman de la Rose* also made use of these sources, but in a different way. And the presence of these influences in no way detracts from Chaucer's originality.

See also: 133

TC—The Themes of Love, Fortune, Religion

123. Andrews, Barbara Hakken. "Value in Love: A Materialist Analysis of Chaucer's *Troilus and Criseyde.*" *DAI* 40(1980):5855A.

The central issue for interpretation in *TC* is the nature and source of human value. The two primary ways in which values are established and tested in the poem are through the use of a significant amount of philosophical material relating to the problem of freedom of the human will, and by the creation of a socio-cultural structure which emerges from the dialectical interaction between the 'courtly love' aspects of the poem and the specific historical setting of the Trojan war. The dynamic of the poem can be described as the interplay between the philosophical and the socio-cultural elements.

124. Frankis, John. "Paganism and Pagan Love in *Troilus and Criseyde.*" In *Chaucer Studies III: Essays on Troilus and Criseyde.* Ed. Mary Salu. Cambridge: Brewer, 1979, p. 57–72.

The pagan references in *TC* perform two obvious functions: they provide local color and they help to delineate character (as in Pandarus' scorn of Troilus—who has just uttered a prayer to several pagan deities—calling him a "mouses hert," III, 736). But, more important, the failure of the love affair and the ultimate failure of the pagan gods to protect the lovers reveals the triviality and transience of various aspects of human experience, while at the same time leaving the reader with an impression of the lasting value of these things.

125. Newman, Barbara. " 'Feynede Loves,' Feigned Love, and Faith in Trouthe." In *Chaucer's Troilus: Essays in Criticism.* Ed. Stephen A. Barney. Hamden, Conn.: Shoestring P, 1980, pp. 257–75.

The dichotomy between *trouthe* (fidelity) and truth (actuality) marks *TC* from the outset. *Trouthe* in love is linked to *routhe* and *kyndenesse*, and on every level is compromised by the characters' feigning. Moreover, the proverbs which are so much a part of the poem, are equivocal inasmuch as they are both prophetic and ironic. The narrator, finally disillusioned with the feigned love and lore, arrives at his own version of *trouthe*.

126. Taylor, Karla. "Proverbs and the Authentication of Convention in *Troilus and Criseyde.*" In *Chaucer's Troilus: Essays in Criticism.* Ed. Stephen A. Barney. Hamden, Conn.: Shoestring P, 1980, pp. 277–96.

In conflating love and poetics in *TC*, Chaucer uses proverbs both to validate truth and to express the limitations of traditional language. The attempt to secure stability through this language and the failure of the attempt are part of Chaucer's deliberate strategy. The conventional language, depicting love as a religious experience and a hunt, is to be seen as different from love itself; and Chaucer finally dissociates himself from the equivocal language of this world which confuses words with reality.

127. Toole, William B., III. "The Imagery of Fortune and Religion in *Troilus and Criseyde*." In *A Fair Day in the Affections: Literary Essays in Honor of Robert B. White, Jr.* Ed. Jack M. Durant and M. Thomas Hester. Raleigh, NC: Winston, 1980, pp. 25–35.

In developing the theme that Troilus values too highly love and beauty in this world, Chaucer throughout *TC* intertwines imagery of Fortune and of religion to describe Troilus' experiences and to characterize Criseyde. Although the depiction of Criseyde is psychologically credible, it also has important figurative implications, for she is linked to intricate image patterns of circularity and turning wheels which are usually associated with Fortune.

128. Wetherbee, Winthrop. "The Descent from Bliss: *Troilus*, III, 1310–1582." In *Chaucer's Troilus: Essays in Criticism*. Ed. Stephen A. Barney. Hamden, Conn.: Shoestring P, 1980, pp. 297–317.

Chaucer is concerned with showing the consequences of the consummation of the love of Troilus and Criseyde as it concerns both characters and narrator. The events following this consummation scene also broadly parallel those in Dante's *Purgatorio* from Canto 19 to the end.

TC—Narrative Technique

129. Boyd, Jessie Mary Heather. "Figurative Patterns in the Poetry of Chaucer with Special Reference to *Troilus and Criseyde* and Selected *Canterbury Tales*." *DAI* 40(1980):4585A.

For Chaucer, a poem was an imaginative focus for the representation of a larger pattern of experience. The patterns created by the opposing figures of speech in his poetry (the concrete and empirical / the archetypal) reflect a complex sense of duality, and are used to create a perspective which is characteristically inclusive, moving from everyday, earthly life to the realm of the abstract and the spiritual. The spiral-like circular pattern in *TC* stands for a view of history and of human experience which is perceived in a series of cycles that do not repeat themselves but move gradually to completion. In *CT*, rhetoric and style work their variations from one teller to the next as each view of experience gives way to another.

130.   Dahlberg, Charles. "The Narrator's Frame for *Troilus.*" *ChauR* 15(1980):85–100.

Opening and closing stanzas of *TC* combine high, epic style with *sermo humilis*, creating a rising and sinking pattern of 'unlikeness.' The verse and rhetoric reflect the meanings, the sublimest points made in simplest statement. The conclusion thus parallels the opening pattern.

131.   McGunnigle, Michael Gerard. "Romanticized History and Historicized Romance: Narrative Styles and Strategies in Four Middle English Troy Poems." *DAI* 41(1980):2616A.

The genres of history and romance in Middle English Troy poems are distinguished by contrasting attitudes towards sources and the historicity of the subject; by a corresponding contrast in attitudes towards the historical distance between past and present, pagan and Christian; and by differences in thematic and structural unity. In Chaucer's *TC*, the historicizing values and strategies of a Christian translator co-exist with the romanticizing values and strategies attributed to the fictional pagan author, 'Lollius.' Chaucer's use of this dual persona is shown to be a technique for reconciling pagan and Christian values and for harmonizing the historicizing and romanticizing tendencies.

132.   McKinnell, John. "Letters as a Type of the Formal Level in *Troilus and Criseyde.*" In *Chaucer Studies III: Essays on Troilus and Criseyde.* Ed. Mary Salu. Cambridge: Brewer, 1979, pp. 73–89.

Trivet's commentary on Seneca's *Hercules Furens*, which Chaucer may have known, reveals that medieval theorists gave weight to the 'formal cause' of tragedy. In *TC*, the interpolated songs, dreams, prayers, and letters may be analyzed as elements that comprise, in part, this 'formal cause.' The letters often follow the prescriptions of the contemporaneous *artes dictaminis*. Letters were considered the repository of the spoken word, and therefore we should not imagine that they would cause any problem in a poem that was doubtless read aloud. They serve to shed light on the characters who composed them, comment on them, or respond to them in other ways.

TC—Characterization

133. Bisceglia, Julie Jeanne. "Paradigms of Personality: Chaucer's *Troilus and Criseyde* and the Traditions of Ovid and Dante." *DAI* 41(1980):258A.

TC can be read with two distinct poetic traditions in mind: the serious, Platonic ideal represented by Dante, which desires absolute truth, purposeful behavior, and an immutable self; and the Ovidian rhetorical ideal which upholds behavior shaped by circumstances and the role-playing self. Chaucer uses his love-story paradigmatically to show how each kind of self acts and reacts. He sets in motion four possible ways to organize the world; Troilus, the unself-conscious, serious, committed self; Criseyde, the unself-conscious, role-playing self; Pandarus, the self-conscious role player; and the narrator, the self-conscious, serious self; and then shows the consequences each one has, both for the individual and those around him.

134. Jimura, Akiyuki. "Chaucer's Depiction of Characters through Adjectives: Troilus and Criseyde." *The Ohtani Studies* (July 30, 1980):1–20.

The admirable and delicate precision with which each character is portrayed in Chaucer's works depends on the poet's skillful use of adjectives and similes. The writer illustrates this fact with particular reference to the descriptions of Troilus and Criseyde.

TC—Criseyde

135. Arn, Mary-Jo. "Three Ovidian Women in Chaucer's *Troilus*: Medea, Helen, Oënone." *ChauR* 15(1980):1–10.

Similarities to Ovid's young Medea give Criseyde's character innocence; to Helen, guile and reluctance to decide; while references to Oënone prefigure treachery in the connection to Paris' betrayal and the war. Ovidian references undercut the action, creating irony and richer narrative.

136. Bowers, John M. "How Criseyde Falls in Love." In *The Expansion and Transformation of Courtly Literature*. Ed. Nathaniel B. Smith and Joseph T. Snow. Athens: U of Georgia P, 1980, pp. 141–55.

The visual image of Troilus on his horse, which Criseyde sees from her window, is connected to the earlier image of Troilus as a horse. The horse image, with its suggestions of lust and pride, is associated with both Troilus and Criseyde.

137. David Alfred. "Chaucerian Comedy and Criseyde." In *Chaucer Studies III: Essays on Troilus and Criseyde*. Ed. Mary Salu. Cambridge: Brewer, 1979, pp. 90–104.

Recently critical emphasis has been upon the sustained irony in the tragic tale of *TC*. Along with it is a peculiarly Chaucerian kind of comedy that may best be labeled 'bodily laughter,' because although it laughs *at* the body, it does so out of sympathy in order to affirm, not to deny, the body's values. Unlike the prototypical Boccaccian heroine, Chaucer's creation is endowed with a sense of humor. Further, the poet makes fun of her quintessential femininity, as it was seen in the Middle Ages, perhaps in stereotype. Even in the increasingly sad Books IV and V, her comic values remain. For a worthy continuation of this kind of comedy we look to *CT* and to *WBP*. Though Alison of Bath is different in many ways from Criseyde, she nevertheless shares many attributes, including the comic-pathetic one whereby both are comic heroines who go round and round on Fortune's wheel and who believe in the future, beating against the current even as they are borne back ceaselessly into the past.

138. Lambert, Mark. "*Troilus*, Books I–III: A Criseydan Reading." In *Chaucer Studies III: Essays on Troilus and Criseyde*. Ed. Mary Salu. Cambridge: Brewer, 1979, pp. 105–25.

C. S. Lewis was right to emphasize Criseyde's timorousness. She is unambitious and moderate, and the cosy, unheroic situation in Troy in the first three books suits her well. It is a slightly childlike and unworldly situation—as contrasted with the adult and urbane world of the Greek camp. Though Troilus may be the titular hero of the poem, surely Criseyde is the more memorable and the more fully developed creation, and much of the strength of the Criseydan strain in *TC* comes from the peculiar affinity of Criseyde and what finally is not just Thesean man, but Chaucerian man. She and not the poem's hero may be the more profoundly autobiographical creation.

TC—Troilus

139. Gaylord, Alan T. "The Lesson of the *Troilus*: Chastisement and Correction." In *Chaucer Studies III: Essays on Troilus and Criseyde*. Ed. Mary Salu. Cambridge: Brewer, 1979, pp. 1–22.

Modernist critics reduce Troilus' experience to sentimentality. They encourage us to pity the hero because he could not do otherwise. The lesson of *TC* is, on the contrary, that the characters in the tale (and we the audience) do indeed have choices to make, and that we can assert ourselves and our reason through action. Despite his prolonged and gnarled disquisition on free will in Book IV, Troilus abandons himself to passivity, as does Criseyde. The 'chastisement' of which Chaucer speaks is a learning process, as the word used in medieval thought had as its root instruction. Thus while the modernists devise complex, balancing structures of dichotomies, they inevitably demean Chaucer's medieval humanism, which was based on an uncomplicated belief in the freedom of the will and the splendor of reason.

140. Mann, Jill. "Troilus' Swoon." *ChauR* 14(1980):319–35.

Chaucer's addition of Troilus' swoon allows reestablishment of *obeisaunce* critical to Criseyde's loving him, and threatened by Pandarus' story of his jealousy and his own inability to refute or continue it. Mutual apologies suggest mutual surrender and Chaucer's attention to the fine points of relationships.

141. Olmert, Michael. "Troilus and a Classical Pander: *TC* III, 729–30." *Chaucer Newsletter* 1,i(1979):18–19.

Troilus' prayer to Mercury is ill-considered. The god's diffident and finally unsuccessful attempt to bed Herse brings disaster to the go-between Aglauros. Further, the reference to this affair draws a pointed contrast between Pandarus and Herse's silent sister Pandrosos.

141a. Taylor, Davis. "The Terms of Love: A Study of Troilus' Style." In *Chaucer's Troilus: Essays in Criticism*. Ed. Stephen A. Barney. Hamden: Shoestring, 1980, pp. 231–56.

In *TC*, Chaucer uses specific stylistic conventions of medieval love poetry (recurrent superlatives, absolute commitments, and extended monologues) to characterize Troilus. Through his use of irony, Chaucer questions the moral and practical implications of Troilus' behavior and language and explores Troilus' believability as a character. Chaucer's conventional rhetoric increases its moral significance when spoken by a lover, Troilus, whose behavior and self-consciousness is consistent.

TC—Pandarus

142.   Cormican, John D. "Motivation of Pandarus in *Troilus and Criseyde*." *USF Language Quarterly* 18(1980):43–48.

Whatever his name may suggest, Pandarus was himself a true lover, holding love and friendship, though subject to the vicissitudes of Fortune, as the highest human values. Endowed with social grace and committed to friendship, Pandarus pretends not to realize that his friend's love affair is ended until Troilus himself gains that insight.

143.   Fyler, John M. "The Fabrications of Pandarus." *MLQ*, 41(1980):115–30.

Just as *TC* is 'distanced' from the reader by its setting during the Trojan War, so too does Pandarus blur the lines between reality and fiction. The 'real' world is an illusion; the little world of the lovers is all that is real. Ironically, Pandarus' fabrications turn out to be true—e.g., the invention of the fictional rival Horaste forces the guiltless heroine to defend herself against a charge that will soon enough be true, when she falls into Diomede's hands. There is a feeling that Pandarus' lies—like the poem itself and like God's own creation—are transitory but nonetheless alluring and delightful.

144.   Slocum, Sally K. "How Old Is Chaucer's Pandarus?" *PQ* 58(1979):16–25.

Evidence suggests Pandarus is a peer to Troilus and hardly older than Criseyde, probably around thirty. The younger age eliminates harsh judgments on his involvement in their love affair and on behavior deemed lecherous in an older man.

Book of the Duchess

145. Ebi, Hisato. "Light and Darkness in *The Book of the Duchess*—The 'Aesthetics of Light' of Gothic Art." *The Journal of The Liberal Arts Department, Kansai Medical University* (December 1980), pp. 15–126.

Pseudo Dionysius Areopagita's theory of "One Light of God" had very much to do with the rich achievements of Gothic art. Consciously or unconsciously, Chaucer was a man in the High Gothic era. In *BD* his aesthetic idea is clearly presented by the fine counterpointing of 'white' and 'black' and the metaphor of 'light.'

146. Ferster, Judith. "Intention and Interpretation in the *Book of the Duchess*." *Criticism* 22(1980):1–24.

The primary mode of discourse, conversation, emphasizes the difficulty of communication. *BD* oscillates between two opposing views: the existence and the dissolution of the self and the other. Chaucer gives the reader an awareness of the conditions that shape interaction; language may cure this isolation or intensify it. *BD* is an account of successful communication between the Black Knight and the narrator.

147. Salter, Elizabeth. "Chaucer and Internationalism." *SAC* 2(1980):71–79.

Chaucer's writing of *BD* in English is not evidence of English nationalism but is "the triumph of internationalism." He adopted "both theory and precedent for the creation of high-prestige vernacular literature" to produce in English the kind of artistic work his contemporaries were producing in French.

148. Shoaf, R. A. "Stalking the Sorrowful H(e)art: Penitential Lore and the Hunt Scene in Chaucer's *The Book of the Duchess*." *JEGP* 78(1979):313–24.

The poet in *BD* takes the role of confessor and *medicus animae* to the Black Knight, whose shrift and repentance return him to the duties of everyday living. The hunt, which sets the scene, is an allegorical image of the process of confession pointing out the obvious ambiguity of the hart/heart imagery.

See also: 10 35 43

Parliament of Fowls

149.   Donaldson, E. Talbot. "Venus and the Mother of Romulus: The *Parliament of Fowls* and the *Pervigilium Veneris.*" *ChauR* 14(1980):313–18.

J. E. Hankins' view of the *Pervigilium Veneris* as a source for *PF* has not caught on because no one has yet found a persuasive verbal echo. Such an echo appears in the list of persons love has destroyed: *PF*, 286–92 has a counterpart in *Pervigilium*, 69–74.

150.   Fujiki, Takayoshi. "Chaucer's 'love' in *The Parlement of Fouls.*" *Shuku-gawa Studies in Linguistics and Literature* 4(1980):1–13.

The puzzling character of the earthly love and life of human beings is what *PF* tries to explore and discover. Chaucer revealed an irrational aspect of humanity in this work.

151.   Olson, Paul A. "*The Parlement of Foules*: Aristotle's *Politics* and the Foundations of Human Society." *SAC* 2(1980):53–69.

The discussion of love between men and women is the vehicle for discussing the nature of society and social love. The parliament itself—a talking together—represents the means provided to fallen man for discovering how to achieve the common profit, natural law's equivalent to charity.

152.   Reed, Thomas L. "Chaucer's *Parlement of Foules*: The Debate Tradition and the Aesthetics of Irresolution." *Revue de l'Université d'Ottawa* 50(1980):215–22.

The bird parliament accords with scholastic and literary forms of the debate, including the terminology which characterizes the tradition. Typical of the literary debate, *PF* ends without any clear decision on either side. The initial *demande d'amour* gives way to the opposition of courtly idealism and bourgeois pragmatism, and the validity of all earthly love is questioned by Scipio's dream. Thus Chaucer turns the debate to refreshingly ambivalent ends.

153.   Tenebruso, Marie Yrsa. "Chaucer's *Parlement of Foules*: An Interpretation Based upon a Structural Analysis of Rhetorical Usage." *DAI* 40(1980):5856A.

In spite of the limitations imposed on Chaucer by virtue of his socially inferior position in relation to his courtly audiences, his thorough mastery of rhetorical principles and techniques allowed him to transmit his *sententia*, namely, the necessity of abandonment of passionate, unreasonable love, as often exemplified in an *amour courtois* relationship, at peril of damnation of one's immortal soul.

154.   Yamamoto, Toshiki. "Chaucer and *The Parliament of Fowls*." *Essays on Classical Studies* (March 1980):40–50.

A discussion of the characteristics of Nature in *PF*.

See also: 10

House of Fame

155.   Hiraoka, Teruaki. "A Japanese Translation of *The House of Fame*, III, 1091–1656." *Mimesis* 12(1980):41–50.

156.   Kanno, Masahiko. "The Meaning of *The House of Fame*." In *Essays in Honour of Professor Hiroshige Yoshida*. Shinozaki Shorin Press, 1980, pp. 47–57.

The narrator of this work, pretending ignorance, is conscious of his position as a poet, and shows a humorous but skeptical attitude towards utterance. Like a nominalist, he examines everyday speech, which is only "eyr ybroken," from the point of view of 'appearence' and 'existence,' solving their contradiction through the natural reconciliation of 'statement' with 'deed.'

See also: 10

Legend of Good Women

157.   Hahn, Thomas. "Natural Supernaturalism in the *Prologue* to the *Legend of Good Women*." *Chaucer Newsletter* 1,i(1979):7–8.

The prologue of *LGW* is a kind of *ars poetica* that contrasts seasonal renewal with eternal regeneration in order to show that poetry can mediate between them and serve as a true guide to love.

158.   McMillan, Ann Hunter. " 'Evere an Hundred Goode ageyn Oon Badde': Catalogues of Good Women in Medieval Literature." *DAI* 40(1980):5437A.

The labels 'antifeminism' and 'courtly love' misrepresent the medieval literary treatment of women. Three types—the chaste wife, the 'manly' virgin, and the martyr of love—dominate the catalogues through the Middle Ages. Chaucer drew mainly upon the idea of love's martyrs from Ovid and Vergil, and the question of what makes a good woman becomes for him an aspect of the larger conflicts between men and women and between authority and experience. In *LGW* and *CT* the catalogues reveal more about their tellers than about women. Chaucer's development of characterization reaches its culmination in Dorigen and the Wife of Bath.

159.   Shigeo, Hisashi. "Chaucer's Idea of 'Love' and 'Goodness' in *The Legend of Good Women.*" *The Meiji Gakuin Review* (October 1980):37–54.

The stories about Hypsipyle, Medea, Lucrece, and Ariadne are treated. In each case it seems that the poet finds feminine virtue in masculine vice. Except for the case of Lucrece, simplicity and flippancy on the part of women are exempted from moral denunciation.

160.   Waller, Martha S. "The Conclusion of Chaucer's *Legend of Lucrece*: Robert Holcot and the Great Faith of Women." *Chaucer Newsletter* 2,i(1980):10–12.

Holcot is a source for the conclusion of *Lucrece*: his *In Librum Sapientie* includes (1) the statement, not in the Gospels, that Christ found greater faith in women than in men, and (2) a catalogue of pagan good women including Lucretia and others in *LGW*.

See also: 87

ABC

161.   Crampton, Georgia Ronan. "Of Chaucer's *ABC*." *Chaucer Newsletter* 1,i(1979):8–9.

ABC is not polite praise of the Virgin or gentle expression of filial love: it is a needy, fearful, grasping cry for her protection, evincing the greed, craft, and importunity of a child seeking its mother's reassurance.

162.   Hagiwara, Fumihiko. "Chaucer's *ABC*—A Japanese Translation." *Prose and Poetry* 35(1980):5.

The first Japanese translation of the work with a brief explanatory introduction.

Former Age

163.   Schmidt, A.V.C. "Chaucer's *Nembrot*: A Note on *The Former Age*." *MÆ* 47(1978):304–07.

Nimrod ("Nembrot") is the only biblical figure in "The Former Age." The detail that he designed the Tower of Babel is traditional, but Chaucer's reference in this poem seems to be derived directly from Walafrid Strabo's *Glossa Ordinaria*.

164.   Witlieb, Bernard. "Jupiter and Nimrod in *The Former Age*." *Chaucer Newsletter* 2,ii(1980):12–13.

Ovide Moralisé is a source for Chaucer's depiction of Jupiter and Nimrod in *Form Age*.

Truth

165.   Gillmeister, Heiner. "The Whole Truth about *Vache*." *Chaucer Newsletter* 2,i(1980):13–14.

In *Truth* the reference to Vache is not to Sir Philip de la Vache but to Chaucer.

240

"Vache, leve" translates the OF phrase "reis, vache!" which is (e)Chavsier spelled backwards. The reversal of letters points to a real conversion in Chaucer.

Romaunt of the Rose

See: 122

Boece

See: 122

Book Reviews

166.   Aers, David. *Chaucer, Langland, and the Creative Imagination.* Rev. Paul Strohm, *Criticism* 22(1980):376–77; Victoria Rothchild, *TLS* Aug. 8, 1980, p. 901.

167.   Boyd, Beverly, ed. *Chaucer According to William Caxton.* Rev. Richard R. Griffith, *SAC* 2(1980):151–53.

168.   Brewer, Derek S. *Chaucer: The Critical Heritage.* Rev. T. A. Shippey, *TLS* Nov. 30, 1979, p. 73.

169.   Burlin, Robert B. *Chaucerian Fiction.* Rev. A. J. Minnis, *MÆ* 49(1980): 145–49; Robert M. Jordan, *Review* 2(1980):49–69; Russell A. Peck, *SAC* 2(1980):154–58.

170.   Davis, Norman, Douglas Gray, Patricia Ingham, and Anne Wallace-Hadrill. *A Chaucer Glossary.* Rev. Basil Cottle, *RES* 31(1980):445–46; T. A. Shippey, *TLS* Nov. 30, 1979, p. 73.

171.   Fyler, John M. *Chaucer and Ovid.* Rev. Elaine Tuttle Hansen, *MLQ* 41(1980): 90–93; Lisa J. Kiser, *MP* 78(1980):167–69; T. A. Shippey, *TLS* Nov. 30, 1979, p. 73; R. W. Hanning, *SAC* 2(1980):159–65.

172. Gilbert, A. J. *Literary Language from Chaucer to Johnson*. Rev. Basil Cottle, *TLS* March 14, 1980, p. 300.

173. Haskell, Ann S. *Essays on Chaucer's Saints*. Rev. Thomas R. Liszka, *SAC* 2(1980):165–67.

174. Jones, Terry. *Chaucer's Knight: The Portrait of a Medieval Mercenary*. Rev. J. A. Burrow, *TLS* Feb. 15, 1980, p. 163.

175. Lewis, Robert E., ed. *De Miseria Condicionis Humane*. Rev. Daniel Silvia, *SAC* 2(1980):167–72.

176. McAlpine, Monica E. *The Genre of 'Troilus and Criseyde.'* Rev. Robert S. Haller, *SAC* 2(1980):172–79.

177. Metlitzki, Dorothee. *The Matter of Araby in Medieval England*. Rev. Edgar Hill Duncan, *SAC* 2(1980):181–87.

178. Miller, Robert P., ed. *Chaucer: Sources and Backgrounds*. Rev. Bruce A. Rosenberg, *SAC* 2(1980):187–90.

179. Möske, Birgit. *Caritas: Ihre figurative Darstellung in der englischen Literatur des 14. bis 16. Jahrhunderts*. Rev. Stephen L. Wailes, *SAC* 2(1980):194–96.

180. Owen, Charles A., Jr. *Pilgrimage & Storytelling in* The Canterbury Tales: *The Dialectic of "Ernest" and "Game."* Rev. Gerald Morgan, *ES* 61(1980):462–65; Thomas J. Garbáty, *SAC* 2(1980):196–202.

181. Rowe, Donald, W. *O Love, O Charite! Contraries Harmonized in Chaucer's Troilus*. Rev. Ralph W. V. Elliot, *ES* 61(1980):367–69; Jörg O. Fichte, *Anglia* 98(1980):489–92.

182. Salu, Mary, ed. *Essays on Troilus and Criseyde*. Rev. T. A. Shippey, *TLS* July 4, 1980, p. 753.

183.   Salu, Mary, and Robert T. Farrell, eds. *J. R. R. Tolkien, Scholar and Storyteller: Essays in Memoriam*. Rev. Emerson Brown, Jr., *SAC* 2(1980): 204–07.

184.   Schaefer, Ursula. *Höfisch-ritterliche Dichtung und sozialhistorische Realität . . . bei Chaucer*. Rev. Howell Chickering, *SAC* 2(1980):207–11.

185.   Tripp, Raymond P., Jr. *Beyond Canterbury: Chaucer, Humanism, and Literature*. Rev. Alan T. Gaylord, *SAC* 2(1980):211–18.

Author Index—Bibliography

Aers, David   166
Ainsworth, Jeanette Therese   117
Andersen, Wallis May   34
Anderson, David   60
Ando, Shinsuke   38
Andreas, James R.   39
Andrews, Barbara Hakken   123
Arn, Mary-Jo   135
Bazire, Joyce   1
Besserman, Lawrence   82
Bisceglia, Julie Jeanne   133
Bowden, Betsy   15
Bowers, John M.   136
Boyd, Beverly   167
Boyd, Jessie Mary Heather   129
Brewer, Derek S.   168
Brown, Emerson, Jr.   5, 6, 109, 183
Brown, Peter   71
Burlin, Robert B.   169
Burrow, J. A.   174
Cahn, Kenneth S.   89
Caluwé-Dor, Juliette de   25
Chickering, Howell   184
Clark, Susan L.   73
Coletti, Theresa   95
Collette, Carolyn P.   99
Cooper, Geoffrey   65
Cormican, John D.   142
Correale, Robert M.   103, 112
Cottle, Basil   170, 172
Crampton, Georgia Ronan   161
Crépin, André   104
Crider, Richard   105
Crisp, Delmas Swinfield, Jr.   50
Crowther, J. D. W.   85
Dahlberg, Charles   130
Dane, Joseph A.   66
David, Alfred   137
Davis, Norman   170
DeWeever, Jacqueline   26

Donaldson, E. Talbot   16, 149
Dulick, Michael George   118
Duncan, Edgar Hill   177
Ebi, Hisato   145
Elliot, Ralph W. V.   181
Farrell, Robert T.   183
Ferster, Judith   146
Fichte, Jörg O.   181
Fisher, John H.   2
Frankis, John   124
Fujiki, Takayoshi   150
Fujimoto, Masashi   92
Fulk, R. D.   110
Fyler, John M.   143, 171
Garbáty, Thomas J.   180
Gaylord, Alan T.   139, 185
Gilbert, A. J.   17
Gillmeister, Heiner   165
Goodall, Peter   67
Graham, Paul Trees   35
Gray, Douglas   170
Griffith, Richard R.   167
Gugelberger, Georg   17
Hagiwara, Fumihiko   162
Hahn, Thomas   157
Haller, Robert S.   176
Hamel, Mary   100
Hanning, Robert W.   61, 171
Hansen, Elaine Tuttle   171
Hardman, C. B.   18
Hardman, Phillipa   87
Haskell, Ann S.   173
Hassan-Yusuff, Z. Dolly   83
Heffernan, Carol Falvo   51, 72
Higgs, Elton D.   52
Hilary, Christine Ryan   40
Hira, Toshinori   41
Hiraoka, Teruaki   155
Hoeber, Daniel R.   62
Ingham, Patricia   170

Ikegami, Tadahiro   3, 8, 19
Ikegami, Yoshihiko   27
Jacobs, Edward Craney   101
Jimura, Akiyuki   134
Johnston, Mark E.   107
Jones, Terry   174
Jordan, Robert M.   169
Jungman, Robert E.   96
Justman, Stewart   53
Kaminsky, Alice R.   114
Kanno, Masahiko   156
Kelly, Henry Ansgar   42
Kern, Edith   9
Kirby, Thomas A.   4
Kiser, Lisa J.   171
Klene, Jean, C.S.C.   43
Knight, Stephen   10
Kossick, S. G.   90
Lambert, Mark   138
Leicester, H. Marshall, Jr.   54
Lewis, Robert E.   175
Liszka, Thomas R.   173
Loftin, Alice   44
Luengo, Anthony E.   113
MacCurdy, Marian Mesrobian   45
Mack, Maynard   20
Mann, Jill   11, 140
Marshall, David F.   111
McAlpine, Monica E.   97, 176
McCobb, Lillian, M.   63
McGrady, Donald   55
McGunnigle, Michael Gerard   131
McKenna, Conán   98
McKinnell, John   132
McMillan, Ann Hunter   158
Metlitzki, Dorothee   177
Middleton, Anne   56, 88
Mieszkowski, Gretchen   119
Miller, Robert P.   178
Mills, David   1
Milosh, Joseph E., Jr.   68
Minnis, A. J.   169
Morgan, Gerald   180
Morgan, Mary Valentina   36
Möske, Birgit   179
Nelson, Joseph Edward   64
Newman, Barbara   125
Nitzsche, Jane C.   69
Olmert, Michael   120, 141

Olsen, Alexandra Hennessey   21
Olson, Paul A.   151
Owen, Charles A., Jr.   7, 48, 180
Palmer, Barbara D.   76
Peck, Russell A.   169
Reames, Sherry L.   108
Reed, Thomas L.   152
Reisner, M. E.   77
Reiss, Edmund   31
Revard, Carter   70
Ridley, Florence H.   12
Robertson, D. W., Jr.   78
Roddy, Kevin   74
Rogers, William E.   13
Rosenberg, Bruce A.   93, 178
Ross, Thomas, W.   28
Rothchild, Victoria   166
Rowe, Donald W.   181
Rowland, Beryl   22
Runde, Joseph   37
Saito, Isamu   32
Salmon, Vivian   56a
Salter, Elizabeth   147
Salu, Mary   182, 183
Scattergood, V. J.   23
Schaefer, Ursula   184
Schleusener, Jay   91
Schmidt, A. V. C.   163
Schulenburg, Jane Tibbetts   79
Schuman, Samuel   46
Shigeo, Hisashi   159
Shikii, Kumiko   57, 102
Shippey, T. A.   14, 168, 170, 171, 182
Shoaf, R. A.   148
Silvia, Daniel   175
Sklute, Larry   59
Sleeth, Charles   75
Slocum, Sally K.   144
Spraycar, Rudy S.   47
Stokes, Myra   115
Strohm, Paul   33, 166
Stugrin, Michael   58
Takamiya, Toshiyuki   29
Taylor, Ann M.   121
Taylor, Davis   141a
Taylor, Karla   126
Tenebruso, Marie Yrsa   153
Terasawa, Yoshio   30
Toole, William B., III   127

Tripp, Raymond P., Jr.   185
Turner, Robert K.   24
Wailes, Stephen L.   179
Wallace-Hadrill, Anne   170
Waller, Martha S.   160
Wasserman, Julian N.   73
Watanabe, Ikuo   94
Weissman, Hope Phyllis   49, 80, 81

Wentersdorf, Karl P.   86, 106
Wetherbee, Winthrop   128
Wimsatt, James I.   122
Windeatt, Barry   116
Witlieb, Bernard   164
Yamamoto, Toshiki   154
Zellefrow, W. Ken   84

Letter From The Editor

This fourth issue of *Studies in the Age of Chaucer* marks the end of my service as editor of the New Chaucer Society's yearbook. I shall be spending the upcoming academic year on sabbatical leave at the University of Queensland in Brisbane, Australia, and at La Fondation Camargo in Cassis in the south of France, and the problems I apprehend in attempting to continue with the editorship under those circumstances have persuaded me that this would be an appropriate time to resign the position and relinquish direction of the journal to my successor. At this moment of leave-taking, I would like to express my appreciation to the large—and necessarily largely anonymous—group of colleagues and friends who in various ways have helped make the rather daunting enterprise of launching a new journal on the long-populated sea of Chaucer scholarship both a profitable and a pleasing experience.

My thanks are due first of all to Professor Paul G. Ruggiers, the Executive Director, and to the initial Board of Trustees of the New Chaucer Society, for appointing me founder editor of the society's journal. I hope that the contribution made to date by the journal in promoting Chaucer studies has been such as to justify their confidence in its potential usefulness. Making some allowance for difficulties inherent in initiating a new venture of this kind, I must admit myself generally well pleased with its achievements. The policy favoring publication of comparatively long articles with a significantly theoretical bias which draw connections between Chaucer's works and their cultural matrix has established *Studies in the Age of Chaucer* as an independently valuable vehicle for the publication of Chaucer research of this nature, and, as the existence of the journal becomes better known among members of the scholarly community, is generating a constantly increasing number of submissions. It was not my intention as editor to exclude from the journal articles which dealt with fourteenth- or fifteenth-century authors other than Chaucer, or in a general way with the concerns of the late medieval English literary scene. That such articles have not appeared reflects the fact that few, if any, have been submitted for consideration, not that they have been systematically rejected. *Studies in the Age of Chaucer*, as its name implies, was conceived to embrace a wider range of interests than specifically and exclusively Chaucerian materials, and I would personally be gratified to see it becoming more catholic in its contents, but the new editor's ability to effect such a change, should he wish to do so, will depend on the willingness of future contributors to furnish him a wider spectrum of submissions from which to make his final selections.

A special debt of gratitude is owed to Professor John H. Fisher, who kindly undertook compilation of the annotated Chaucer bibliography, and to the numerous workers in this particular vineyard who volunteered assistance with the unglamorous task of writing annotations. They performed their assigned duties diligently and conscientiously. Their reward is most meaningfully to be found in the enthusiastic appreciation expressed by the Chaucer scholars who have profited from the results of their endeavors. I would also like to thank those colleagues who responded with such gracious cooperativeness to my invitations to review books, or who gave their time and special skills to evaluate manuscripts. Finally, it is my pleasure to acknowledge that without the contribution of editorial expertise and secretarial assistance from my wife Christine, *Studies in the Age of Chaucer* would undoubtedly have fallen far short of the professional standards of production on which she patiently but firmly insisted.

It remains to wish the new editor and the journal itself every success in the future.

Roy J. Pearcy
University of Oklahoma

Abbreviations for Chaucer's Works

ABC	An ABC
Adam	Adam Scriveyn
Anel	Anelida and Arcite
Astr	A Treatise on the Astrolabe
Bal Comp	A Balade of Complaint
BD	The Book of the Duchess
Bo	Boece
Buk	Lenvoy de Chaucer a Bukton
CkT	The Cook's Tale
ClT	The Clerk's Tale
Compl d'Am	Complaynt d'Amours
CT	The Canterbury Tales
CYT	The Canon's Yeoman's Tale
Equat	The Equatorie of the Planets
Form Age	The Former Age
For	Fortune
FranT	The Franklin's Tale
FrT	The Friar's Tale
GP	The General Prologue
Gent	Gentilesse
HF	The House of Fame
KnT	The Knight's Tale
Lady	Complaint to his Lady
LGW	The Legend of Good Women
MancT	The Manciple's Tale
Mars	The Complaint of Mars
Mel	The Tale of Melibee
MercB	Merciles Beaute
MerT	The Merchant's Tale
MilT	The Miller's Tale
MkT	The Monk's Tale
MLT	The Man of Law's Tale
NPT	The Nun's Priest's Tale
PardT	The Pardoner's Tale

249

ParsT	*The Parson's Tale*
PF	*The Parliament of Fowls*
PhyT	*The Physician's Tale*
Pity	*The Complaint unto Pity*
PrT	*The Prioress' Tale*
Prov	*Proverbs*
Purse	*The Complaint of Chaucer to his Purse*
Ret	*Chaucer's Retraction*
Rom	*The Romaunt of the Rose*
RvT	*The Reeve's Tale*
Ros	*To Rosemounde*
Scog	*Lenvoy de Chaucer a Scogan*
SNT	*The Second Nun's Tale*
ShT	*The Shipman's Tale*
SqT	*The Squire's Tale*
Sted	*Lak of Stedfastnesse*
SumT	*The Summoner's Tale*
Th	*The Tale of Sir Thopas*
TC	*Troilus and Criseyde*
Ven	*The Complaint of Venus*
WBT	*The Wife of Bath's Tale*
Wom Nob	*Womanly Noblesse*
Wom Unc	*Against Women Unconstant*

General Index

Abelson, Paul 36n
Ad C. Herennium 35, 36, 45
Alan of Lille *Anticlaudianus* 37, 103n
Albiruni 66
Albohazen Haly *De judicijs astrorum* 66n, 82
Alcuin 37, 38
Alfonso X, King of Castile 60
Anne of Bohemia 6
Aquinas, Saint Thomas 38
Arn, Mary-Jo 109n
Arzachel 60
Atkins, J. W. H. *English Literary Criticism: The Medieval Phase* 39n, 116n
Augustine, Saint 38, 117, 118; *De doctrina Christiana* 34, 36, 38
Auerbach, Erich *Literary Language and its Public in Late Latin Antiquity and in the Middle Ages* 42
Ayers, Robert W. 118n
Baker, Donald C. 34n
Bassett, Samuel E. 106n
Baum, Paull F. *Chaucer's Verse* 88n
Beauchamp, William 7
Benoît de Saint-Maure *Roman de Troie* 118n, 127
Bergen, Henry 23n
Boccaccio, Giovanni 110n; *Corbaccio* 48n; *Filostrato* 109, 127, 129n, 130; *Genealogie Deorum Gentilium Libri* 113n, 114n, 124, 125, 129n, 130n; *Teseida* 115; *Amorosa Visione* 123n
Bolton, W. F. 33n
Bowden, Betsy 46
Boyd, Beverly 11n
Bradley, Henry 14
Brae, A. E. 84, 85
Branca, Vittore 110n
Brembre, Nicholas 12
Brewer, Derek S. 10n, 17, 33n, 34n
Bronson, B. H. 33n

Browning, Robert 48
Brusendorff, Aage *The Chaucer Tradition* 5n, 21n
Bukton, Peter 6–12 passim
Bukton, Robert 12
Burke, J. J. 133n
Cambyses 32
Capella, Martianus 36, 38
Caplan, Harry 35n; *Of Eloquence* 38n
Cassell, Anthony K. 48n
Cawley, A. C. 87n
Caxton, William *Mirror of the World* 40
Cejador y Frauca, Julio 48n
Chambers, E. K. *The Mediaeval Stage* 42
Charland, Th. M. 39n
Charles d'Orleans 19
Chaucer *CT* 5–28 passim, 48, 49, 87–107; *GP* 44, 45, 57, *KnT* 5–25 passim, 49, 50, 57; *MilT* 24–31 passim, 49, *RvT* 49; *MLT* 13, 24, 25, 53–55, 58, 76–84, 112n; *FrT* 24, 45, 46, 90–103 passim; *SumT* 24, 46; *ClT* 24–31 passim; *MerT* 25, 56, 57; *SqT* 24, 25; *FranT* 24–26, 31, 53, 58–69, 76, 90–103 passim; *PhyT* 25, 49; *PardT* 24–27; *ShT* 24–27; *PrT* 24–31 passim, 49; *Th* 25, 94n; *Mel* 5, 7n, 16, 24–27, 31; *MkT* 24–27, 90–102 passim; *NPT* 45, 90–102 passim; *SNT* 24–27; *CYT* 24–27 passim; *MancT* 24, 25; *ParsT* 5, 24–27, 54, 55; *BD* 6, 16; *HF* 123n; *Anel* 21, 22; *PF* 10; *Boethius* 5, 7n, 21; *TC* 5, 12, 14, 23, 46–48, 109–33; *LGW* 6, 10, 16, 44; *Pity* 22; *Mars* 22, 58, 69–76, 82, 128; *For* 22; *Truth* 11, 22; *Gent* 11, 22; *Ven* 22; *Scog* 7–16 passim; *Buk* 13, 16; *Purse* 9n, 16, 22; *Astr* 80

Chenu, M.-D. *Nature, Man, and Society in the Twelfth Century* 116n

Christine de Pisan 10, 11; *Lavision-Christine* 10n

Cicero, Marcus Tullius 36–40 passim; *De Oratore* 35, 45

Clerval, Alexandre; *Les Écoles de Chartres* 42n

Clanvowe, John 6–14 passim; *The Boke of Cupide* 6, 10n

Clanvowe, Thomas 10

Clemoes, Peter *Liturgical Influence on Punctuation in Late Old and Early Middle English Manuscripts* 87n

Clifford, Lewis 6–14 passim; *Book of Tribulacion* 10

Clogan, Paul M. 109n, 114n, 120n; *The Medieval Achilleid of Statius* 124n

Coghill, Nevill 33n

Cohen, Ralph 3n, 4n

Comestor, Peter *Historia Scholastica* 117n, 122n

Conrad of Hirsau *Dialogus super Auctores* 113n

Constans, Léopold 117; *La Légende d'Oedipe* 117n

Costantini, Aldo Maria 110n

Crow, Martin M. *Chaucer Life-Records* 9n

Curry, Walter Clyde *Chaucer and the Medieval Sciences* 81n

Dame Sirith 42

Dante Alighieri *Commedia* 47, 123n; *Convivio* 114n

David, Alfred *The Strumpet Muse* 7n, 13, 16n, 28n

Davis, Norman *A Chaucer Glossary* 122n

Dederich, A. 130n

Deschamps, Eustache 6, 9

Dictys Cretensis *Ephemeridos Belli Troiani* 130n

Diomedes 104

Donatus, Aelius 104

Doyle, A. I. 87n, 88n

Dugdale, William *The Baronage of England* 9n, 10

Dunn, Peter M. 48n

Ebel, Julia 132n

Edward III, King of England 31

Edward, Duke of York *Master of Game* 21

Eisner, Sigmund 54n, 84

Erdmann, Axel 20n

Eusebius *Chronicon* 111–18 passim, 124n

Faral, Edmond 34n, 39n

Ferrand, Gabriel *Instructions nautiques et routiers arabes et portugais des XVe et XVIe siècles* 55n, 66n

Fisher, John H. *John Gower: Moral Philosopher and Friend of Chaucer* 13

Floris and Blancheflour 25

Floure and the Leafe 47

Fortunatianus, Chirius 36

Francis of Assisi, Saint 41

Frinchele, John 23

Froissart, Jean 9

Furnivall, F. J. 10, 17n, 21n

Fyler, John M. *Chaucer and Ovid* 109n

Gaertner, Otto *John Shirley: Sein Leben und Wirken* 20n, 21n

Garbáty, Thomas J. 94n

Gaylord, Alan T. 88n

Geoffrey of Vinsauf *Documentum de Modo et Arte Dictandi et Versificandi* 34, 35; *Poetria Nova* 39–45 passim

Gerritsen, W. P. 43

Gower, John 6–15 passim; *Confessio Amantis* 13; *Cronica* 13

Gransden, Antonia *Historical Writing in England, c. 550–c. 1307* 113n

Grant, Edward *A Source Book in Medieval Science* 62n

Green, Richard Firth *Poets and Prince-pleasers* 7n, 17–21 passim

Gretton, R. H. *The English Middle Class* 29n

Grierson, Herbert 32n

Guido delle Colonne *Historia Destructionis Troiae* 113n, 127, 130n

Guiraud, Pierre *La Versification* 106n

Gybbon-Monypenny, G. B. 48n

Halm, C. 36n, 37n

Haskins, C. H. *Studies in the History of Medieval Science* 113n

Hauser, Arnold 4, 5

Hawes, Stephen *The Pastime of Pleasure* 40

Helm, R. W. O. 111n

Henry IV, King of England 9–19 passim

Henry V, King of England 16–19 passim

Henry VI, King of England 8, 16

Henry of Hesse *Ars Predicandi* 38

Hermann, J. P. 133n

Higden, Ranulph 38; *Polychronicon* 10n, 110–13 passim

Hinckley, H. B. 64; *Notes on Chaucer* 64n, 66n

Hoccleve, Thomas 6–17 passim; *Male Regle* 17; *Complaint* 17; *Letter of Cupid* 19

Hodgson, Phyllis 59, 64

Holgrave, William 23

Holtz, Nancy Ann 69n

Horestes 32

Howard, Donald R. *The Idea of the Canterbury Tales* 49n

Howell, Wilbur Samuel 37n; *Logic and Rhetoric in England, 1500–1700* 39

Hugh of St. Victor 38, 116n

Hulbert, James *Chaucer's Official Life* 12n, 31n

Humphrey, Duke of Gloucester 8, 17

Hungerford, Walter 23

Huygens, R. B. C. 113n

Interludium de Clerico et Puella 43

Isidore of Seville *Etymologiarum* 37, 116

Jacob, E. F. *The Fifteenth Century* 11n, 15n, 16

Jameson, Fredric *The Political Unconscious* 4n

Jauss, Hans-Robert 3, 4

Jean of Angoulême 23

Jeffrey, David L. 42n

Jennings, Margaret, C.S.J. 38n

Jerome, Saint 111, 117

John of Garland 38

John of Gaunt 6

Johnson, Richard 37n

Juvenal *Satire VII* 124n

Kean, P. M. *Chaucer and the Making of English Poetry* 16n

Keil, Heinrich 105n, 106n

Kibler, William 5n

Kingsford, C. L. *Prejudice and Promise in Fifteenth Century England* 30n

Kittredge, George L. 12n; *Chaucer and His Poetry* 48n

Krüger, Karl H. *Die Universalchroniken* 113n

Krul, Leopold 39n

Kuhl, Ernest P. 12

Lawler, Traugott 38n

Lenaghan, R. T. 7

Lettenhove, Kervyn de 9n

Lindsay, W. M. 37n, 116n

Little, Lester K. 116n

Livre des Estoires 117n

Livy 116

Lote, Georges *Histoire de Vers Français* 106n

Lubac, Henri de *Exégèse Médiévale* 116n

Lucas, Peter J. 87n

Lumby, J. K. 10n

Lydgate, John 17, 20, 22; *Siege of Thebes* 20n, 21n, 117n, 118n; *Invocation to St. Anne* 21; *Complaint of the Black Knight* 21; *Departing of Thomas Chaucer* 21; *Dream of a Lover* 21; *Troy Book* 23

Magoun, Francis P., Jr. 121n

Manheim, Ralph 42n

Manly, John M. 22, 23n, 29, 102

Margarita philosophica 53

Marshall, Mary H. 43n

Mazzotta, Giuseppe *Dante Poet of the Desert: History and Allegory in the Divine Comedy* 116n

McCall, John P. 123n, 133n; *Chaucer among the Gods* 129n

McCormick, William *The Manuscripts of Chaucer's Canterbury Tales* 22n, 23n

McFarlane, K. B. *Lancastrian Kings and Lollard Knights* 8–10 passim, 31

McGregor, James H. 33n

Mead, William Edward 41n

Meek, Mary E. 113n

Meyer, Paul 117n

Middleton, Anne 7

Miskimin, Harry A. 29n, *The Economy of Early Renaissance Europe* 29n

Mitchell, Jerome 14n

Montagu, John 7–15 passim

Montaiglon, Anatole de 42n

Morgan, Margery M. 87n

Murphy, James J. 38n, 39n, 87n

Muscatine, Charles   20; *Chaucer and the French Tradition*   42n
Mustanoja, Tauno F.   88n
Neckham, Alexander   113n
Nicholas of Lynn *Kalendarium*   54, 83–85
Nims, Margaret F.   39n
North, J. D.   57n, 60n, 69n, 73n
Norton-Smith, John *Geoffrey Chaucer*   43n
Olson, Clair *Chaucer Life-Records*   9n
Orosius, Paulus *Historia Contra Paganos*   117, 118n
Osgood, Charles G.   *Boccaccio on Poetry*   124n, 125n
Ovid *Metamorphoses*   126n, 127n, 131n
Owen, Charles A., Jr.   24, 27
Padoan, Georgio   110n
Paratore, Ettore   124n
Parkes, M. B.   33n, 87n, 88n
Parlement of the Thre Ages   47
Parr, Johnstone   69
Pearsall, Derek   6, 7, 33n; *Old and Middle English Poetry*   7, 17n, 19n, 20
Petrarch, Francis *Seniles*   124n
Pirenne, Henri   29n, 30n
Plato   45
Postan, M. M.   29, 30
Preston, Raymond   27n
Quintillian, Marcus Fabius   36
Raby, F. J. E.   *A History of Christian-Latin Poetry from the Beginnings to the Close of the Middle Agess*   41n
Rackham, H.   35n
Ramsey, Roy Vance   88n, 90n
Rand, E. K.   43n, 114n, 130n
Raynaud, Gaston   10n, 42n
Regula Sacerdotis   21
Remigius of Auxerre   43
Renoir, Alan   120n
Richard II, King of England   6–16 passim, 31
Richard III, King of England   23
Rickert, Edith   11, 15, 22, 23n, 29, 102
Robbins, Rossell Hope   5, 8n, 19, 21, 43n
Robert of Basevorn *Artes praedicandi*   38, 39

Robertson, D. W., Jr.   *Chaucer's London*   133n
Robinson, Ian   88n
Roman de la Rose   9
Roman de Thèbes   117, 120n
Romano, Vincenzo   113n
Root, Robert K.   109–27 passim
Rowland, Beryl   22n, 49n, 88n
Rudisill, George   133n
Ruggiers, Paul G.   87n
Ruiz, Juan *Libro de Buen Amor*   47, 48n
Sacrobosco *De Sphaera*   78, 79
Said, Edward   7n
Saint-Hilaire, Le Marquis de   10n
Salter, Elizabeth Zeeman   33n, 51n, 87n
Scattergood, V. J.   10
Schipper, Jakob   88; *A History of English Versification*   89n
Schoeck, R. J.   27n
Scogan, Henry   6–17 passim; *Moral Balade*   11, 15, 19
Seneca, Lucius Annaeus *Hercules Furens*   43, 131n
Sergius   104, 105
Servius Honoratus, Maurus   114n, 130
Shirley, John   8–23 passim
Silvia, Daniel S.   22n, 24
Simonelli, Maria   114n
Skeat, Walter W.   10, 56n, 64–71 passim, 84
Smith, J. C.   32n
Smith, M. Bentinck   89n
Sotheworth, Richard   23
Southworth, James G. *Verses of Cadence: An Introduction to the Prosody of Chaucer and His Followers*   88n
Spearing, A. C. *Criticism and Medieval Poetry*   34n
Spitzer, Leo   47
Stahl, W. H.   37n
Statius, Publius Papinius *Thebaid*   109–33 passim
Stone, W. G.   21n
Stopyndon, John   23
Strode, Ralph   6–15 passim
Sturry, Richard   9, 14
Sutton, E. W.   35n
Sweeney, Robert D. *Prolegomena to an Edition of the Scholia to Statius*   114n

Swift, Jonathan *Gulliver's Travels* 48
Tale of Beryn 21n
Taylor, Jerome 27n, 116n
Taylor, John *The Universal Chronicle of Ranulf Higden* 113n
Ten Brink, Bernhard 88; *The Language and Metre of Chaucer* 89n
Terence 43
Theorica Planetarum 62
Thompson, J. W. *Economic and Social History of Europe in the Later Middle Ages* 30n
Thorndike, Lynn 79n
Tout, T. F. 7, 12; *Chapters in the Administrative History of Medieval England* 16
Towner, Sr. Mary Louis 10n
Traversagni, Lorenzo Guglielmo *Nova Rhetorica* 40
Trevet, Nicolas 112; *Expositio Hercules Furens* 43; *Historia ab Orbe Condito ad Christi Nativitatem* 112n
Trevisa, John *Nichodemus* 21
Tuckerman, Bryant *Planetary, Lunar, and Solar Positions, A.D. 2 to A.D. 1649* 70n
Usk, Thomas 6–15 passim; *Testament of Love* 14
Ussani, V., Jr. 43n

Ussery, Huling E. *Chaucer's Physician: Medicine and Literature in Fourteenth-Century England* 49n
Vache, Philip de la 6–14 passim
Veneto, Paolino 110n
Victor, Julius 36, 37
Victor, Sulpitius 36
Victorinus, Marius 104–06
Vincent of Beauvais *Speculum Historiale* 111, 113
Virgil *Aenid* 114–30 passim
Watson, Andrew G. 88n; *Catalogue of Dated and Datable Manuscripts* 103n
William of Auvergne 38
Williams, Raymond *Marxism and Literature* 4n
Willis, Raymond S. 48n
Wilson, R. M. *The Lost Literature of Medieval England* 43n
Wise, Boyd A. *The Influence of Statius upon Chaucer* 109n, 119n, 132n
Wood, Chauncey *Chaucer and the Country of the Stars* 58n
Wordsworth, William 48
Wright, Thomas 37n
Wyclif, John 12
Wynkyn de Worde 94n
Young, George *An English Prosody on Inductive Lines* 89n